Drew Pearson:

An Unauthorized Biography

HARPER'S
MAGAZINE
PRESS

DREW PEARSON

AN UNAUTHORIZED BIOGRAPHY

BY OLIVER PILAT

HARPER'S MAGAZINE PRESS

PUBLISHED IN ASSOCIATION WITH HARPER & ROW

NEW YORK

FIRST EDITION

Designed by Sidney Feinberg

Library of Congress Cataloging in Publication Data

Pilat, Oliver Ramsay, 1903-
  Drew Pearson: an unauthorized biography.
   I. Pearson, Drew 1897-1969.
PN4874 . P38P5   070'.92'4 [B]   72-79719
ISBN 0-06-126499-7

Contents

A section of illustrations follows page 144.

Acknowledgment

The relatives, friends, enemies and more or less impartial colleagues of Drew Pearson proved generally accessible and helpful during the decade-long preparation of this biography. They are too numerous to list here and in some instances they were promised immunity from mention. I wish particularly to thank Drew's sisters, Mrs. Gordon C. Lange and Mrs. Lockwood Fogg, Jr.; his cousins, Miss Dorothy Pearson and Mrs. Josephine Arnold; Dorothy Detzer Denny, national secretary of the Women's International League for Peace and Freedom, who for decades played a constructive role in Drew's life; George C. Vournas, his closest friend; Marian Canty, his office manager and confidential secretary; Colonel Robert S. Allen and Jack Anderson, Pearson's columnar partners; Herman Klurfeld, his ghostly collaborator; Faith and William Neel; and Margaret and Alan McSurely.

If a man is to write *A Panegyrick,*
he may keep vices out of sight;
but if he professes to write *A Life,*
he must represent it really as it was.
—SAMUEL JOHNSON

DREW PEARSON:

AN UNAUTHORIZED BIOGRAPHY

CHAPTER I

A Scourge in Washington

JOURNALISTS OFTEN CREATE A GREAT STIR as they pass through life, but nobody bothers much about them after they are gone. Even those who hailed Drew Pearson as phenomenal and unique no longer remember precisely what he accomplished or how he looked and sounded in action. Yet he was the greatest controversialist in the United States during the first two-thirds of the century. His equal in affecting the flow of events is not likely to be seen during its remainder.

Pearson extended his influence steadily without a setback or a break despite a decline in the number and economic condition of American newspapers and a general flight from argument on the air. During his last thirty-seven years he produced eight syndicated newspaper columns a week (one column for weeklies and seven for dailies) for six hundred clients with a total circulation of forty million. Each column ran about eight hundred words. Including at least twenty million listeners on radio—where his wordage was high because of the speed of his delivery—he possessed a long-term audience of at least sixty million.

Moreover, he went on news-gathering expeditions abroad; he crisscrossed the country on lecture tours; he maintained contact by mail and telephone with a coast-to-coast net of tipster-supporters;

he kept a captious eye on the New York newspaper syndicate in which he held a controlling interest; he owned a small motion picture company making foreign films; he gave rare interviews; he produced articles and books with or without the help of ghost writers; and he issued a $50-a-year confidential weekly business-and-economics newsletter called *Personal from Pearson*.

In a career spanning nine Presidents, his millions of words reached more Americans regularly than those of any other journalist, novelist, entertainer, preacher or politician. He was known around the globe not only because his column appeared in such countries as Canada, Mexico and England and in cities like Rio de Janeiro, Honolulu, Havana, Athens and Madras, but also because of the international impact of his exclusives. By manipulation of his trips he gave an illusion of being on or near the scene whenever news broke.

"I've always gone for the action," he liked to say. He could not be defined simply as an extrovert or an introvert; he was more what Ed Murrow used to call an ambivert. Like Winston Churchill and Norman Mailer he insisted on a role in the history he wrote.

In an original, not always scrupulous fashion, he crusaded for peace, integration, civil rights, domestic welfare programs, foreign aid and East-West détente. He opposed censorship, corruption in government and the military-industrial complex. He harried racketeers, racists and Red-baiters; Birchites, Klansmen and neo-Nazis; plutocrats who received tax favors or otherwise evaded their taxes; and the anarchists and revolutionaries who emerged from the ranks of disaffected youth during his closing years. He supported reformers, from Woodrow Wilson to Ralph Nader.

Because his audience included middle-of-the-roaders and conservatives Drew Pearson disguised his partisanship. His best stories, he declared in one interview, came through accurate tips, diligently followed up, or through doping out a scandal in his mind and confronting somebody to see if it ticked. "I operate by sense of smell," he liked to say. "If something smells wrong, I go to work."

"It's the job of a newspaperman," he said on another occasion, "to spur the lazy, watch the weak, expose the corrupt. He must be the eyes, ears and nose of the American people. Yes, the nose is important for no matter how much stench a newspaperman is exposed to, he must never lose his smell."

Pearson's stress on his nose for news was overdone. Most of his historic exclusives were thrust into his hands as a reward for taking part in public quarrels with a high ideological content.

"I've always tried to emphasize the personal side of journalism," he declared in a third interview. "It makes my points about clean government more effective and it does not put people to sleep the way some of my thumb-sucking colleagues do." (In the lexicon of the trade, thumb-suckers are pundits who analyze conditions without much factual ribbing.)

Once again Pearson's words were deceptive. He did not as a rule accuse liberals or radicals of anything; he accused conservatives. His anticorruption stance was a passport to acceptance by supporters in the hinterlands who did not invariably share his politics. Though he came to embody the national distrust of politicians, he was in fact the most consummate of politicians himself.

Pearson gave the impression that he knew everybody of importance and that everybody knew him. Nobody, it seemed, could fool him or buy him off. Nobody owned him. An illustration of this occurred in 1942 when he was being called a Communist because he campaigned for unstinted aid to the Russian ally in the war. He was attending a dinner in honor of Constantine Oumansky, the Russian Ambassador, at the palatial home of his mother-in-law, Mrs. Eleanor (Cissy) Patterson, the Washington newspaper publisher.

Oumansky was a verbose boor. After listening to his pomposities for a while Pearson conspicuously closed a wooden matchbox on loose skin above his right wrist. Making the matchbox dance by clenching and unclenching his fist, he said quietly to the Ambassador across the table: "That's you when Stalin speaks!"

In his style of writing Pearson was strictly a journeyman. He complained to friends at times about his inability to produce fancy language, but to some extent this also may have been camouflage. By high factual content and sparing, subtle use of clichés and platitudes, he wrote what Washington insiders considered sophisticated commentary, at the same time reaching around them to the small-town residents of the Middle America from which he sprang.

Though the big-city liberals whose causes he espoused often took Pearson for granted, the citizens in the hard-dirt boondocks relished his columnar menu of exposé garnished with historical analysis, reminiscence, predictions, sentimentality, gossip and corn. They respected and trusted Pearson; in many cases he was the only Washington correspondent they knew by name. From stray references to family solidarity, common sense and the flag they recognized him as one of themselves and were willing to listen occasionally to populist opinions which they would not tolerate from anybody else.

Unlike Jack Anderson, a former Mormon missionary who became his journalistic pupil and junior partner in later years, Pearson was at all times heavily involved with friends and enemies. Anderson believed in keeping his distance from politicians— "standing back a bit and growling," as he put it. When he took over the "Washington Merry-Go-Round" after Pearson's death, he instructed his assistants to avoid White House soirees, cocktail parties and meals with informants lest they be unduly influenced.

Anderson did well with the column for a while. By producing exclusives ranging from the Pentagon Papers to President Nixon's private bias in the Indian-Pakistani war, he retained and even extended the circulation he inherited. In only one instance—his account of the domestic and foreign maneuvers of the International Telephone & Telegraph Corporation—has he donned, briefly and tentatively, the knight-errant mantle of his predecessor. Without it he will never be more than half the man Pearson was. He will remain Jack Anderson, muckraker, compared to Drew Pearson, muckraker-crusader.

2

Pearson's reach for the throat of an adversary in print or on the air used to be a favorite topic in Washington salons. No agreement on this or any other aspect of his character was easy because public quarrels tended to obscure the private man. Was he really "the Savonarola of U.S. journalism" or "the Robespierre of our society"? Not at all. Those who applied such phrases were taking an oblique stand for or against somebody being pounded by the columnist. They were not seriously comparing Pearson with the fifteenth-century Florentine friar who crusaded against corruption or the bloody dictator of the terrorist party in the French Revolution.

A visitor from New York who arrived in the middle of one of these discussions retold the fable of the scorpion who hitchhiked a ride on the back of a frog. Halfway across a pond, the scorpion stung. As the frog and the scorpion began to sink, the frog said: "Why did you do it? Now we'll both drown," and the scorpion replied: "It's my nature."

"That's Pearson for you," said the outsider. "The Scorpion-on-the-Potomac!"

A local admirer of Pearson pointed out that he was a Quaker and a pacifist. Religion, rejoined somebody else, did not prevent Cromwell from wrenching arms off the bodies of enemies on the battlefield. Eventually, a majority of those present inclined to the view that Pearson was personally peaceful and professionally warlike, a confusing formula which would serve until the next discussion.

Although half his college class got into combat during World War I and eight of them died, Pearson avoided active military duty. After the war, he worked two years without pay with an American Friends Service Committee reconstruction unit in Serbia. Then he became a free-lance foreign correspondent who slanted his dispatches in favor of disarmament, world peace and noninterference by large nations in the affairs of small ones.

Having gained a foothold in Washington through marriage, Pearson joined Bob Allen, a stocky, truculent Kentuckian working for the *Christian Science Monitor,* in writing their celebrated critical books about the Hoover administration: *Washington Merry-Go-Round* and *More Merry-Go-Round.* Just before the start of the Roosevelt administration they launched a joint syndicated newspaper column in the same name and vein.

According to Dorothy Detzer, a fellow pacifist who saw a great deal of Pearson during this period, he was a "disarming ginger-haired young man who walked with a swift swinging lope." His "frequent smile," she said, "pleated his eyes into narrow slits." Though large, well built and strong, he had the look of somebody who never delivered a blow in anger. This seemed also to be his nature.

President Hoover's Secretary of War, Patrick J. Hurley, was described in the first *Merry-Go-Round* book as a flamboyant character who practiced his social entrances and exits before a mirror. Finding Pearson alone in a side room at a party, Hurley called him every foul name he knew to provoke a fight. Pearson endured it and walked out. His memory, however, was excellent. When Hurley ran for U.S. Senator in New Mexico seventeen years later, Pearson went down there, hired time on a statewide radio network and presented a devastating summary of the former War Secretary's record. Hurley was defeated.

Allen and Pearson, according to a version current among New Dealers, operated like a pair of detectives breaking down a suspect by alternate menace and sympathy. Allen would surge into a Congressman's office and demand information. If it was not forthcoming, he would romp around and make threats before leaving. Next day Pearson would arrive, suavity itself, to deplore his partner's vehemence and extract facts painlessly from the relieved legislator. In later years, Allen denied the legend. He never needed help to get a story, he would say grumpily, but there may have been something to it. Certainly, Pearson was the smoother member of the team.

At one party given by Pearson and his first wife, Felicia, a Capitol Hill reporter for the Associated Press named Francis Stephenson became tipsily belligerent toward his host. When Pearson failed to rise to the challenge, Allen escorted Stephenson out into the garden, gave him a beating and helped him get home.

An early "Merry-Go-Round" column exposed a Baltimore-Washington bootlegging operation. Pearson got the tip and insisted on using it despite Allen's feeling that it needed checking. Two days after the story appeared, a leathery-faced little man slid into Allen's twelfth-floor office in the National Press Building to announce: "I'm going to kill you." Allen whirled in his chair. "Why, you son-of-a-bitch," he shouted. "So many people want to kill me! You got to wait in line for your turn." The howling frightened off the intruder, but Allen had a chunk of lead in his hand ready to throw if necessary.

Allen did not relish being the butt of his partner's rashness. He tried to stay out of sight while he concentrated on orthodox news beats. Pearson, on the other hand, kept his name and address in the telephone book. He liked to receive and explore the tips against bureaucrats which were stimulated by the column's anti-establishment tone. His name appeared first in the joint byline. For these reasons much of the abuse began to focus on him. Hoarse voices shouted insults over the phone, letters brought crude drawings of a coffin and other threats. He did not seem to mind.

In the journalistic phrase, Pearson "wrote hard." He made the most of his material regardless of risk, whereas Allen, a former reporter for the United Press, retained a touch of wire service caution. Because libel suits were provoked by Pearson they became his responsibility. The first overpowering suit—for $1,750,000 at a time when the column was barely meeting expenses—was brought by General Douglas MacArthur, on whom Pearson had been picking ever since *More Merry-Go-Round* featured his eviction in July, 1932, of twenty thousand homeless, hungry, unarmed veterans who had been encamped on the Anacostia Flats in a vain effort to persuade Congress to vote them a bonus.

The description was maliciously graphic. It cited the delay in proceedings while an aide went to the General's mother for his dress uniform and medals. It isolated significant details, such as the Negro wrapped in an American flag who was ridden down by an unswerving line of cavalry and the blind veteran whose ear was sliced off by an impatient soldier's sword. Finally, there was the triumphant talk by the man-on-horseback, telling reporters about the gratitude of Washington residents for his "liberation" of their town.

MacArthur's vanity was wounded. Nevertheless, he took no action. He would probably never have sued except for President Roosevelt, who soon found the column disrupting his unorthodox processes of government. The President hinted to the General that he could have another four years as Army Chief of Staff if he stopped the "Merry-Go-Round" column. MacArthur took the hint and filed suit.

Pearson, in defense, utilized his network of informants to reach the General's former Eurasian mistress. With her help he forced

MacArthur to abandon the suit. The unexplained rout of the country's chief military figure created an aureole of deadliness around Pearson's head, which deepened with the years.

After a man's first public quarrel—or his first intense love affair—psychologists say that subsequent ones tend to repeat it. In retracing the MacArthur pattern Pearson became bolder. It was characteristic of the partners' attitudes that when an increase in syndicate sales permitted a modest expansion in staff, Allen hired a reporter as his assistant whereas Pearson employed a former prohibition undercover man as an investigator.

The forbidden taste for warfare brought into his life by libel suits induced Pearson to defend his turf. Ernest Cuneo, a lawyer and family friend, liked to tell of an incident at a garden party given by Drew and his second wife, Luvie (pronounced "Loovie"), in the late 1930s. The women wore picture hats and in some cases carried parasols against the spring sun. The air was heavy with the smell of roses in the colonial garden. Coming up to Cuneo, Luvie said: "Ernest, do you know the man Drew hit on the head with a flowerpot?"

Taking an inclination of Luvie's blond head as guidance, Cuneo trotted from the garden where the party was being held around a projecting rear building into a lesser garden also owned by the Pearsons. Drew was standing alone by the gate, carefully wiping his hands on a handkerchief. "A process server," he explained briefly.

Pearson was still more or less committed to nonviolence personally, but his political pacifism underwent a shift after the capitulation of Chamberlain to Hitler in Munich in 1938. Leaders in the movement to keep the United States out of the tightening struggle in Europe—men like Professor Charles A. Beard and Harry Elmer Barnes—could hardly credit the news.

"Drew thought Hitler was going to put his mother in a gas oven" was the unpleasant later explanation of John T. Flynn, in reference to the little-known fact that Pearson's mother was a Jewish convert to Quakerism. Flynn was an America First leader who had been on close terms with Pearson when he taught briefly at Columbia University.

Despite various other surmises, the largest discernible factor

in the columnist's decision was what happened in Spain. George
C. Vournas, U.S. lawyer for the Spanish Loyalists, Pearson and
other local left-of-center zealots in Washington tried desperately
first to upset, then evade, the American ban on arms to Spain,
which was hurting only the legally elected government. The in-
surgent Nationalists and clerical Fascists were getting plenty of
military help from the German and Italian dictators.

In the end, of course, the Loyalists lost. After that experience
Pearson was willing to concede a point in the affairs of nations and
men at which aggression could no longer be tolerated. President
Roosevelt's policy of collective security, he concluded, might be
the best way to avoid another world war. Once committed to this
course, Pearson outdid his colleagues in ripping the more conspiratorial American isolationists, including rabid anti-Semites.
Much of his material about the lunatic fringe came from the secret
files of the Anti-Defamation League of B'nai B'rith. It tended to
discredit by association some of his former fellow pacifists who
were not reactionary or racist.

Pearson acquired a whole new set of friends and enemies as
a result of his switch on foreign affairs. Outraged isolationists and
their friends belabored him with verbal violence surpassing anything he had known. Under the pressure he lost his pleated smile,
and it never returned.

Curiously enough, it was a nonpolitical situation—a reported
threat on his life by his second wife's first husband—which led
Pearson to apply for a permit to carry a pistol. The application
was denied when the man making the threats convinced the police
he did not own a gun. Since anybody can get a weapon if he wants
one badly enough, Pearson hired a bodyguard in self-defense and
practiced shooting with the guard's revolver.

One of Pearson's new allies was Walter Winchell, the Broadway
columnist. They both took tips from the ADL and from FBI
Director J. Edgar Hoover, who was harassing isolationists under
orders from the White House. On the anti-Hitler issue, Winchell
and Pearson made similar frenetic remarks in their columns and
on radio, a high-pressure medium into which Pearson had succeeded in dragging Bob Allen.

In the fall of 1939, Winchell and Pearson happened to travel to Hollywood on the same transcontinental train. Hearing of his ally's presence on board, Winchell instructed Ed Weiner, his publicity man and bodyguard, to locate the other commentator and invite him for a companionable drink. Weiner went to Pearson's compartment and knocked on the door. Getting no answer, he repeated his knock. He pushed the door cautiously open. There in a crouch against the far wall was Pearson with wary blue eyes and the muzzle of a businesslike revolver focused unwaveringly on Weiner's stomach!

3

Newspapers and radio-TV stations discourage publicity about libel suits for fear of stimulating new ones. Pearson operated on the same principle. He talked vaguely, if at all, about the subject; he kept no count of the suits in which he was engaged; and he warned John Donovan, his personal and libel lawyer, against making any list. "If you make a list," he stressed, "it will get out sooner or later." No complete list is yet available, but Donovan estimates that at least 275 suits seeking more than $200 million in damages were filed against Drew and his journalistic clients! That probably establishes some kind of world record in legal combat for a newspaperman. Certainly nobody during Pearson's lifetime envisaged so much money at stake in so many suits.

"There are two means of fighting, by means of law and by means of force," wrote Machiavelli. "The first belongs properly to man, the second to animals." Pearson did not need the comfort of any such dubious distinction. To him legal actions which at times were directed at the annihilation of an opponent were onerous yet somehow exhilarating necessities. He came to believe that he was defending the right—his right—of public discussion. He took pride in having lost only one of all the suits against him which came to trial. In that single defeat he agreed reluctantly to pay $40,000 instead of appealing a $50,000 jury verdict. The payment amounted to 1/50 of 1 percent of the estimated total damages sought from him over the years.

Pearson's profile in libel is more revelatory than traditional gauges of personality and purpose, such as the sequence of romances given by female novelists or the education-and-work record known to personnel managers as a curriculum vitae. It demonstrates that from Huey Long and his Every-Man-a-King movement during the 1930s to Robert Welch and his Birch Society during the 1960s Pearson lavished his roughest language on right-wing radicals. His particular concern during the early days of the New Deal was the Rev. Charles E. Coughlin, Detroit's silver-throated priest, with whom other commentators feared to tangle at first because of his cloth.

Pearson had an advantage in dealing with Coughlin. Bob Allen's legman, Tom McNamara, was a former Washington correspondent for *Social Justice*, Coughlin's widely circulated magazine. Disillusioned by the priest's weekly radio tirades against Wall Street and the Jews, McNamara was willing to comply with Pearson's request for background information on his former boss. A series of biting personal items convinced "Merry-Go-Round" readers that Coughlin was marked for destruction.

Tips flowed in, one of which referred to an affidavit on file in the Internal Revenue Bureau that the priest had given $68,000 to a physician of Royal Oak, Michigan, as compensation for alienating the affections of his wife. When Pearson aired that story, he and WABC were sued by the wife for $225,000 on the ground that she had been portrayed as "unchaste."

Father Coughlin gave a formal statement to lawyers for the plaintiff. Asserting that some aspects of his relationship with a parishioner were confidential, he did not take the ordinary oath to "tell the truth, the whole truth and nothing but the truth." As a result the priest's deposition is referred to as "suppressed" in the court papers still on file but it is not available for inspection. The physician's wife lost her suit after two jury trials.

Pearson widened his anti-Coughlin campaign to include a right-wing Congressman from Ohio named Martin L. Sweeney. He accused Sweeney of being "Washington representative" for Coughlin's Christian Front. He labeled Sweeney an "anti-Semite" on the basis of his opposition to the appointment of a Jewish judge. Bob Allen, who during his decade (1932–1942) of association with the "Washington Merry-Go-Round" never got it into a libel suit, scented danger. He implored his partner to talk to Sweeney or let him talk to Sweeney. Pearson refused; he declined the Congress-man's telephone calls and tore up his letters unread.

The result was chain libel—the bugbear of the newspaper-syndicate business—in which separate suits are brought against every newspaper carrying a specified column. Nearly 150 suits seeking damages in excess of $20 million in separate jurisdictions were filed by Sweeney. Many were knocked out on the proceedings or through legal devices improvised by Pearson's lawyers. Specially selected trial counsel won those cases which came to trial, with invisible extralegal assistance from Pearson's investigators.

Pearson specialized in campaign exposés of reactionary candi-dates for public office on every level, national, state and local. Chain libel on radio—which is to a single-station libel suit what nuclear war would be to conventional war—was provoked by his assertion in 1949 that F. Napoleon Howser, a conservative Attorney General of California running for re-election, was the tool of gamblers.

Howser first brought a $300,000 suit in Washington for national libel by the column. In extending his attack to radio stations he announced he would turn over the money he collected to charity. Pearson worried more over Howser than over any other plaintiff because he did not quite have his gambling charge nailed down. It had come to him as a tip from his son-in-law, George Arnold, and had not been adequately confirmed.

Continuation of the attack against Howser brought another tip, this one from a lawyer in Seattle. John Donovan went out to Chicago and persuaded a small-time mobster to sign an affidavit that he had handed twelve hundred-dollar bills to the Attorney General as a payment from gamblers. On top of this, one of Pearson's friends and informants in the U.S. Attorney General's office agreed to testify about a secret federal investigation into California gambling. The combined information cracked the California politician like a nut.

Legal actions by Pearson against others were on a lesser though also unlisted scale. They were primarily defensive in nature. Thus Pearson sued Howser for $300,000 because the Attorney General made slanderous remarks about him during a pretrial hearing, open to the press, in Arnold's law office in Los Angeles. The Pear-son counteraction and Howser's appeal from his lower-court defeat were jointly dismissed in the wake of the Attorney General's political eclipse.

In 1966 Pearson reminded voters in California—on another George Arnold tip—that George Christopher, a Republican Mayor of San Francisco running for Governor, had been convicted twenty-six years earlier as a milk distributor for watering his milk. Though this was solidly backed by court records, Christopher sought $6 million for the inopportune mention of his ancient misdemeanor. He was sued back for $2.6 million. The suits canceled out after Christopher lost in his campaign.

An earlier offset suit involved Vivien Kellems, the Connecticut cable-grip manufacturer who became nationally known as a foe of the withholding tax and later as a right-wing aspirant for public office. She filed for libel because the column portrayed her amour-by-mail with a Nazi diplomat in Argentina during World War II.

Miss Kellems' reaction to the advertisement of her flirtation with an enemy in wartime was sufficiently sulphuric to call for a return suit. She could not question the authenticity of the printed excerpts. They came from copies of letters leaked from the U.S. Censor's office. Pearson probably had the better position on the legal chessboard, but he chivalrously consented to a draw after the military hostilities (and the romance) were over.

Considering the way he shredded the reputations of others, Pearson was incredibly thin-skinned. In 1948 he instructed Donovan to bring a nuisance suit against *Time* for one of its typical pert phrases. A settlement worked out by Morris Ernst, his New York lawyer, arranged for his picture to appear on the cover of the magazine. In 1963 Pearson collected a small but gratifying sum of money from a California publisher who called him a Communist after he had enjoyed the first of several exclusive talks with Nikita Khrushchev.

One purpose of such legal forays may have been to convince critics that he was dangerous to affront. Long after this was generally conceded, Pearson sought $176,000 for damage to his feelings when C. W. Snedden, editor of the Fairbanks (Alaska) *Miner*— daily circulation, 9,950—described him as "the garbage man of journalism." Pearson had annoyed Mr. Snedden by claiming that

Ernest Gruening, a Democrat running for U.S. Senator, was the true father of Alaskan statehood rather than "a lot of Johnny-come-latelies such as Mike Stepovich," the Republican Governor.

An anomalous slur circulated obscurely up near the Arctic Circle might have been shrugged off by anybody but Pearson. The defense tried to laugh him out of court by stipulating that garbage was a literary term for trash and demanding: "How many garbage pails must a person empty to be called a garbage man?"

Pearson was deadly serious. He induced his friend Wayne Morse to travel to Fairbanks to testify at the trial that he was not, indeed, a worthless or filthy fellow. He submitted affidavits from former President Truman, James Roosevelt and others attesting to his achievements and character. In the end the local judge ruled that a Washington writer who intervened in an Alaskan political row might reasonably expect a retaliatory slap or two.

Pearson was so determined to expunge this smutch on his escutcheon that he overruled his lawyers and insisted on appeal to a higher court. There he lost all over again.

4

Long before this, Pearson had put aside his youthful precept about treating others as he wanted to be treated. He felt obliged to employ extreme tactics against confirmed enemies to prevent them from using extreme tactics against him. "People forget that I'm trying to do something for the country and the world," he said. He may or may not have been justified, but for him the adage about bad means spoiling good ends did not apply. He was dealing with politics, and in politics questionable means are often employed for desirable goals. How otherwise can anybody defend diplomacy, espionage or war?

Scarcely a week went by that Pearson did not eat breakfast, lunch or dinner with John Donovan in town or at the farm. He held periodic conferences with two, sometimes three, investigators who kept busy on assignments in the field. He discussed strategy with some of the most distinguished lawyers in Washington, men like F. Joseph (Jiggs) Donohue, who handled the Coughlin case; Colonel William A. Roberts, who disposed of Miss Kellems; and

William P. Rogers, later a Secretary of State, who humbled F. Napoleon Howser. To avoid payments to opponents over the years he spent hundreds of thousands of dollars in legal fees to trial counsel. He attended pretrial sessions and the trials themselves.

There was one small amusing aspect to all this nonjournalistic activity. Just as he sold himself on his flair for merchandising farm manure, Pearson came eventually to believe that he had unsuspected talents as a lawyer. One year when his Buick with the lucky license plate, E 13, was demolished as it sat parked outside the Mayflower Hotel, he insisted on handling the negligence suit. Since the damage had been caused by a runaway car from a garage across the street, the case seemed open and shut. In examining the jury before trial, however, Pearson let slip the fact that his own car was insured. To his dismay this caused a mistrial.

Pearson's lavish expenditure of time, effort and money on litigation familiarized him with the art of sustained hostility. Contrary to the advice of psychologists, who urge the dropping of personal anger as soon as possible before it can harden into hatred, he let quarrels torment his mind over extended periods of time. Some of them, such as his ten-year feud with Nicolae Malaxa, Rumania's No. 1 industrialist, perceptibly affected his feelings.

Malaxa reached the United States as a refugee in the late 1940s. He was denounced by the "Washington Merry-Go-Round" as an anti-Semite who had collaborated with both Nazis and Communists in his country. On the advice of Rabbi Paul Richman, Washington representative of the Anti-Defamation League of B'nai B'rith, Pearson backtracked. Though still suspicious of Malaxa, he went so far as to write that there seemed to be no legal reason why the Rumanian should not become an American.

Pending final determination of his status by the immigration authorities, Malaxa settled on the outskirts of Whittier, California, Richard Nixon's home town. There, in 1951, with the help of Nixon's law firm, he set up the Western Tube Corporation. The Nixon connection revived Pearson's earlier doubts. He obtained a copy of an unpublicized investigation of Malaxa which had been made by the House Un-American Activities Committee. On the basis of the report, but without disclosing his source, Pearson charged that Malaxa had secured his first-preference visa by concealing patches of discreditable activity in his career. Malaxa sued for $5 million in damages.

Pearson had harried four House Un-American Activities Committee chairmen—Hamilton Fish, Martin Dies, J. Parnell Thomas and John Wood—but he collaborated confidentially with the latest HUAC chairman, Representative Francis Walter (D–Pa.). Weren't they both brawling with Vice President Nixon? What better basis for friendship than a mutual antipathy?

Edmund G. (Pat) Brown, the Democratic Governor of California, supported Pearson's anti-Malaxa drive. So did groups of left- and right-wing Rumanian-Americans. Malaxa was denied re-entry into the United States after a South American business trip. In time his lawyers upset revocation of his re-entry permit. As soon as he got back in the country, Malaxa sued Pearson for an additional $45 million to cover loss of an Argentine contract for locomotives.

Malaxa's tug-of-war with the immigration authorities and his $50-million libel suit dragged on during the Eisenhower years. From time to time Pearson lashed out at Malaxa without decisive effect. An inconspicuous bill to award citizenship to the wealthy Rumanian gained ground in Congress. Tipped off by the veteran chairman of the House Judiciary Committee, Representative Emanuel Celler (D, L–N.Y.), Pearson was able to block its passage by charging that Vice President Nixon was its hidden sponsor.

When John F. Kennedy became President, Pearson asked his friend, Secretary of Labor Arthur Goldberg, to file a demand for Malaxa's deportation with Attorney General Robert F. Kennedy. Goldberg was unwilling to initiate such an action. He would do it, he said, only if a reputable organization like the Anti-Defamation League certified Malaxa as an anti-Semite.

Pearson approached Herman Edelsberg, who had succeeded Paul Richman as Washington representative of the ADL. He suggested a letter to Goldberg describing Malaxa as "the Krupp of Rumania, the wartime partner of Albert Goering, brother of Field Marshal Goering and financier of the Iron Guard at the time it was mass-murdering Rumanian Jews."

Edelsberg declined to send such a letter. He had copies, he said, of letters from the Chief Rabbi of Rumania and the Israeli

Minister to Holland indicating that the industrialist had secretly protected Jews from the Iron Guard. Edelsberg conceded that Malaxa had "compromised himself" by making deals to survive, first with King Carol and his mistress, Madame Lupescu, then with the Nazi masters of Rumania and, when they were kicked out, with the Communists, but he would not concede that Malaxa was a killer or an anti-Semite.

Pearson never spoke again to Edelsberg. He requested his staff members to avoid any contact with the Washington representative of the ADL. He complained about Edelsberg to the national ADL office in New York. In a formal memo Edelsberg defended himself by saying he had "gone to the edge of conscience for a friend" —Pearson—by asking government agencies to provide whatever investigative material they had about Malaxa's career but that he did not feel he could go any further. Malaxa was simply not an anti-Semite, he said.

With Edelsberg's permission, the national ADL office sent a copy of the memo to Pearson to show support for its representative in Washington. More determined than ever, Pearson carried his campaign to large individual contributors to B'nai B'rith with whom he enjoyed a personal relationship. The national office, though distressed, stood firm.

Partly because of the continuing strain, Edelsberg took a leave of absence to become executive director of the U.S. Equal Opportunity Commission. As he was driving home one evening, he turned on the car radio. Drew Pearson was criticizing Franklin D. Roosevelt, Jr., chairman of the new commission, for picking an executive director "with a record of being soft on Fascists"!

Over the years the ADL had helped Pearson enormously. It had provided information he could not obtain elsewhere, backed his lecture tours, even assisted in the circulation of his weekly newsletter. Though he continued to treat its Washington office as hostile territory, he mended his fences with Arnold Forster, its general counsel. In an emergency he would visit Forster in New York or reach him for advice by telephone. Thus he avoided a complete break with the ADL.

When the Malaxa case was called for trial, Jack Wasserman, lawyer for the Rumanian industrialist, arose in open court and withdrew the action. He also agreed to pay costs. John Donovan, Pearson's lawyer, was stunned. There had been no formal agreement of any kind between the parties.

Malaxa was in his mid-seventies. At that age he might have been reluctant to face a public review of the accumulated compromises of a lifetime. He told Wasserman, however, and later Edelsberg, that his purpose was merely to avoid deportation. Pearson had gone beyond Arthur Goldberg in bringing pressure on Attorney General Kennedy. Malaxa knew that Senator Estes Kefauver was one of several influential politicians acting in Pearson's behalf. So far Kennedy had not yielded—one of Pearson's subsequent complaints against the President's younger brother was that "Bobby failed to act on Malaxa"—but Malaxa could not be sure that his resistance would continue.

Having by bluff and intrigue nullified the $50-million libel threat, Pearson stopped pushing for deportation. Malaxa became a citizen. Every once in a while, however, the "Washington Merry-Go-Round" would take a new swipe at him to remind the public that he remained in the category of General Douglas MacArthur: somebody who had earned no exemption from criticism by canceling a legal mistake!

CHAPTER II

Astride the Capitol and
the White House

NOBODY EVER HIT CONGRESS HARDER or more persistently than Drew Pearson. His exposés sent four Representatives—Ernest Bramblett of California, Walter Brehm of Ohio, Andrew May of Kentucky and J. Parnell Thomas of New Jersey—to jail for fiscal mischief. He reported that one Congressman from North Carolina carried a dead man on his payroll, that another from Pennsylvania had a son involved in a paternity suit. He did not hesitate to name U.S. Senators influential in shaping foreign policy who had mistresses inserted under them by British intelligence. He even named the mistresses.

For disclosing in great detail in 1966 how Senator Thomas J. Dodd of West Hartford and Representative Adam Clayton Powell of Harlem and Bimini played fast and lost with the public funds, Pearson was voted a Pulitzer prize in reporting. This top journalistic award, obviously earned by him several times in the past, had always been jerked from his grasp by publishers whose business interests or sensibilities had been wounded by his crusades.

Once again it happened: the Pulitzer trustees reversed their editorial committee at the last minute and gave the prize to somebody else. This time other correspondents and the public itself howled at the Pulitzer trustees. Pearson's reputation as a national political cop had grown to the point where the prize needed him more than he needed the prize.

Ordinarily Pearson went easy on minority-group politicians, but he had rapped Powell for asserting his right to the vices rather than the virtues of his white colleagues. He began to regret his attack; Powell, he wrote, only did openly what unpunished whites did furtively. The change of heart came too late: Powell lost his House seat before Dodd was censured by the Senate.

Congress was run, Pearson wrote, "by a gaggle of old men from small towns . . . a council of elders whose only claim to power is their ability to outlive their colleagues." The seniority system, he pointed out, gave control over the committees and their legislative output to men without reference to "ability, honesty or senility." He abused particular committees, such as the House Un-American Activities Committee and the Senate Internal Security Subcommittee, for generating much of the irresponsible anti-Communism in Congress. Annually, for purposes of public ridicule, he compiled a list of Old Codgers from among the more objectionable committee chairmen.

No liberal legislator classed as an Old Codger. To Pearson age was another convenient stick to belabor those who disagreed with his left-of-center views. In addition to citing legitimate offenses—excessive campaign expenditures, subservience to lobbyists, conflicts of interests and right-wing extremism—he attacked Congressmen on a variety of pretexts: ghost-voting (arranging to be improperly recorded on a bill when not present or paired), personal violence, junketing, absenteeism and alcoholism.

Pearson's reason for using a pretext could usually be discerned. Thus his columnar rebuke of Senator Kenneth McKellar (D–Tenn.) for brandishing a clasp knife at Senator R. S. Copeland (D–N.Y.) was obviously based on McKellar's harassment of the Tennessee Valley Authority, prized by Pearson as an historic experiment in the production of public power.

Taking to the Senate floor, where he could not be sued for libel, McKellar made vituperative response. Pearson, he said, was "an infamous liar, a revolving liar, a pusillanimous liar, a lying ass, a natural-born liar, a liar by profession, a liar for a living, a liar in the daytime, a liar in the nighttime, a dishonest ignorant corrupt and groveling crook. . . ."

Warming to his task, the choleric old Senator ground out fresh insults minute by minute, postponing the call of nature for relief so long that when he finished and tottered out into the cloakroom, he fell to the floor in a faint. To his additional discomfort, as much of his tirade as could be accommodated in a single column appeared with minimal editorial comment in the "Washington Merry-Go-Round" several days later.

Blanket denial was a favorite Congressional reaction to a columnar charge which was true in the main but included one or two inaccurate details. Thus Senator Walter George of Georgia, accused of favoring subsidies for large oil companies and opposing them for poor farmers in his home state, called Pearson "an ordinary, congenital, deliberate and malicious liar." Faced with a comparable allegation, Representative Philip Bennett of Missouri described the columnist as a "dishonest, unreliable, vicious character assassin."

"He will go down in history," sputtered the racist Senator Theodore Bilbo of Mississippi, "as Pearson-the-sponge because he gathers slime, mud and slander from all parts of the earth and lets them ooze out through his radio broadcasts and through his daily contributions to a few newspapers which have not yet found him out." Archconservative Senator William Jenner of Indiana rivaled that by calling Pearson a "filthy brain-child conceived in ruthlessness and dedicated to the proposition that Judas Iscariot was a piker." Other familiar epithets included journalistic mad dog, polecat, skunk and rattlesnake.

Senator Strom Thurmond of South Carolina, a segregationist leader instrumental in Richard Nixon's election as President in 1968, acquired a twenty-two-year-old bride that year, when he was sixty-six. Soon after the nuptials Pearson noted that "Strom and his Nancy are spatting." With a slight touch of originality in a desert of repetitive insult, the Senator declared that the columnist had contracted "a case of journalistic leprosy."

Pearson did not complain about the oratory in the pages of the *Congressional Record*, but he became upset whenever a legislator filed a libel suit. He tried to discourage such suits by building a reputation for implacability. In one case he followed a litigious enemy right into the grave.

"An important part of the Great Society program," he wrote

during President Johnson's administration, "the cleaning up of American waterways, got a boost when a member of Congress was killed in a July 4th accident on a North Carolina throughway. He was Rep. T. Ashton Thompson, Democrat of Louisiana, who had many fine qualities. In the opinion of the big chemical companies, one of his finest was his opposition to cleaning up water pollution. . . ."

Behind his smokescreen of *ad hominem* attacks, Pearson pounded away at the desirability of reforms—Medicare, better meat inspection, oil-pipeline safety, some kind of health warning against cigarettes, to mention a few—until he created what Ralph Nader called "a climate of inevitability" for their passage. Like other pressure groups ranging from the U.S. Chamber of Commerce and the American Legion to the AFL-CIO and the *New York Times*, he sometimes introduced his own bills through favorite Congressmen, whom he then praised for initiative.

Sharp essays on pending legislation in the "Washington Merry-Go-Round" were timed to appear before crucial committee meetings. Pearson's legmen would warn committee members of reprisals if they voted wrong. Those recorded against aid to Appalachia or the urban slums might find themselves listed by name in the column, along with provocative comment about other misdeeds, such as loading a nephew on the payroll, touring the Paris nightclubs at government expense or chasing a secretary around a table in the office. Ignoring several warnings might install them on the column's blacklist for periodic drubbing.

Pearson's campaigns earned him no kudos in Congress. More lawmakers than were generally suspected cooperated with the column out of self-preservation, but they sought no recognition for their public service. The prevailing attitude toward Pearson among their colleagues was too hostile.

At times Pearson intervened personally in the legislative process. During the late 1940s he exposed organized crime in Louisiana, New York, Chicago and elsewhere before large law-enforcement agencies were quite willing to concede the existence of the Mafia. He was delighted when Senator Estes Kefauver (D–Tenn.) introduced a resolution to investigate the rackets on a national scale. The resolution having stalled for lack of support from Senate Majority Leader Scott Lucas (D–Ill.), Pearson went to Lucas to remind him of rumors that he had received large campaign contributions from Chicago gamblers.

"It will look bad," he assured the Senator, "if you continue to block Kefauver's investigation."

Lucas yielded. Kefauver's probe was solidly prepared. (Some of its most sensational revelations were exclusively leaked in advance to the "Merry-Go-Round.") The dramatic handling of major underworld figures at hearings converted Kefauver overnight into a presidential possibility. The data amassed during his investigation also provided a base for various subsequent inquiries.

Since Pearson never wrote about Lucas' rumored underworld contacts, he was eventually asked if he had not in effect blackmailed the Senator. "Nonsense," he replied with equanimity, "Scott is a friend of mine."

Though Congress normally allows a President to choose his own advisers, Pearson decided to buck tradition when President Eisenhower nominated Lewis L. Strauss as Secretary of Commerce. He blamed Strauss, a former Atomic Energy Commission Chairman, for "capitulating to Joe McCarthy" and driving out of public life Dr. J. Robert Oppenheimer, the scientist who supervised production of the atom bomb at Los Alamos. Strauss had also been responsible, Pearson believed, for the Dixon-Yates deal which, had it not been exposed and defeated, would have destroyed the public-power principle of the Tennessee Valley Authority and cost consumers hundreds of millions of dollars.

The key to any campaign against Strauss was Senate Majority Leader Lyndon Johnson. For months Johnson had been under attack in the "Washington Merry-Go-Round" as "Lyin' Down Lyndon" for his subservience to the oil lobby and his refusal to challenge Joe McCarthy.

"How would you like to get Drew off your back?" inquired Jack Anderson during an unexpected visit to Johnson's office.

"Who do I have to kill?" demanded the Senator.

"Strauss."

"No, no, no," said Johnson, batting his head with his hands. Anderson was almost at the door before the Senate Majority Leader called him back. "Let's talk about it," he said. A dinner meeting was held at Drew's house at which Johnson and other Senators made plans.

Strauss was a Wall Street investment banker with a title of admiral. When hearings began on his fitness to become an Eisenhower cabinet member, Pearson appeared with CIO National Secretary James B. Carey and other opposition witnesses. "Strowse," charged the columnist, feigning ignorance of the banker's preference for "Straws," had recently sought confidential information from the Atomic Energy Commission to "smear" one of his critics, a young Chicago nuclear physicist.

Strauss entered a flustered denial. "Put the Admiral under oath," demanded Pearson. "He'll change his story or you'll have a perjury case on your hands!" Everybody in the room began shouting at once. When the excitement subsided, Strauss had been defeated for confirmation as Commerce Secretary.

2

He had more enemies to the square inch in Congress, Pearson liked to say, than anywhere else. The concentrated hostility on Capitol Hill did not disturb him unduly with two possible exceptions: when Senator Joseph McCarthy made him a primary target in the 1950s and a decade later, toward the end of his life, when Senator John McClellan (D–Ark.) obtained documentary proof of Pearson's dalliance with a former secretary.

Joseph R. McCarthy was a demagogic genie out of a bottle. His background provided small clues to his incendiary gifts. He had been a chicken farmer in Appleton, Wisconsin. He ran unsuccessfully as a Democrat for District Attorney in his home county. Switching to the Republicans, he became a lawless Circuit Court judge. Campaigning on a spurious war record, he won election as a U.S. Senator in the fall of 1946.

Pearson followed Senatorial campaigns closely. He knew that McCarthy had upset Senator Robert M. La Follette in the Republican primary in Wisconsin partly by praising Stalin as a man of peace to encourage the Communist-controlled CIO in that state to knife Young Bob. In the general election McCarthy swung right to overwhelm a liberal Democrat with help from the Chicago

Tribune and its adjunct, American Action, Inc. From Pearson's point of view, La Follette Progressivism had been a liberating force in the country for forty-five years. He was prejudiced in advance against the opportunist who had killed it off.

Jack Anderson, less sophisticated politically, was attracted by the personal charm which was not the least of McCarthy's assets. The two men became friendly soon after McCarthy arrived in Washington in 1947. They double-dated on occasion. When Anderson married Olivia Farley, a former FBI employee, in 1949, the Senator was conspicuous at their wedding reception. On the theory that McCarthy was looking for a constructive legislative role, Anderson wrote a populist agricultural speech or two for him to deliver.

Pearson did not permit Anderson or anybody else to determine "Washington Merry-Go-Round" policy. He found fresh reasons to slap McCarthy, including association with White House wheeler-dealer John Maragon, running errands for the real estate lobby and cheating on his income taxes. He responded quickly in 1950 when McCarthy chose anti-Communism as a major issue and made his first charge about "205 members of the Communist Party . . . still working and shaping policy in the State Department." By meticulous checking, Pearson was able to show that the loyalty of only three persons on the McCarthy list could be questioned. Two had resigned from the State Department four years earlier. The third had never worked there.

After months of hearings a Senate subcommittee under Senator Millard Tydings (D–Md.) dismissed McCarthy's State Department charges as "a fraud and a hoax," but by then the Senator had found other situations to exploit. When the next Senatorial elections rolled around, McCarthy and the Washington *Times-Herald* helped to unseat Tydings, a conservative Democrat, in a campaign featuring a composite or false photograph of Tydings in company with Earl Browder. McCarthy's shadow lengthened as he took political revenge against other critics.

Public hysteria had been created by the Korean War, development of atomic weaponry by the Soviet Union and revelations of earlier Stalinist burrowing within the New Deal. McCarthy took advantage of it with the flamboyant callousness of a Huey Long.

Many liberals helped him by their cowardice. On the theory that anybody who had ever associated with a party-liner or held a pro-Soviet, pro-Chinese or pro-Socialist opinion was suspect, they disarmed themselves and left the country almost at the mercy of McCarthyism.

Unbothered by feelings of guilt, Pearson opened the column to the complaints of local and Wisconsin enemies of McCarthy. The response was overwhelming. For every sensation of the Senator, Pearson produced a countervailing personal exposé. In addition to being physically strong, with a reputation during his farm days for lifting a mule in his arms, the ham-handed McCarthy had a volcanic temperament. He told friends he was wondering "whether to kill Pearson or just maim him."

As Pearson related to the writer some time afterward, he had an intimation of personal danger as he stood in line at a Gridiron Club dinner and later at the Sulgrave Club.

> McCarthy came up beside me and snarled: "I'm going to break your arm. You've done me a lot of damage." Except for the tone of his voice I would have thought he was joking. I had just written a story of how he took $10,000 from a housing organization for a report a few pages long. It was obviously a concealed payment for his vote on the Banking and Currency Committee.
>
> Some time after that Joseph B. Keenan [a former Assistant U.S. Attorney General] telephoned saying he wanted to talk to me. He came by immediately. The night before he had been at Georgetown University when Joe McCarthy spoke to several others about mutilating me. The idea was to put me out of commission and make me an invalid for life. I told Joe Keenan I thought he was too much alarmed but I wrote a memo on the conversation.
>
> The Sulgrave Club incident took place on Dec. 13, 1950. Dec. 13 is ordinarily a lucky day for me because it is my birthday. Instead of giving me a birthday party my wife told me she was taking me to the club to a dinner being given by Mrs. Louise Ansberry. Nothing could have pleased me less. Mrs. Ansberry was noted for having a lot of punks at her dinner parties, particularly right-wing punks whom I did not like.
>
> On this occasion I found myself seated beside Mrs. William A. McCracken, whom I do like. Her husband was Assistant Secretary of Commerce for Air under Hoover. Across the table was another

man I like, Congressman Charlie Bennett of Florida, who had polio and uses crutches.

It was one of those supper-dance parties where people dance between courses. Joe McCarthy was sitting at the other end of the table next to my wife. He told her he was going to make a speech attacking me the next day which would cause a divorce in the family. During an intermission he came down to my end of the table and told me the same thing, that he was going to put me out of business with a speech on the Senate floor and that there would be nothing left of me professionally or otherwise when he had finished. I listened for some time. Then I said: "Joe, have you paid your income taxes yet?"

He got very sore and challenged me to come outside. Charlie Bennett, the cripple, held on to me. Bill McCracken came by and restrained McCarthy. Nothing happened. I spent the rest of the evening dancing with Mrs. McCracken, who was indignant over the incident, having listened to a good part of it.

As the party broke up I went downstairs to check out my overcoat. McCarthy came up halfway behind me and pinned my arms down on each side. He claimed afterward I had my hand in my side pocket getting a gun. Actually I had a hole in my pants pocket which my wife had forgotten to mend so I was keeping change in the coat pocket. He proceeded to kick me in the groin with his knee. Richard Nixon came up and pulled us apart. As he did so McCarthy took a swing at my left ear which landed but not with any damaging effect. Nixon had some pacifying words to say that we shouldn't embarrass our hostess. I picked up my coat and left, keeping a wary eye to my rear. . . .

McCarthy denied using his knee. He slapped rather than punched, he said. "I never saw a man slapped so hard," Nixon told his biographer, Ralph de Toledano. "If I hadn't pulled McCarthy away, he might have killed Pearson."

Pearson taunted him at the dinner table, McCarthy declared. "He said the column had more circulation than the *Congressional Record*. If I made my speech, he said, he would go after me, adding: 'I haven't gone after a man yet that I haven't got in the end.' "

McCarthy delayed his speech by twenty-four hours. A friendly fellow Senator, he said on the Senate floor, had warned him: "Don't do it, McCarthy. It will be like standing in the mouth of the Cloaca Maxima and trying to stop the flow. You will be inundated by slime and he will go on every day polluting the airwaves."

After this delicate opening the Senator described Pearson as "the diabolically clever voice of international Communism," a "Moscow-directed character-assassin," a "journalistic fake and prostitute," a "degenerate liar" and a "twisted, perverted mentality." There was an odd sexual flavor to many of the epithets. McCarthy hinted at scandal in Pearson's boyhood—something treated more explicitly by Senator Dodd eighteen years later—but the speech did not lead Mrs. Pearson to file for divorce.

Conceding that the columnist was not a Communist Party member, McCarthy charged that "one of Pearson's No. 1 jobs" was to "destroy Chiang Kai-shek . . . and create Red China." A special assignment from Stalin, he said, was to control the flow of information to the American public. The public took the charges seriously, pro or con; nobody was capable of impartiality during the McCarthy era. Such a sensible gentleman as Senator Ralph Flanders (R–Vt.) became so upset over McCarthy's gabble about mass infiltration of the State Department by homosexuals that he made comments about McCarthy's supposed sexual interest in his own male staff members.

Whether Joe McCarthy believed his own charges is debatable. Richard Rovere, an authority on the subject, maintained that the Senator was a thug who fell short as a revolutionary because he did not take himself seriously enough. He did intend to destroy Pearson. He sent copies of his opening and later Senate speeches to "Washington Merry-Go-Round" subscribers in a not particularly effective drive to induce cancellations. By threatening a patriotic boycott of sponsors he forced Pearson off network radio. Among his Congressional allies and journalistic flunkies he created the atmosphere of a lynching bee.

Back in World War II a Southern Congressman named Ned Patton, annoyed over Pearson's criticism of General George S. Patton—no relative—waved a knife beerily under the columnist's nose in the House restaurant. Representative Maury Maverick (D–Tex.) came along just in time to divert his unsteady colleague. There had been no subsequent physical gestures against Pearson on Capitol Hill.

A couple of weeks after the Sulgrave Club incident Pearson encountered in the Mayflower Hotel lobby Charles Patrick Clark, $100,000-a-year lobbyist for Franco Spain. Furious over stories that he had paid off Senator Owen Brewster of Maine and Representative Eugene Keogh of New York, Clark unleashed a wild one-two punch which floored Pearson. Clark was fined $25 in court for assault. Overnight he received more than $400 in small cash gifts from McCarthy admirers who urged: "Hit him again for me!" A favorite Congressional joke was that a license to slug Pearson could be obtained for only $25—which was a bargain!

George E. Sokolsky, a right-wing counterpart of Walter Lippmann, wrote anti-Pearson speeches for McCarthy. (It may have been Sokolsky who coined "left-wing mockingbird" as an epithet for Pearson.) A dozen other conspicuous publicists were inspired by McCarthy to try their controversial skills against Pearson.

Fulton Lewis, Jr. was a nuisance because he had a five-day-a-week radio program on top of a syndicated Washington newspaper column and a Washington newsletter called *Exclusive*, but Westbrook Pegler and Walter Winchell were the most persistent and troublesome. Using three dots in a way which made his sentences sound more disjointed than they actually were, Winchell went yippety-yap in print and on the air at Pearson, who had once been his ally:

> Everybody makes mistakes . . . but this S.O.B. makes a racket, a business, a mint of money writing fiction in the guise of news reporting. . . . We have known him a long time. . . . We started playing "lose me" when we wearied of his tantrums and demands that we assist him in assassinating politicians and others who stepped on his toes. . . . We kept playing "lose me" when we learned from the public prints that at one time or another his staff included Pinkos and Reds who were scared away by the blinding light of pub-louse-ity.

Pegler conveyed menace in long, rumbling sentences:

> I cannot substantiate McCarthy's charge that Pearson conducts his lying campaign from Moscow but I do urge those who have confidence in my work and my integrity to resist the campaign to discredit McCarthy and thus to whitewash Pearson . . . a slippery

devious fellow absolutely insensitive to the inhibitions of truth and ethics as I intend to prove if he ever brings to trial a suit which he filed for the purpose of muzzling me in my determined campaign to expose him and break his sinister power.

Though he ignored Winchell, Pearson brought several lawsuits against Pegler. The first one asked $25,000 in damages when Pegler, who was too shy for radio, called him a "miscalled newscaster specializing in falsehoods." He withdrew that suit when Pegler made a reluctant apology under pressure from his syndicate. He filed a second suit, this time for $500,000, after Pegler called him several varieties of blackguard and liar.

By 1951 Pearson felt vulnerable. He was by no means alone in fighting McCarthy, but he occupied the most isolated spot in Washington. To many observers it seemed that if he faltered and fell, an antidemocratic tide would sweep across the country. For public-relations reasons more than anything else, he brought a $5.1-million suit against Joe McCarthy, Westbrook Pegler and nine others for conspiracy to drive him out of business.

Lewis, whom Pearson had rocked with disclosure of a document from Spain describing him in 1940 as "an admirer of Hitler," was still bothersome enough to be included in the suit. So were the Washington *Times-Herald* and a former *Times-Herald* city editor named Morris Bealle, who had investigated Pearson for McCarthy. Once again Winchell, to his fury, was ignored.

A loose conspiracy to ruin Pearson did exist, but it was difficult, almost impossible, to prove. Some of the defendants in the suit did not know each other. Nevertheless, publicity over the case and its pretrial hearings kept McCarthy under pressure until his fate could be settled in the natural arena of Congress.

Eugene Meyer of the Washington *Post* and Dorothy Schiff of the New York *Post* sharply aligned their newspapers against the Wisconsin demagogue. The *New York Times*, the St. Louis *Post-Dispatch*, other publications and a wide range of liberal writers and radio-TV personalities like Elmer Davis and Ed Murrow joined in a campaign to stop what was considered to be a totalitarian movement. In fact, McCarthy hesitated and then backed away from overt fascist tactics like organizing uniformed storm troopers on the Hitler model.

Before and after his election as President in 1952, General Eisenhower felt obliged to make concessions to Joe McCarthy. Meanwhile, Senate Majority Leader Lyndon Johnson was waiting for the Republicans to take the lead in disciplining their party's leading maverick. Despite the bipartisan temporizing, Pearson never let up. He followed McCarthy relentlessly, and he anointed with praise every new head raised in opposition to the Senator.

To discourage direct or indirect violence against himself, Pearson printed the warning from former Assistant U.S. Attorney General Keenan. Though Keenan promptly repudiated his own confidential tip, the story served as a form of protection. Pearson also gave Anderson time off from his column duties to write a book-length exposé of McCarthy in collaboration with Ronald W. May, a United Press reporter from Wisconsin.

Anderson made available his files, including dubious unpublished material, to Hank Greenspun, the crusading publisher of the Las Vegas *Sun*, whom McCarthy by a slip of the tongue had called "ex-Communist" when he apparently meant "ex-convict." The Las Vegas *Sun* comments on McCarthy were so shocking, according to the Denver *Post*, "that nobody dared to utter them above a whisper."

Publication in the "Washington Merry-Go-Round" of exclusive details about the favoritism shown by the Army to David Schine, a rich hotel man's son and intimate of Roy Cohn, counsel to Senator McCarthy's Senate Investigating Committee, helped to bring the struggle to a focus. When McCarthy tried to brazen out his blackmail of the defense establishment to such small purpose, President Eisenhower decided on a test of strength over the integrity of the country's military forces. As soon as the President's followers swung into action, Lyndon Johnson led the Democrats in a belated charge up, down and around Capitol Hill. Joseph Welch stripped McCarthy of pretensions during nationally televised committee hearings and it was all over—except for the shouting.

The reversal of opinion was exemplified by Senator Arthur Watkins (R–Utah). After the Sulgrave Club incident he had wired Joe McCarthy, noting that there were two newspaper versions as to where Pearson was hit—and he hoped both were right. Yet it was Watkins, four years later, who chaired the committee recommending Senatorial censure of McCarthy.

Once repudiated by his colleagues, McCarthy had no political future. He ceased to be newsworthy. More and more he stayed by himself, drinking. Shortly before he died of cirrhosis of the liver in the spring of 1957 he phoned Pearson, to whom he had not spoken since the encounter at the Sulgrave Club. The Senator wanted to explain that he had put into the *Congressional Record* a "Merry-Go-Round" analysis of the double-cross of Israel over the Gulf of Aqaba and the Gaza Strip.

"I haven't always agreed with your column," said McCarthy in historic understatement, "but in this case I'm sure it's completely accurate. I'm telling you in advance what I've done so you won't faint."

Reporting this in a columnar obituary after McCarthy's death, Pearson suggested that the Senator must have been haunted by those whose lives he had destroyed with false charges. He added:

> I suppose no one newspaperman suffered more economically than I did from Joe McCarthy, but I felt sorry for Joe in these latter years. He had been so famous once. He was so lonely later. . . .
>
> I'm afraid Joe wanted to die. He would not have stuck to his diet of whiskey had he wanted to live. . . . Had he been content to be just another Senator he might have undone the harm he did and become a Senator who truly deserved fame.

3

Controversies in Congress or elsewhere in the national capital tend to creep into the White House. The President faces inevitable pressure to intervene in any local quarrel. If he takes an open, or even a concealed, stand, it is usually with decisive effect. Thus Drew Pearson made no great headway in his long campaign against James V. Forrestal until the Defense Secretary gambled on a Dewey victory in the 1948 presidential election. When the mentally troubled Forrestal balked at resigning after losing his electoral gamble, Pearson received a green light, and perhaps some backstage assistance, from President Truman in a renewed columnar barrage which led to Forrestal's ouster and death.

Pearson got the Indian sign on Forrestal back in 1944 when Franklin D. Roosevelt was finishing his third term. Forrestal, then Under Secretary of the Navy, brought Frank Knox, the Navy Secretary; William C. Bullitt, former Ambassador to France and Russia; and Admiral Ernest King with him to the White House to present proof that Pearson had bribed a Navy clerk to get classified information.

FDR roared with laughter at the idea of prosecuting the columnist. "We've got Pearson!" he said, putting the papers into his office safe. "From now on, he'll be my hatchet man!"

Two weeks later the "Washington Merry-Go-Round" began with these arresting words: "Very few people knew of an incident which occurred a little more than a year ago at Forrestal's Georgetown mansion—but the President did!" Forrestal's guests at that time, he said, included Presidential Adviser Bernard Baruch, Assistant Secretary of War Robert Patterson and "one or two" high-ranking Army officers critical of civilian control over the War Production Board.

The deliberations of this "Council of War," continued Pearson, were overheard. Charles E. Wilson, Vice Chairman of the WPB, had a new listening device developed by the General Electric Corporation, of which he had formerly been president, which could "pick up conversations as far as three miles away" without requiring a microphone in the room under surveillance.

With the help of this miraculous device, it seemed, Wilson heard Baruch "taking some rough raps at his old pal, FDR. As Baruch is deaf, the others talked in rather loud voices, among them Forrestal, who gave out his share of presidential criticism. In fact, the criticism of the Commander-in-Chief was so vigorous that Wilson and Donald Nelson [WPB Chairman] took a transcript to the White House."

After listening to the record, according to the columnar account, President Roosevelt placed it in his safe, chortling: "Now we've got them where we need them! They'll have to do what we want."

Wilson denied knowing about the existence of any such device. In what was supposed to be a retraction, delivered on the air as well as in print, Pearson said the purpose of his account had been to emphasize that President Roosevelt "forgave" Forrestal for his disloyalty. Since Wilson did not object to the part about a report on the Forrestal meeting reaching the President, the implication was that somebody, somehow, did inform FDR about the "Council of War."

Forrestal had to absorb the unsettling news that he was less secure at the White House than he had supposed. More devastating was the fact that FDR reacted identically in two instances. Could Pearson have been told what happened during the Forrestal appeal and shifted the dialogue to the Wilson-Nelson appeal? Could Roosevelt and Pearson be toying with him? Forrestal could not answer these disturbing questions. Without the answers he was psychologically unprepared to sue Pearson when the latter raised a false accusation of personal cowardice against him.

President Roosevelt needed James Forrestal and other conservative recruits from Wall Street to give a bipartisan flavor to the war effort, but he had no illusions about them. Forrestal was less essential in his scheme of things than Drew Pearson. Back in his first term FDR had learned that (a) any prosecution of the columnist would be interpreted as an infringement on the freedom of the press; and (b) efforts to knock out Pearson by proxy (through somebody like General MacArthur) were unlikely to succeed. Thereafter he had been making use of Pearson in his own intricate fashion.

According to the diaries of Secretary of Interior Harold L. Ickes, Roosevelt was willing occasionally to provide Pearson with damaging exclusives on politically disloyal members of his administration, such as Vice President John N. Garner and Postmaster James A. Farley. When one of those worthies complained, the President would denounce the columnist privately for irresponsibility or hint that this or that other cabinet member might have been responsible for the leak.

"Washington Merry-Go-Round" items about which FDR openly complained were usually trivial: a statement, for example, that he shouted in 1944 from a Hyde Park voting booth, "This damned thing don't work." He never said "don't," he pointed out. "That was ungrammatical; I said 'doesn't.'"

Early in 1944 the column carried secret letters received by FDR the previous July from William Phillips, the President's temporary personal representative in India. Ambassador Phillips had informed Roosevelt that his speeches and the Atlantic Charter had inflamed India's desire to be free; that the Indians were increasingly restive under British rule; and that their restiveness hampered American military efforts in that part of the world. A pledge that independence would be granted after the war, the Ambassador reported, was likely to throw thousands of additional Indian soldiers into the war.

After completing his mission Phillips had returned to Europe as political aide to General Dwight D. Eisenhower, Supreme Allied Commander. A few months later Phillips was dropped from that post as *persona non grata* to the British. Roosevelt was annoyed at British Prime Minister Churchill's retaliation over Phillips' suggestion about India. He considered officious Churchill's objections to the renomination of Henry A. Wallace as Vice President because he had taken an anti-British stance, or the appointment of politician Edward J. Flynn as U.S. Ambassador to Australia. Though Wallace and Flynn were dumped by the White House, relations between the British and American war leaders were at a temporary low.

Churchill bellowed like the caricature of the John Bull he resembled when the "Washington Merry-Go-Round" carried the Phillips letters and the reason for Phillips' demotion. Churchill could not challenge the authenticity of the columnar material, but he could and did ask President Roosevelt to locate and punish the person responsible for the leak.

What happened next was high comedy: The President had distributed twenty copies of the letters among top advisers. He requested that each copy be returned to the White House within twenty-four hours. The missing copy, presumably, would point to the culprit. Surprisingly, twenty-nine copies were received! An American investigation began, at which Pearson, as chief witness, testified he got the letters "from an Indian." His memory could not be stimulated beyond this vague phrase.

British intelligence, the best in the world, came to the rescue in a sticky situation. It confirmed that an unnamed Indian military attaché had been sent home from Washington, assigned to

front-line war duty and killed in action. Though the British inquiry had not been pushed to the hilt, the British seemed suddenly
anxious to forget the whole incident. Had they learned the real
source of the leak?

No columnist could stay in business if he revealed the origin
of an exclusive of such magnitude, yet vanity required an invisible
signature of some kind on the exploit. Pearson claimed to have
Indian blood. He was an expert on Indian lore. Since the President of the United States was the Great White Father of all the
Indian tribes, wasn't it reasonable from Pearson's point of view
to refer to him as an Indian, in fact *the* Indian? *Of course it was,*
concluded the astute Washington grapevine, closing the case.

4

Because of political bias, Pearson bore down more heavily on
Republican than on Democratic Presidents. Around the time of
the publication of the Phillips letters, he was queried by one
of his editors about a rumor that President Roosevelt was critically
ill. By careful checking, Pearson established that the President had
been scheduled for a serious operation but that the operation had
been put off because of a worsening heart condition. He did not
write the story. Had he done so, there might have been no fourth
Roosevelt term.

In contrast with this defensible restraint, Pearson created an
unnecessary sensation in 1956 by reporting a collapse of President
Eisenhower on the campaign trail. He was contradicted at every
turn. *Time* magazine described him as "more irresponsible than
Walter Winchell," a charge which Winchell promptly enlarged
upon by producing a whole column of abuse of Pearson. Lamely,
Pearson told friends that he had exaggerated a tip out of a feeling
that Eisenhower's health, after a heart attack and intestinal sur-
gery, was not adequate for a second term. A private remark to him
by the President that he intended to serve only one term had also
stuck in his mind, he said.

General Eisenhower "lost his head and heart to a British
WAC" during the Second World War, was talked out of getting
a divorce by General Omar Bradley, and was yanked home from

Europe by President Truman to terminate the affair, Pearson wrote on one occasion. On the other hand, after Harry Truman displayed a brace of dueling pistols in a side drawer of his desk in the White House and promised to use them if he saw any more false stories in the "Washington Merry-Go-Round" about his wife, Bess, and his daughter, Margaret, Pearson ceased to write about Truman's family.

No President was more humiliated by Drew Pearson than John F. Kennedy. This intellectually arrogant man forced himself in the spring of 1960 to make a pilgrimage to the columnist's office-home in Georgetown in search of an endorsement for the Democratic nomination for President. Pearson received him courteously —and came out for Lyndon Johnson!

Pearson could not easily separate John Kennedy from his younger brother Bobby, who twice worked for and never repudiated Joe McCarthy, and their father, Joseph P. Kennedy, an unscrupulous economic royalist and former isolationist who had put friends and fortune at the disposition of the family political ambition. Pearson inclined to the view that the Kennedys as a group were more dangerous than McCarthy, though he respected John for his intelligence and for some gestures he made in the field of foreign policy.

On his part President Kennedy tried to keep the difficult columnist at arm's length. Except for the curiosity he showed about Pearson's exploratory talks with Nikita Khrushchev in 1961 and 1963, the President avoided Pearson in person. Columnar requests for information were referred to one of the three S's— Schlesinger, Sorensen and Salinger. If the request was deemed reasonable, it was fulfilled in routine fashion.

At any moment a "Merry-Go-Round" bomb was likely to rock the White House. One column would recall nostalgically that Joe Kennedy, the President's father, acted as a "bagman" for his father-in-law, the corrupt Mayor John F. (Honey Fitz) Fitzgerald of Boston when Joe was a Harvard student. If that seemed impossibly long ago, a subsequent column might come sharply up to date by blaming John Kennedy's Catholicism for current increases in American military assistance to a Catholic puppet regime in South Vietnam.

A series of columns which excessively annoyed the sensitive man in the White House dealt with Peter Lawford, the Hollywood actor who had married John's sister Patricia. In view of his professional prominence, Lawford resented persistent press identification of himself as the President's brother-in-law. Since he came frequently without advance notice to see Jack and Jackie at the White House—"unshaven, sockless and in sandals"—he had been turned away at least once by Secret Service men as a suspicious character.

On an airplane trip to Florida, Lawford was snubbed by John and flared up at the President in return, according to the "Merry-Go-Round." On another occasion Lawford was rebuked for teaching young Caroline Kennedy a parody of a nursery rhyme: "There was a little girl / Who had a little curl; / She slipped on the grass / And fell on her ass." The very sight of Lawford "bored the President to tears," the column declared in an oblique understatement of the tension between the two men.

With four children after a decade of marriage, the Lawfords were separated and headed for divorce. This would be the first divorce in the very Catholic family of Joseph P. Kennedy. Since it would embarrass the whole family and particularly Patricia's brother in the White House, every effort was being made to keep the situation under cover and postpone any decisive action.

"Now that Peter and Pat are having a tough time," John F. Kennedy told Paul B. Faye, Jr., a nonpolitical friend from Navy days who later quoted the remark in a book of reminiscences, the "Merry-Go-Round" columns were "just plain cruel. Here I am, President of the United States, and I can't do anything to stop Drew Pearson."

Because of Pearson's presumptuous use of his power, White House occupants called him names with bipartisan lavishness. At least four Presidents described him as various kinds of a liar, but the only epithet which lodged under his skin was a traditionally American, biologically impossible and faintly humorous insult applied by a Democratic President with whom he ended on friendly terms.

"No S.O.B. like Pearson," snapped President Truman in reply to suggestions that he fire his bumbling military aide, General

Harry H. Vaughan, "is going to prevail on me to discharge anyone by some smart-aleck statement over the air."

In the disproportionate excitement aroused by this remark, Pearson tried to be insouciant. The initials, he said, stood for Servant of Brotherhood. "S.O.B.," replied Truman scornfully, "is as simple as A.B.C." In an effort to disinfect the phrase in the way he had disinfected "muckraker" by flaunting it, Pearson wrote a series of three articles for the *Saturday Evening Post* under the title "Confessions of an S.O.B.," but the obloquy persisted. Every new antagonist threw *le mot Truman* in his face.

Toward the close of his life Pearson agreed to write his biography under a title devised by Joseph Borkin, a former Department of Justice official who was one of his friends: "Memoirs of an S.O.B." He never got around to writing the book. According to Borkin, a letter addressed to "The S.O.B."—with no name, street address or even "Washington, D.C." on the envelope—was duly delivered to the controversialist's office-home in the Georgetown section of Washington.

Pearson's aggressive indiscretion in dealing with public officials and his accumulation of personal problems had gradually tightened the screws on his nerves. He could no longer relax at his Georgetown office-home. The only place where he could still rest, he said, was his large and lovely working farm in Potomac, Maryland, eighteen miles northwest of Washington. He wanted to be buried out there, he announced, under the inscription "Here Lies an S.O.B.," but he failed to make the necessary arrangements.

CHAPTER III

The Young Lion

DREW PEARSON'S FONDNESS for farming dated back to boyhood. Starting when he was nine or ten, he spent a number of summers on Kansas farms belonging to various cousins. These were visits classified as vacations, but he worked because it was the thing to do and he could do it well. He earned his keep and received a token dollar or two at the close of each season.

Naturally sturdy and outgoing, he throve on the outdoor life. He made friends with the livestock. He accepted the ammoniac odor of manure as part of the warm, friendly atmosphere of the barn. He loved the smell of hay. Harnessing a horse and driving a horse and buggy with milk to the main house early in the morning before the dew was off the grass he found an exhilarating experience.

Drew's tasks fell within the limits of his strength and enthusiasm. In picking strawberries for the table it was understood that he could eat as many as he chose. He picked up potatoes until he tired. Gradually, he learned to do his share of the milking, to weed in the family garden with one knee on a potato sack for protection. He hoed corn with farm hands who went down the rows together and paused at the end of each row to hitch up their pants and joke a little. They acted gingerly with this relative of the boss until

40

they realized he could be relied upon not to talk about what he heard.

Acceptance by grownups was a heady satisfaction in itself. Intrigued by the endless farm talk of buying and selling, Drew made an investment, the first of his life, in what could be called an agricultural growth industry. With money from home he purchased a pregnant sow.

This profit-laden animal, he was told, would cost nothing to maintain since garbage was available for food. It would eventually produce up to a dozen piglets, each worth a handsome price at market, and he would still have the sow. His stock, unfortunately, did not live up to expectations. It produced fewer piglets than it should, ate half of them, rolled on the rest and had to be given away because by this time its youthful owner was back East in Illinois, unable to locate a suitable purchaser.

Drew's farm experiences had indirect nonfinancial benefits. The solid diet, the deep nights of sleep and the sweaty daily exercise in those sun-drenched Midwestern fields—on top of his robust constitution—combined to give him the physical basis for sailing through crises which overwhelm lesser men. Summers in Kansas also brought the boy into contact with family traditions dating back to prerevolutionary days.

Through Andrew Jackson Cameron, his great-grandfather on the Pearson side, he was, he learned, named after President Jackson. On his mother's, the Wolfe, side, he could claim Indian blood. The Wolfes had settled in the Midwest in 1730. Back about the time they founded Fort Olentangy, which became Columbus, Ohio, one of their females was captured by an Indian chief and returned later to the whites with a half-Indian son.

The anecdote fascinated Drew. When he attended his first Wolfe family reunion at Parsons, Kansas, at the age of eight, he fully expected to see braves in regalia. To his disappointment, none appeared. Even so, he was sufficiently impressed by the legend of consanguinity to become an expert on Indian lore as an adult.

Family reunions were an important part of the frontier tradition, for self-protection and reassurance in a largely hostile country. The Wolfes, mostly French in origin, adhered to the tradition as strongly as the Cameron-Pearsons, who were of Scots, English and German stock.

Both families were long-lived as well as large. Grandpa Morris Wolfe and Grandpa Samuel Pearson each had eleven brothers and sisters, most of them still visible when Drew was a boy. Grandpa Wolfe lived to be eighty-six and Grandpa Pearson to be seventy-six. During his first trip to Kansas, Drew met his great-grandfather and namesake, Andrew Jackson Cameron, who lived to be ninety-seven. From him he heard anecdotes about General Jackson's exploits during the siege of New Orleans in the War of 1812 and an account of the footrace which Andrew Jackson Cameron's mother —when she was one hundred!—ran with her own daughter. The mother lost the race and out of humiliation, it was said, died three years later.

Those who attended the family reunions counted on enjoying themselves, boasting a little, exchanging experiences and anecdotes, getting help if they needed it. At that first Wolfe family reunion attended by Drew, Grandpa Wolfe noticed that his daughter Edna looked thin and tired. He knew her husband went out every summer on the lecture trail and that her son Leon had been left home with one of his usual colds.

Concluding that the rambunctious Drew and his sickly brother were too great a drain on his daughter's strength during the summertime, Grandpa Wolfe arranged for Drew to come the following summer to the farm of his brother Charles near Ottawa, Kansas. This was a large farm, so profitable that Charles had acquired the first automobile ever seen in Ottawa.

Through similar negotiations Drew was later installed on farms of other relatives near Cherryvale and Humboldt. He learned to make trips back and forth from the East by himself. "I started to travel young," he said later in life, "and I've been on the go ever since."

Family influences on the personality of an individual are as diverse and hard to disentangle as the influences in and out of the White House on a single presidential decision. Nevertheless, Drew's paternal grandparents in Kansas, Samuel and Ellen Cameron Pearson, taught him some things about business and personal morality which stuck in his mind.

Grandpa Pearson was a farmer who to escape attacks of asthma left the soil to tend store in Cherryvale, Kansas, and later in Osa-watomie, Kansas, which John Brown made famous. Samuel lost his store in Cherryvale, as well as his home, because he stubbornly honored his $10,000 note to underwrite construction of a hotel which failed, though the note's four cosigners put their property in their wives' names to escape their share of the debt. In Osawa-tomie he persisted in selling groceries to scabs during a strike and was boycotted out of business by the union. In each case he made a comeback.

Grandma Pearson was a Methodist of such probity that she used no brandy in her mincemeat. Her list of deadly sins included dancing and playing cards. She did not permit her husband to smoke in the house. If Samuel wanted to smoke, he could always go down to the barbershop. He was not permitted to open his store on Sundays, though his competitors did.

Even in the formidable presence of Samuel and Ellen Pearson, Drew was not invariably tractable. His father, Paul, had to be informed by mail that the boy had done some skylarking in the store and had reacted violently to a threat of physical punish-ment.

"Be careful with yourself," Paul wrote Edna in response to complaints that her son got on her nerves. As a partial solution he added: "Lock Drew up for half a day."

Samuel's quickness awed Drew. At home one day somebody hurriedly closed a drawer on a mouse. Reopening the drawer, Grandpa Pearson caught the mouse in his hand as it jumped. (He could swat a fly on the wing!) At home and at the office he told broad, hilarious stories. Some relatives argued that anybody living with Ellen needed a sense of humor to survive; others accused him of buying a jokebook.

In between jokes Samuel expressed a cracker-barrel philosophy based on his experiences. To explain his selling to all comers at the store, strike or no strike, he said: "It's a free country, isn't it?" Without blaming those cosigners who had left him in the lurch, he formulated a primary business maxim: "Never endorse any-body's note." Having never gone beyond third grade in school and having married a woman without money, the otherwise extremely estimable Ellen Cameron, Samuel urged his son Paul and later his grandson Drew to acquire education and a well-to-do wife.

"Be sure to marry for love," he said, "but marry the girl that's got the money!" Both Paul and Drew obeyed this golden rule.

2

Paul Martin Pearson, Drew's father, was a short, round-faced fellow who in repose was believed to look like Napoleon. He was rarely in repose. His burbling friendliness concealed an invincible determination to get ahead according to the paternal plan. He worked his way through Baker University in Kansas by peddling popcorn balls made by his mother to train passengers while the locomotives took on water. With help from his father he earned money by staging recitals and entertainments. He was a senior at Baker when he noticed a shy freshman named Edna Wolfe and decided to marry her.

A thin blue-eyed girl wearing thick blond hair in long braids down her back, Edna was almost as tall as Paul. She dressed distinctively, drifted through her courses at the university and showed some talent for poetry and painting. Neither she nor her well-to-do father, Dr. Morris Wolfe, a balding, bearded six-footer who had been the first dentist in territory which became Oklahoma and who had branched out into business since coming to Kansas, was impressed at first by the talkative youngster from Osawatomie.

Dr. Wolfe was unobtrusively Jewish. There were not many Jews in the Midwest in those days. Synagogues were almost unknown. As a Methodist Ellen Pearson was not sure what her proper reaction to a Jew should be. She neither encouraged nor discouraged her son's preference, but he received covert support from his father. Before Edna's graduation from Baker University, Paul proposed. Partly perhaps for religious reasons, since he was serving as a Methodist minister in an East Kansas circuit of small communities, Edna turned him down.

Paul was not one to let small obstacles stand in the way of his purpose. With Edna's approval, he gave up preaching and enrolled for graduate study at the School of Speech in Northwestern University, Evanston, Illinois, then the mecca for aspiring lecturers from all over the country. He tutored students and filled overnight speaking engagements to defray his expenses, while continuing his courtship by mail and an occasional visit. Two years later, when he was teaching elocution and English at Northwestern, he and Edna were married.

Andrew (long for "Drew") Pearson arrived in Evanston during a blizzard on Monday evening, December 13, 1897. His middle name of Russell, which he later discarded, was the maiden name of Dr. Wolfe's wife Abigail.

According to his father's diary, Drew was a "lusty child—if one were to judge from his first cry." Active and healthy, he seemed to have that excess energy that psychologists call drive. His favorite diversion was being hauled across a room on a small rug, gesturing and crowing like a miniature demagogue. Drew was a regular lion, said his father, who referred to him at times as "the lion."

A second son, Leon Morris Pearson, was born twenty-two months later. Edna, her doctor revealed, had been in trouble during both births and would probably be unable to bear any more children. For the next decade she was rarely well and often a semi-invalid.

Leon was small and frail, gentle and intuitive and talented in his mother's image. During his early years he stumbled from one physical handicap to another. When whooping cough invaded the neighborhood, he almost died from it, whereas Drew had only a mild case. Next Leon contracted spinal meningitis. For a week it looked as if he would not pull through. When he did recover, his right arm was partially paralyzed for a while, and shrunken. The disability put him at a disadvantage with other children. On the surface, at least, there was no sibling rivalry. From the beginning Leon looked to Drew for comfort, protection and direction.

Because Leon saw apparitions at night, Edna slept in a room with him, while Paul slept in a room with Drew. Awaking on farm schedule, Paul would be greeted with childish cries of "Tares, tares!"—Drew's early word for "stories." Paul's morning stories at home were more dramatic and colloquial than his Bible readings at Sunday school. Drew never tired of hearing about the journey of the Three Wise Men on their camels through the desert in search of the newborn Christ. When he grew up, the boy vowed, he would become a camel driver.

Paul also read nursery rhymes and poetry. Since Drew was not invariably obedient, the first reading which remained in his memory was a poem from James Whitcomb Riley's *Little Claude* book:

> When Little Claude was naughty wunst
> At dinner-time, an' said
> He won't say "Thank you" to his Ma,
> She maked him go to bed
> An' stay two hours an' not git up—
> So when the clock struck Two,
> Nen Claude says, "Thank you, Mr. Clock,
> I'm much obleeged to you!"

Across Maple Place in Evanston lived the family of a younger brother of Paul named Andrew Cameron Pearson. This additional namesake of President Jackson was known as Uncle Drew. He had two pretty daughters—Dorothy and Josephine—in the Drew-Leon age range, and the four children played together.

The difference in temperament between Drew and Leon was illustrated when Uncle Drew purchased a Russian wolfhound named Czar. At first sight of this huge lovely dog, Drew shouted in delight and rode it like a horse. It wasn't a camel, but it would serve! Leon, however, cowered in such fear of the dog that Czar broke into a fury of barking at him.

Drew was not immune to peril. At the age of three or four he dressed as Santa Claus for a Christmas party at his uncle's house. His flimsy costume ignited from a candle on the tree. While Dorothy and Josephine screamed and Leon stood petrified, Uncle Drew rolled the boy in a rug and smothered the flames.

The ever-ambitious Paul Pearson took the family from Evanston to Cambridge, Massachusetts, in the fall of 1901 so he could enroll for postgraduate study at Harvard. To defray family expenses, he tutored students and lectured indefatigably on the side. One day he took Drew to see the Bostwick Circus in Boston. This eye-opening experience forced the boy to revise his boyhood ambition of becoming a camel driver. On close acquaintance camels proved to be such shaggy and smelly beasts! It might be better, Drew decided, to become a clown in a circus.

On the basis of his Harvard training Paul received an offer from Swarthmore College, a Quaker institution in Pennsylvania, to

teach English and public speaking as an assistant professor at
$1,200 a year. Because of the rank and the prospect of tenure, he
felt obliged to accept, though the salary was not high. For protec-
tive coloration he decided to join the Society of Friends.

The prospect of a more settled existence in Swarthmore pleased
Edna, but she fretted over the kind of social life she would find
among the austere Quakers and, by implication, how she would
be received as a Jew in that closed campus atmosphere. Despite
the reassurances of her husband, her doubts deepened. She decided
to take the boys for a visit to her parents in Kansas.

The fall term had already begun, and Paul's colleagues at
Swarthmore kept asking about the absent Edna. Rumors spread
through the family that she might not return East at all. Marriages,
however, did not dissolve easily in those days. After Paul had
rented a house, remodeled and refurbished it even to the installation of bookshelves, and hired a housekeeper, his wife and sons rejoined him. They all became Quakers.

3

Drew Pearson was reared in the belief that he owed a debt to his
parents and to humanity. His mother had risked her life and
damaged her health in bringing him into the world. He could repay her by taking care of his brother. His father had labored to the
limits of his strength to raise a family on a small college salary. He
could repay his father by displaying the same kind of industry and
good character.

Drew tried to meet the family requirements. He cherished his
brother. He was rarely idle as a boy, and as an adult he usually
worked sixteen hours a day. When he came to write his share of
the hurriedly produced book which first brought him to public
attention—*Washington Merry-Go-Round*—he mentioned no fewer
than three times, each time with wonder and respect, that Dwight
Morrow's father, as president of Marshall College, had raised five
children on a salary of $2,400 a year.

Paul Pearson believed that a man could do anything he wanted
if he tried hard enough. Edna was endlessly inquisitive. She always wanted to know why people said what they said and why they

did what they did. The family was so close that Drew absorbed his father's idealism and his mother's curiosity.

Swarthmore turned out to be a nice town to grow up in. Drew was shy at first. When visitors came to the house, he hid behind his mother's skirts. Several years later, when he and Leon took to selling butter and eggs to the neighbors, he would ring the doorbell and step aside to let Leon deliver the sales pitch. Nevertheless, he could become obstinate or truculent without warning when his feelings were aroused.

Drew and Leon liked school. They conformed to the meditative customs of the Quiet People. They enjoyed the literary flavor of life in their Swarthmore home. James Whitcomb Riley and other writers celebrated in Paul's standard lectures on "American Poets," "American Dramatists" and "American Humorists" had become family friends. When the Whitney brothers, the best quartet on the Lyceum, came for a visit, the two boys would insist on a private rendition of the musical version of their favorite Eugene Field verse:

> I'm a beautiful red, red drum,
>   And I train with the soldier boys;
> As up the street we come,
>   Wonderful is the noise!

After supper one evening Edmund Vance Cook was asked by Leon how to write poetry. "That's easy," said Cook, "*you* start with something and *I'll* keep going." Leon started with "I'll be glad when Christmas comes," and Cook kept going: "With its trumpets and its drums,/With cakes and sugar plums. . . ." Thereafter Leon wrote verse.

The sons of faculty members who were also Quakers came into contact with each other naturally through a series of close-knit organizations. Drew and Leon became Knights of Nottingham Forest. Drew was large enough for his age to qualify as Little John. Unfortunately, Robin Hood's Merry Men were dispossessed from their headquarters, an empty house, so that it could be converted into a new home for the college president.

The Pearsons were invited to a formal dinner at the home of Dean and Mrs. A. A. Wright. All went well until their host made a clumsy joke about the eviction of the Knights from the president's home. Drew stiffened and blurted that the beefsteak on his plate was "tough as elephant meat." Was he changing the subject or talking in the authentic voice of Little John confronting the Sheriff of Nottingham? Nobody knew, any more than they knew whether elephant meat was really tough.

Paul Pearson spanked the boys, he said, only when they needed it. He considered the remark a spankable offense, but his elder son no longer took kindly to corporal punishment. When the family got home, Drew was told to go to his room and stay there until he had composed a suitable apology to the dean. Instead, he went on strike, refusing all food until his mother persuaded his father to deliver a conciliatory speech. The retraction was forgotten.

Another showdown occurred one morning when Drew failed to take out the furnace ashes. He did not have time, he said. His father told him not to come home until he was ready to perform his delayed daily chore. Drew did not come home for supper. The hours went by. Toward midnight, Paul and Edna enlisted neighbors in a search for their missing son. They found him seated calmly at the base of a large willow tree facing Crum Creek, which meandered through the woods that bordered the campus.

A somewhat older boy, the son of the chief engineer of the Pennsylvania Railroad, helped the followers of Robin Hood to build a wooden shack in an old cow pasture beside Crum Creek. A museum featuring arrowheads and birds' nests was created, which adults paid a penny or two to see. Frogs were displayed in an enclosure covered with mosquito wire.

A concrete pond was built for perch and sunfish and a few goldfish, most of which died. Learning to distinguish between poisonous and nonpoisonous snakes by the shape of their heads, the boys found nonpoisonous black, water and garter snakes and kept them as pets. Drew was always surprised how cold they felt in his hands. Using a homemade glass furnace, the boys melted lead obtained from plumbers working on local houses. They saved the lead on the theory that it would come in handy someday. It never did. They tried without success to emulate the Biblical feat of making bricks without straw.

A so-called Lead, Brick and Skin Company was organized. It made some money by trapping. In nearby woods called Whiskey Run, the boys caught various small animals. Drew volunteered to go to St. Louis on a railroad pass to dispose of the pelts. From a firm named Funkhauser he received $5 each for skunks, $8 for a single mink—"We were gypped, I guess, on that one"—and nothing for numerous rabbit skins. The transactions were recorded in the *Crum Creek Club News,* founded and edited by Drew Pearson.

Paul Pearson had found the local public school "too common" for Drew and Leon. Under an arrangement whereby he delivered lectures to defray their tuition, he shifted them to the Swarthmore Preparatory School. There Drew was inspired one day to place the bagged innards of a skunk behind a classroom radiator—with predictable results. Only the eloquent pleading of his father prevented his immediate expulsion.

Mrs. Pearson's health was improving. Her emaciated appearance had yielded to a modest increase in weight and she seemed more relaxed. Having ever since her marriage lived in a series of rented houses, she insisted on buying a more commodious place suiting her requirements. In 1911 she gave birth to a daughter, whom she named Barbara after Babbie in the Barrie play *The Little Minister.* A year later she bore another daughter who was called Ellen, a name as popular among the Pearsons as Andrew. That rounded out the family.

Making Drew responsible for Leon had worked out well. (The older boy had to regulate his own conscience in the process of supervising his brother.) Since her husband was away from home so often or busy with new lecturing projects, Edna extended her older son's jurisdiction to the girls.

Drew took his duties seriously. At the earliest possible age he went to the girls' room to recite nursery rhymes, like "Hickory Dickory Dock," which he had learned from his father. When Barbara got a splinter in a finger, Big Brother removed it. When the infected finger continued to ache, Drew sat up half the night reading aloud to her from *The Wizard of Oz.* When Ellen at the age of four burst into tears at the first frightening sight and sound of a fire engine, he picked her up, placed her on his shoulder and marched her home. In the role of regent for his father, he spoiled his sisters outrageously enough to earn their lifelong devotion.

4

"Dr." Paul Pearson—the doctorate came from Baker University in the form of an honorary Lit. D. as "an interpreter of literature" —had been working on the idea which became his monument. It concerned Chautauqua, which began in the 1870s as a Methodist summer camp. At first this was merely a semireligious, semi-intellectual gathering of good people in a kind of compound on the shores of Lake Chautauqua in upper New York State. By the time Paul graduated from Baker University it had become a nationally recognized educational movement with a heavy emphasis on uplift.

Throughout the Midwest and the Far West Chautauqua took the form of groups which stayed a week in each of a number of small towns on a circuit. Though the East had spawned Chautauqua, it had never tried the traveling groups. It was Dr. Pearson's exciting idea to bring this movable feast to the many isolated small towns along the Atlantic seaboard.

The first Swarthmore conference on the subject was held in 1909. Three years later the first circuit was launched in New Jersey, Pennsylvania, Maryland and Delaware. It lost $15,000 the first season, made $600 the next, and thereafter expanded from year to year on a nonprofit basis until three seven-day circuits and two five-day circuits extending from eastern Canada down into North Carolina were grossing $1 million a year.

Everybody in the Pearson family worked. Drew and Leon became unpaid clerks in the office which mushroomed in their home. At the age of three Barbara informed visitors that her baby sister was named "Ellen Cameron Pearson Chautauqua." Years later she became her father's driver and star actress in Chautauqua plays. When Ellen became old enough, she allowed herself to be sawed in half by a magician in one of the vaudeville acts which Dr. Pearson audaciously introduced.

Drew went into the field as tent boy in 1913 when he was fifteen, and attained the responsibility of tent captain the following year. Except for one messy incident which he never discussed, Drew reminisced freely in later years about his adventures as tent captain. After seven days in some town with a population generally ranging between one and two thousand it was his duty to load everything into a railroad baggage car in a single night, starting around 10 P.M. and running as late as 6 A.M.

There being no motorized trucks in those days, teams of drays brought the tents, chairs and other equipment to the railroad yards. One night a drunk lay down in front of an approaching team. The horses shied away. The drunk arose and began singing "Needles and Pins" in a hoarse voice. He was harmless but annoying. Drew always remembered that the drayman spat full in the drunk's face.

Early that summer William Jennings Bryan, then Secretary of State, was scheduled to talk at the Galeton, Pennsylvania, stop on Drew's circuit. The Great Commoner, a favorite with Drew because of the lung power which enabled him to be heard distinctly a block away in those pre-loudspeaker days, did not appear. Some Archduke had been shot in Sarajevo. Nobody knew where Sarajevo was or what the shooting was about, but that was the start of the First World War.

Dr. Pearson modernized Chautauqua. First he devised lecture-recitals, which combined biographical detail with readings from the works of a single author, such as James Whitcomb Riley or Edgar Allan Poe. Next he ventured into staging plays, such as *The Little Minister*. Finally, he tried light operas, including, to Drew's delight, one called *Robin Hood*. In earlier days such innovations would have been considered subversive, but Paul kept program control in his own hands by requiring the leading businessmen of the visited towns to guarantee expenses in advance.

Chautauqua gradually made Paul a celebrity. When he and Edna returned from a vacation cruise to Puerto Rico, they were given an unexpected welcome-home party to which everybody in Swarthmore came. Magazine articles appeared about the president of the Swarthmore Chautauqua. Newspaper articles referred to him erroneously and embarrassingly as the president of Swarthmore College. Actually, Professor Pearson had taken a leave to concentrate on winter preparation for a summer schedule which was climbing toward its peak of one thousand towns in thirteen states. In time he cut loose entirely from the college.

For his final years of preparatory school Drew went to Phillips Exeter Academy. Despite his father's improved financial and social position, the boy still had to scrimp. The academy granted scholarships to promising new students, subject to revision according to academic performance. Drew soon earned the highest scholarship. In addition, he baby-sat at 25 cents an hour—a chore for which his services at home had eminently qualified him. To meet a language requirement for graduation, he took two years of French in one. It was at Exeter, he always said, that he really learned to study.

The academy emphasis on foreign affairs in the curriculum and in extracurricular debates gave Drew a new goal in life. He would put aside his childish dream of becoming a circus clown, he decided, and qualify as a diplomat dressed (like a circus ringmaster?) in striped pants, cutaway and high hat.

Edna Pearson traveled alone to Exeter—Paul and Leon being busy with Chautauqua—to watch her son graduate in 1915. He was already taller than his father, very thin, but fit and obviously pleased with himself. He had done well in sports and achieved a variety of academic honors.

To entertain his mother, who was dressed for the occasion and who suddenly seemed beautiful to him, Drew hired a horse and buggy for half a day. As they drove through the New Hampshire countryside, he pointed out the spick-and-span white clapboard houses along the roads with their piles of firewood stacked neatly in the rear, and wound up at the Swampscott River, where he sometimes went canoeing.

"It's a shame," he added in self-congratulatory vein in the diary he kept according to family custom, "that boys never spend as much time with their mothers as they should when just a little thoughtfulness makes their mothers so happy."

The relationship between Drew and Edna stayed on this elevated plane. That fall he matriculated at Swarthmore College. Though he continued to test himself against obstacles, it did not occur to his mother that he could do any wrong. When he climbed the firehouse steeple at night to ring out a college sports victory— a prank for which he was arrested—she noted merely that he was a surefooted boy. When he drove a car thirty-five miles or so an hour, a suicidal speed in those days, she remarked that Drew was really a fine driver.

Edna Pearson gardened indefatigably. Her recipes for creamed chicken for two hundred and punch for two hundred won praise at Quaker quarterly meetings. The Friends Hospitality Committee, which she headed, brought smiles and flowers to new arrivals. Notwithstanding her good works, some neighbors were surprised over her casual reaction to news that her seventeen-year-old black houseworker had become pregnant. She arranged for the delivery of the child, then allowed it to be brought up by the young mother in the Pearson household. "That was the beginning of integration," Drew once said dryly.

Edna Pearson was more curious than ever about small things. When she visited a female relative, it was said, she trotted uninvited to the hostess' closets to inspect any new clothes. With the years she put on weight, became less careful how she dressed. Increasingly, she focused on her painting. Small annoyances triggered artless comments about events, friends and relatives, even Chautauqua, which she said had taken her husband from her.

The rest of the family agreed that she must be joking, though she possessed no sense of humor at all. How could she criticize Chautauqua without criticizing her husband? With his wavy, prematurely gray hair, dominant stance, sonorous voice and easy assumption that people would do what he wanted them to do, he somehow personified the movement.

Big-city sophisticates decried Chautauqua as smug and corny. They assumed that Paul Pearson was hypocritical or sanctimonious, though he had real integrity. They dismissed devotees of Chautauqua as rubes or dolts. This also was unfair. For those who took it straight, Chautauqua had a mildly civilizing influence. It taught people to question dogmas, to respect learning and to become more aware of the larger world. It opened the door slightly to populist, reformist, even socialist views.

Dr. Pearson's lecturers ranged from Judge Ben B. Lindsey, who advocated companionate marriage, to the radical Midwestern Senator, Robert M. La Follette, Sr., but his own style, illustrated by his favorite ethical appeals—"The Joy of Living" and "Who Is Great?"—was traditional. In "Who Is Great?," endlessly repeated in public and in private, he said: "Service to humanity is the greatest requirement for greatness. The man who looms greatest is the one who, when he knows he is right, has the courage to do what everybody says must not be done and not to do what everybody says must be done."

5

As a Swarthmore undergraduate Drew was demonstrably more affected by Chautauqua than by his courses, his experimental romances or the war. He served his father as motion picture operator, advance man and lecturer. During his sophomore year he held the post of superintendent for a whole circuit, canvassing and hiring talent during the winter and setting up the summer schedule. In this capacity he encountered a bouncy blond drummer girl known as Bootsy who played once a week with an orchestra.

Bootsy was a girl without money or much education, but her physical charms induced Drew to cut classes. When he talked about marriage in disregard of Grandpa Pearson's guideline, Dr. Pearson became concerned. With unexpected guile he arranged a scholarship for Bootsy at Baker University. There would, he said, be no obligation on her part; time would determine the relationship between her and Drew. Nevertheless, the romance ended at that point.

War fever swept the campus in 1917. Half of Drew's class rushed into uniform to fight the Kaiser. Some were killed in combat. Drew felt obscurely guilty, though he was too involved with Chautauqua to consider leaving.

The onset of war brought a great deal of soul-searching within the Society of Friends. The earliest Quakers spoke of being compelled to bear witness to their principles. They knew what they opposed—personal violence, war, exploitation of man by man, injustice, intolerance and dishonesty—but since they rejected formal creeds and catechisms, the method of opposition was left to the individual conscience.

The momentary confusion among Quakers, which was not confined to Swarthmore, was resolved in 1917 by the establishment of the American Friends Service Committee as a social action agency of the church. This Committee enlisted thousands of college students for humanitarian work overseas as an alternative to military participation. Drew, though interested, felt obliged to remain with his father.

Early in his senior year—on October 25, 1918—Drew's draft number came up. Three days later he obtained deferment by enrolling in the Student Army Training Corps, whose members did close order drill on campus. Army men joked that SATC stood for "Safe at the College," but Drew took his military career as seriously as anything else. When the war ended in a couple of weeks, he had risen to corporal. He was discharged from the Army on November 20.

For years he had seen a great deal of Mary Hull, the girl next door. Mary, called "Ski," was a member of the Clothier department store family. She went to Vassar. Her father taught at Swarthmore, and her mother was national president of Jane Addams' Women's International League for Peace and Freedom. Nobody in the Pearson family objected when Drew talked of becoming engaged to "Ski" Hull, but she turned him down.

Dr. Pearson's dutiful elder son emerged from Swarthmore in a burst of achievement. For not having smoked or taken a drink up to the age of twenty-one he had received a promised $100 from his father. His other credits included: star swimmer and soccer player at Swarthmore, president of his fraternity, editor of the college weekly and member of Phi Beta Kappa, the national scholastic fraternity. He had played the lead role of George Washington in the senior play, and he had won the state oratorical contest with an address entitled "Our Debt to Humanity."

There were final chores to perform before he began paying his debt to humanity. He had signed up for two years as a member of an American Friends Service Committee unit assigned to an area in Serbia which had been terribly devastated during the war. In July he drove part of the New England Chautauqua for Dr. Pearson, going as far north as St. John before returning to Swarthmore. The sober-sided young man of promise composed a farewell letter to his family to be read if he died in a foreign land.

DEAR MOTHER AND FATHER, LEON, BARBARA AND ELLEN:
It is very hard for me to write this because as I sit here at my desk with Mother downstairs and the children playing in the street the possibility of your reading this seems so remote. . . .

They say that no boy ever appreciates what his family, what his parents and especially what his mother means to him until it is too late. I know that I am like others in that respect; but I do hope not quite so much. At Exeter, at college, I tried to keep before me the Mother and Father who had given me my opportunities. At home—I know I was so often cross and irritable—I guess I didn't show much appreciation. And I have regretted it all the time. . . .

Mother, I was reading in the *American Magazine* the other day Dr. Frank Crane's "Ten Ways to Test Fineness of Character," and it made me think how well you answered them all. Read them over and consider as you do that I am holding you as the ideal. I can't say much more. During my life I have tried to make you proud of the son for whom you risked your life, lost much of your health, cared for so faithfully and have done almost too much. Your love was far more than I ever deserved.

Father, I have always felt that if I could ever attain your generosity, your consideration and tenderness, your sense of the square deal, your personality and strength, that I could wish for no more in life. Kipling's "If" has been often quoted and misquoted but I never hear it without thinking of you. . . .

Leon, old boy, be worthy of your Father and Mother. I know you will. . . . Let it be enough that I and other people say, "You're like your pa."

Little Sisters, it has been wonderful to watch you grow and develop into fine big girls. When I remember how I used to rock you and sing you to sleep and take care of you, it makes me mighty sorry to leave you. But then I don't intend to leave you for long. Take good care of Father and Mother. Keep them young just as you have kept us all young. . . .

Well, my beloved family, be of good cheer. . . . Remember that I am leaving you for a great cause. Remember that whatever happens I'll finish strong and it's "not the fact that you're dead that counts, it's only how did you die." . . .

> "Sunset and evening star,
>   And one clear call for me!
> And may there be no moaning of the bar
>   When I put out to sea."

Goodbye my dear family.
DREW

CHAPTER IV

Man on the Make

For a young man who will require exceptional vigor it is an obvious advantage to have been reared in a relatively sheltered middle-class home. Unlike those who come from the ranks of manual laborers, he has not prematurely exhausted his energies. He possesses capabilities of which he is only half aware.

Judging from his farewell letter, Drew was frightened by what he might face in Serbia. It did not occur to him that he had held his own within the family, at school and on the farm. Chautauqua and the domestic mixture of discipline and freedom were excellent training for more formal cooperative effort. In any case he had no alternative; it did not occur to him to question the family decision.

Serbia had been badly mauled during the war. When the Austrian Army poured down from the north and the Bulgarians roared up from the south, much of the rural population was squeezed westward toward the Adriatic, taking their livestock with them. In one of the cruelest migrations in history, a million and a half men, women and children and uncounted animals perished before the survivors reached the foothills at the juncture of Montenegro and Albania. The human beings were homeless, impoverished, undernourished and without hope. Many had typhus.

The Friends from America pitched their tents in Peć, Pegi or Pech, depending on which language was used. They erected barracks for the refugees and a hospital. In time three walled villages were constructed, from which the goats and cattle could be let out by day and brought back at night.

Members of the Quaker unit received no salary but were allowed $10 a month each for food and clothing, plus special allowances for travel. Drew was habitually thrifty—during his senior year at Swarthmore he had met all his expenses and emerged with a surplus of $700—so money was no problem. He and his companions wore military uniforms with regulation cap and Sam Browne belt. As associates of the Red Cross they carried Red Cross patches on their shoulders as well as the Friends insignia on their left sleeves. They drew their side arms only for shooting at the wolves in the brush outside the walled villages.

Though they had independent status, the American Friends leaned on the Serbian Army for help in re-establishing sanitary conditions and on governmental bureaus for other types of assistance. They obtained grain from Herbert Hoover's European relief mission and surplus trucks and horses from U.S. Army headquarters in Vienna. Red Cross medical supplies arrived by pack train from the Adriatic. The water buffalo and oxen used locally for transport, Drew noted in letters to his family, were as picturesque as the camels he had heard about as a boy.

That winter Paul Pearson visited England, Belgium and France, then Berlin, accredited as Captain Pearson of the American Red Cross, at a time when no civilians were supposed to cross the border into Germany. Drew was not surprised. It was an article of faith with him and Leon that their father knew everybody of importance and could do anything he wanted to do.

Drew's previous experience on farms gave him an advantage in Serbia. Others in the unit found the primitive conditions unbearable. They resigned and went home. Within a few months young Pearson was asked to assume command of the unit, consisting of a dozen members, all older than himself and most of them women. He grew a rather frail mustache in an effort to look old enough for the responsibility entrusted to him.

The European headquarters of the American Friends Service

Committee in Vienna received impressive reports on Drew's performance. He had shared his personal rations of bully beef and beans with the starving peasants when he first arrived and had performed other "sacrificial acts." References were made to him as "the Saint of the Serbian Mountains."

It was true that as unit chief Drew worked harder than anybody else. Operating on the assumption that the others would do what he wanted, he experienced no personnel problems. Except for a rare glass of Roja, the plum brandy which customarily lubricates business deals in Serbia, he did not drink. He did not smoke and he had no diversions. Night after night he could be found in his tent moving from one troublesome detail to another as if, in a friend's phrase, "each was a newspaper deadline."

As soon as the arrangement could be made, he imported Andrew Simpson from the United States. Simpson, known as "Andy," was a former Swarthmore College classmate who since graduation had been employed as an engineer by General Electric. At Swarthmore he had been captain of the soccer team on which Drew played and assistant editor of the *Halcyon*, the yearbook, of which Drew had been editor. Drew figured, accurately, that his friend would be just the man to get the ruined local hydroelectric plant functioning again.

In a reunion over Roja the two Andrews renamed the unit outhouse in honor of Phi Kappa Psi, the Swarthmore College rival of their fraternity, Kappa Sigma. Then they settled down to work. Thinking about those days later, Andy Simpson could recall only two other social events at the camp during more than a year: a wedding between two members of the unit, at which Drew was best man, and a costume party. If he dropped around to Drew's tent for a chat, there were a hundred interruptions. Drew ran a tight ship. Nothing came ahead of his work.

Drew found it necessary to make trips to Belgrade, the capital of the new kingdom of the Serbs, Croats and Slovenes known as Yugoslavia. There he met the Beach girls: Sylvia, secretary to Helen Scott Hays, chief of the Red Cross Nursing Service, and her sister Holly (short for Hollingsworth), a typist in the Red Cross office. Though Sylvia was several years older than Drew and Holly older than Sylvia, the three got along well. They found time to visit places of interest in the countryside, such as Sarajevo, where the war had started.

The Beach girls were daughters of Dr. Sylvester Woodbridge Beach, then pastor of the First Presbyterian Church of Princeton, New Jersey. They were polylingual, having been brought up in Paris when their father was pastor of the American church there, and having driven ambulances in Italy during the war. They considered themselves self-sufficient and worldly-wise.

Though they traveled pretty much as a team, the sisters displayed different styles. Sylvia, a small, dark-haired girl, babbled innocuously about her "hopeless passion" for a Major Edwards, the Red Cross medical officer in Belgrade. Holly, larger and more reserved, tried as a suffragette to convince her boss, Captain Herbert O. Robinson, the Red Cross Commission comptroller and office manager, that women were superior beings.

During the winter of 1919–1920 Sylvia resigned from the Red Cross to open an American bookstore on the left bank in Paris. Her Shakespeare & Co., as the bookstore was called, became an intellectual rallying point and home away from home for James Joyce, George Antheil, Jo Davidson, F. Scott Fitzgerald, Ernest Hemingway, Gertrude Stein, Ezra Pound and other creative expatriates from the United States in the era between the world wars.

Holly went to Italy to conduct a special Red Cross survey of children made homeless by the war. When she returned to Belgrade, Sylvia came down on visits from Paris. They and a third sister, Cyprian, were always very close.

Mary Heaton Vorse often came with Sylvia. She passed as an American magazine writer until Holly in her outspoken fashion identified her as an international Communist organizer. Reminiscing years later in St. Petersburg, Florida, after his retirement as a colonel, Herbert Robinson said: "That Vorse woman scandalized Belgrade not only by smoking—which was not done by women in those days—but by chain-smoking in public. She actually ate with a fork in one hand and a cigarette in the other! She would leave Hostess House in the evening to address meetings, taking the Beach girls and Drew Pearson with her.

"Holly would invite me to see what was happening 'out in the world,' as she put it, but I was engaged to marry my assistant, Stella Kinnamon, so I had other interests. From what Holly told me they were sowing the seeds of hate which later ripened into the harvest of Tito. I can't say Pearson attended revolutionary meetings, but he left and returned with the others."

Mary Heaton Vorse drew a picture of the good life in faraway Russia, which was soon going to be shared by the world. With much talk about an individual's right to love and to be loved, she described an ideal society which through socialism would be less oppressed, less insecure, less miserable. Since the experiment in Russia was in its pre-Stalin phase, it sounded impressive.

Drew lacked the family emotional hangups which impel most young recruits into Communism. He had no intention whatever of putting any political philosophy ahead of his absorbing job in Peć, but he heard little in Vorse's propaganda to conflict with his earlier religions of family, Chautauqua and the Quakers. Even her muted talk of eventual revolution in the Balkans seemed not entirely implausible in the light of his developing troubles with the bureaucrats in Belgrade.

Drew wanted to introduce the mass production of crops as he had known it in Kansas. At his request, the government had expropriated land on the plains near Peć, but the plots allotted to individual families, each with its new dry-brick house, proved distressingly small—too small to warrant the use of modern machinery. He could not manage to persuade the government to enlarge the plots or induce the peasants to join in cooperatives.

The Serbian refugees, at first so docile because of their lowered vitality, had found their voices. Because tractors had a way of plowing under the stones which served as the sole boundaries of each plot, the farmers became embroiled in disputes with their neighbors. Unsettled complaints went over Drew's head to politicians in Belgrade, who were not invariably patient with a presumptuous and reportedly radical foreigner.

The American reconstruction effort was drawing to an end. In the sense that it had restored hope to people who had been apathetic it could be considered successful. Under his two-year contract with the Friends, Drew was entitled to first-class passage home from anywhere in Europe. He surprised his colleagues by insisting on

Alexandria, Egypt, which was across the Mediterranean in Africa, as his point of departure. Simpson went home by way of Vienna.

Speculation over Drew's plans grew when it was learned that the Beach girls were going with him. In a misguided gesture of emancipation, one of the girls told friends that the purpose of the trip was to obtain an abortion in Alexandria. Overnight the American colony in Serbia rolled this tasty morsel of gossip on its tongue. Sylvia was generally believed to be the girl in trouble and Drew was presumed to be the man responsible, but nobody could be sure because the three travelers turned angrily secretive under questioning.

The abortion rumor, amply documented by people who were at Peć and in Belgrade, cannot be ignored. It is too important in any analysis of Drew's character. To judge from reports about Bootsy back in Swarthmore, there was a trace of a Galahad in Drew. He was a responsible youth; if either one of his only two close female associates in Serbia was in trouble, he might have wanted to help regardless of the source of the trouble. Yet he was dealing with well-educated, sophisticated girls who prided themselves on their independence. Would they have brought him into the situation unless he was responsible?

Many years later, in the early 1960s, in fact, Drew told successive personal secretaries at his office about an unnamed girl whom he had loved and lost long ago in Serbia. Their relationship, apparently, had been incandescence at first sight. The girl meant more to him than any other. However, she had an established position in Europe which she could not give up for marriage to a young American without money, a job or prospects. They had parted, never to see each other again. He made it all sound attractively star-crossed and forlorn.

Sylvia Beach never married. Several years before her death she produced an autobiography, which concentrated on her famous bookstore. She did not mention Pearson. Holly married some time after leaving the Red Cross. Failing in health but mentally competent, she was approached by her adopted son in a Connecticut nursing home in 1971 and asked if she remembered Drew Pearson in Serbia.

"I never knew him," she said distinctly, and would say no more.

2

Like many a returning war veteran, Drew found things out of kilter when he arrived home. Swarthmore seemed smaller and uncomfortably quiet. The prospects it offered did not match his feelings. Family alignments were different: Leon had moved into the Big Brother void; Barbara and Ellen presented an affectionate united front against their alternately too-tolerant and nagging mother. After the first flush of welcome Drew wondered if any of them except his father understood or cared about what was happening in Serbia.

At Dr. Pearson's suggestion, he had prepared an illustrated lecture on Pearsonavatz—the name given temporarily to one of his three walled towns—for Chautauqua. He brought back Boshidar Barkitch, a young Serbian friend, to operate a slide projector during his lecture. That summer he and Barkitch worked under the general direction of Leon, who as his father's field superintendent was responsible for "making the contract"—that is, producing sufficient revenue to repay the guarantors of a particular circuit.

Leon had developed during Drew's absence. He was socially more adept. He still kept his shriveled arm out of sight as much as he could, but he used it to shake hands and to type. He had equaled Drew in academic honors during his final year at Swarthmore, from which he graduated in June, 1920, only a year behind Drew though he was nearly two years younger. He had gone on to Harvard with a fellowship. When he received his master's degree—it was generally agreed in the family—he would marry Anna Mary Brown, his "junior leader" or assistant in Chautauqua, start teaching and raising a family.

Drew also should marry and settle down, said Dr. Pearson. Nobody would have him, Drew joked. To become a diplomat—still his official ambition—he would need a rich wife. He promised to look for one, but the family got the impression that he was avoiding eligible young women.

Dr. Pearson wanted Drew to become his chief assistant and eventual successor in running the Swarthmore Chautauqua, which was experiencing a modest postwar revival. Drew avoided that proposal, too. In the face of urgent world problems Chautauqua sounded tinny and discursive to him. Lacking any better alternative, he accepted a job that fall teaching industrial geography at the University of Pennsylvania—almost at home, since Philadelphia was only eleven miles from Swarthmore—as an assistant to an old family friend, Dr. J. Russell Smith.

What about Boshidar Barkitch? Dr. Pearson offered him a scholarship at Baker University. Barkitch was willing. Like Bootsy, he went to Kansas for a college education and, like Bootsy, he soon dropped out of classes. Humiliated by his failure, he enlisted in the Army and thereafter made his way apart from the Pearsons.

During visits to Washington that fall Drew confirmed what he suspected: the standards of the American Foreign Service were so high and the pay so low that only bright young men with wealthy parents could afford a diplomatic career. He began to think of alternatives. To test his capacity, he covered the Washington Disarmament Conference late in the year for a string of college newspapers which he had induced to accept his dispatches.

Secretary of State Charles Evans Hughes electrified the conference by announcing that the United States would stop building warships and scrap existing vessels if Great Britain, Japan, France and Italy took similar steps.

Spectators broke into spontaneous applause. Tears of joy rolled down the cheeks of William Jennings Bryan, former Secretary of State, who was reporting the event for a newspaper syndicate. Pearson noted that the promised reductions in armament meant nothing without international supervision, which was impossible because Congress had already pulled away from the League of Nations.

To accommodate conflicting pressures within the family, Drew established for himself a hybrid profession, that of lecturer-correspondent. His Uncle Drew (Andrew Cameron Pearson), who had gone to New York and made money publishing trade newspapers, persuaded Lewis Pierson, a bank president, to underwrite a world trip by his nephew as a free-lance correspondent.

Paul Pearson insisted that the trip be made to pay for itself by a lecture tour. Having in hand somebody else's Chautauqua speech on "The Japanese Menace," which could be converted into a sure-fire lecture in Australia, he approached Ellison & White, of Seattle, which operated Chautauqua circuits in Australia and New Zealand as well as in the United States. Drew had worked part-time one winter for Ellison & White, which enjoyed reciprocal relations with the Swarthmore Chautauqua. They were delighted to book him for a six months' tour Down Under.

Drew's promotional brochure went as follows: "Drew Pearson has visited all three continents. Africa and Europe are familiar fields to him. Drew Pearson has an international point of view as a lecturer on international politics. He is encircling the globe by airplane, automobile, steamship and train; on foot, on horseback and on camel. . . ." Lest somebody miss the point, it was headed: "Around the World With Drew Pearson." It carried a warning: "Confidential—Not for Publication."

Since his previous farewell letter, opened despite his failure to die, had become a family legend, a repeat performance was almost obligatory. This one was shorter:

> Hundreds of times, I have promised myself that I should choose between work on the one side and family and friends on the other —and let the former go hang! But I know that a combination of the two is best if only the proper balance can be kept. I am a firm believer that we live to do what we will to do. Therefore this is not a farewell but a milepost where I record the passage of time, the changes in my life. . . .
>
> I am sorry and glad that I do not still come to Father for as much advice as I once did. His advice is better than ever and I need it perhaps more than ever but I am gradually growing to fight my own mental battles. Sometimes I am on the verge of changing my mind in an instant and remaining at home. There is nothing I should rather do than to settle down, marry and help Father with Chautauqua. But I have my own life to live and my own ideas to work out—and after trying them, I shall come back and do what I have long wanted to do.
>
> I find it harder and harder to leave. Little Sisters, do you be better than your big brother—and take care of your mother. I know you will. All that I have said in my first letter I feel again and with the deeper feeling of three added years.
>
> > My family goodbye,
> > DREW

Instead of mailing his promotional brochure to newspaper editors, Drew delivered it personally with a sales pitch as he traveled by day coach from city to city on the way to Seattle.

A number of editors agreed to accept his dispatches and to pay for those used. In Seattle he was turned down for a sailor's job. Realizing that he did not look the part, he got his chest tattooed with the Greek letters of his college fraternity and returned to lounge about a hiring hall with open shirt. This time he was taken on as an ordinary seaman on a passenger vessel to Japan.

In Yokohama he jumped ship. With help from American correspondents stationed in Japan, he produced a reasonable amount of copy before moving on to Siberia. There he was jailed for taking pictures. Upon his release he interviewed a General Teronim Uborievitch, who was later shot by Stalin. He saw enough of Russian living conditions—families living in a *ugolok*, or corner, of a room shared with other families; no bathrooms worth mentioning and toilets that leaked and stank; people subsisting on black bread and standing in line for various scarce commodities— to realize that Mary Heaton Vorse must have been talking about some other country.

Australia came next. There his status as a lecturer and the familiar language yielded more stories than he could use. He wrote feature articles for several Australian newspapers. On the way home he stopped off in India to interview Mahatma Gandhi. Unfortunately, Gandhi was in jail.

Traveling third class by ship across the Mediterranean to keep expenses down, Pearson received an unexpected wireless message from an American newspaper syndicate, offering $2,000 in expenses plus pay on publication for interviews with "Europe's Twelve Greatest Men." He accepted and obtained the interviews, ranging from Mussolini to Lord Balfour. Then he sailed home first class on the *Aquitania*, lolling on the soft cushions in the men's lounge and reminding himself to eat lobster at least once a day— his definition of luxury.

The entire trip had taken a year and a half. When the delayed checks rolled in, he had $714, compared with the $700 rainy-day fund he had maintained since college days.

He tried to establish himself in the domestic free-lance market by turning out a few more great-man interviews, Burbank, Edison and Ford among them. Since he had saved his background material on Gandhi, he combined it with his firsthand stuff on Ford in an article for the magazine *Asia* contrasting the different approaches of the two men toward the decentralization of industry. If obtrusive local color about India and quotations from Gandhi implied personal contact with a world leader he had never seen, that came under the head of journalistic enterprise.

Drew was satisfied with his performance. Having lived on the dangerous edge of things, he felt competent to tackle any journalistic assignment. None came his way at home or in the foreign field. That fall he took refuge once again with Dr. J. Russell Smith, this time as an instructor in commercial geography at Columbia University.

3

Mrs. Eleanor Medill (Cissy) Patterson, a very wealthy divorced woman with the power and the itch to manipulate people, encountered Drew Pearson in the spring of 1924. More accurately, he encountered her by turning up at one of the celebrity-studded dinners she gave regularly in her marble-and-mahogany palace on Dupont Circle in Washington. According to her biographer, Alice Albright Hoge, Cissy Patterson was something of a "female Don Juan" during this period, but she was also making a determined, if not entirely successful, bid to become Washington's leading hostess, which required the evaluation of guests on grounds other than sex.

Drew's credentials for attending the party were adequate. He had been spending the weekend at the Washington home of William Hard, a former classmate of Dr. Pearson at Northwestern University and a frequent Chautauqua speaker.

Hard, a well-known Washington correspondent, had written a biography of Senator Joseph Medill McCormick, who, like Eleanor Medill McCormick, was one of the four privileged grandchildren of Joseph Medill, founder of the Chicago *Tribune*, America's most profitable newspaper. The Hards often dined with Mrs. Patterson. This time, when he came down with influenza, his wife drafted Drew as her escort, knowing that Cissy preferred a vouched-for stranger to a last-minute vacancy at table.

If experience is the commodity for which a man exchanges his youth, Drew at twenty-four—eighteen years younger than Mrs. Patterson—could not be considered young. He had learned to use the world. He avoided the journalist's favorite mode of wisecracking. He lacked that overknowing air which spoils so many correspondents. He did not dress or talk well. Yet to Cissy, a connoisseur in such matters, he had an actor's size and presence, "the aura of an adventurer and a heart to give and take blows." He brought to mind her elder brother Joe—Captain Joseph M. Patterson—whom she idolized.

It was Joe whose childish slurring of "sister" gave Eleanor Patterson the nickname which became public property. Joe left Yale in his junior year to write about the Boxer Rebellion in China for the Hearst chain of newspapers. He was a Socialist before he served with distinction as an Army officer in World War I. From Lord Northcliffe of England he acquired a journalistic formula which he had applied to the *Daily News,* a postwar tabloid founded by him in New York, and which was pushing its circulation beyond that of any rival.

Cissy had a weakness for reporting and for reporters. Like Joe, she had ignored the struggle between Hearst's Chicago newspaper, the *Herald and Examiner,* and the Patterson-McCormick trust established by Joseph Medill to keep the Chicago *Tribune* intact after his death.

She had covered a Republican National Convention in Chicago for Hearst. She was on good terms with Hearst, with Arthur Brisbane, his editorial adviser, and with Tom White, his general manager. Through them she intrigued for the acquisition of a Washington newspaper, which was to make her, in the words of a later *Collier's* magazine article, "the most powerful and perhaps the most hated woman in America."

Of the twelve persons at that first Dupont Circle dinner, Drew remembered Cissy and her daughter, Felicia; Eugene Meyer, a banker who wanted to buy a newspaper; and Elmer Schlesinger, a forty-three-year-old lawyer who was aggressively attentive to Cissy. Felicia was the only child of Cissy's marriage to Count Josef Gizycki, a fortune-hunting Pole whom she met at the Austro-Hungarian court when her uncle, Robert S. McCormick, was the Ambassador there. The Count had delayed the marriage ceremony until he got his dowry, he had raped his bride (so she said) on their wedding night, he had beat her to her knees when she complained about his extramarital adventures and he had extorted an extra $200,000 before he conceded divorce.

From a sullen, neglected child Felicia had blossomed into a gorgeous blonde of eighteen who could no longer be ignored if only because, in her mother's words, she was "harder to handle than a team of bull moose." Though she was a big girl, Felicia was intensely feminine, sweet and elusive. She had no intention of getting married, she said. She refused a social debut, she went for solitary walks in the rain, she criticized her mother's guests. "You'd think I was running a bad house and that all my friends were trollops, which they are, God bless them," Cissy said indignantly.

Cissy Patterson, who could not consider remarriage with Felicia on her hands, lied about her daughter's age in a vain effort to diminish her own. She made fun of Felicia's generous figure.

Drew Pearson was not the first bachelor to whom Felicia had been exposed by abrupt command: "Put on a dress and come down to dinner, a woman dropped out." This time she had wobbled on the verge of defiance. She was still "too troubled in her mind" over the quarrel with her mother, she confided later, to focus on the dinner.

The stranger next to her kept his distance. She was not sure of his first name. "It's Lion," he said, explaining that he had "roared" as a baby. He retrieved her napkin when it fell off her lap. She dropped her handkerchief, and he picked that up, too. "Oh, Lord, she drops things all the time," he complained to himself. Felicia laughed. Somewhat to her surprise, she found herself telling him she wanted to become a writer.

After the dinner she had contradictory opinions. "He's a stick-in-the-mud," she told one friend, "older than God and he's got a mustache, ugh." To another she confided that he seemed strong in a world of weak men. She treasured a note he had sent with her handkerchief.

Cissy Patterson's reaction was important. Inducing Drew to talk a little about himself, she had been pleased by his ingenuity and persistence as a free-lance correspondent. She invited him to stay at "The Dupont Circle," as her mansion was known within the family, whenever he came down from Columbia University. There would be no difficulty putting him up, she said. (The Dupont Circle had a staff of ten, including a couple of footmen in green livery, and thirty rooms on four floors for guests who could reasonably expect terrapin on silver plates, champagne and dancing to Meyer Davis' orchestra.)

The Patterson showplace had been built two decades earlier to designs by Stanford White as a social refuge for Cissy's mother, who was estranged from her husband, Robert Patterson, editor of the Chicago *Tribune*.

When the elder Mrs. Patterson suffered a stroke, divided her huge estate between Cissy and Joe and retired to live in a Chicago hotel, Cissy took over and modernized The Dupont Circle. She derided her home as "a movie palace" because of the semiprecious stones used as doorknobs and other forms of Hollywood ostentation, but she found it useful for bringing the local bigwigs within her orbit.

On his second visit Drew took Felicia, at Cissy's suggestion, to her first nightclub. They had a planter's punch apiece in a hot crowded room before he called it an evening. "Drink up, my child," he said firmly, "and let's go." On the way home he found occasion to kiss her and complained that she must be made of ice. Thereafter he began to commute fairly regularly between New York and Washington. Felicia's wariness did not put him off. When he could not see the daughter, he willingly settled for the mother.

With her blunt features and too-small, imperious head on its narrow column of neck, Cissy Patterson could not be considered beautiful, but her white skin and red hair, her soft husky voice, her slenderness, graceful carriage and theatrical clothes dazzled men of all ranks and ages. Elmer Schlesinger was the latest in a series of admirers which had included Count Johann von Bernstorff, the German Ambassador; William E. Borah, the shaggy-maned Western Senator; Tom White of the Hearst organization; and an uncouth Westerner or two on the ranch in Wyoming where she lived for extended periods.

Schlesinger had been pursuing Cissy since he came to Washington in 1921 as counsel to the U.S. Shipping Board. In his infatuation he had divorced his wife in Chicago, though they had teen-aged children. Cissy valued him, she said, as a "good money maker, a vulgar and charming man who makes me feel physically desirable," but she was not sure she wanted to marry him, if indeed she wanted to marry anyone again.

Out of a sense that Pearson was complicating his courtship of Cissy, Schlesinger subtly backed the young instructor as a possible husband for Felicia. That summer Drew sold syndicated newspaper features on the road for $100 a week, plus payment for whatever acceptable great-man interviews he could arrange and write in transit. At Schlesinger's suggestion, Cissy invited him in July to spend a month at the Flat Creek Ranch in Woods Hole Valley in Wyoming.

Considering the invitation a sign of Felicia's esteem, Pearson rearranged his affairs and hurried to the ranch. When he arrived on horseback, he found the atmosphere full of static. Schlesinger was trying frantically to avoid another in a series of "roundups," or quarrels, between Cissy and Felicia. Drew's arrival was hardly noticed. The tension snapped when Cissy's Swedish maid, Aasta, resigned, and Cissy told her to find her own transportation back to town.

Railing at her mother as a "slaveholder," Felicia offered to carry the maid back to civilization on her pony, a gift from Cal Carrington, the eccentric former cattle rustler who managed Cissy's ranch as if he owned it, but the maid wept and declined, fearing horses. The argument continued until Felicia decided to leave home for good.

Disdaining saddles and bridles since they belonged to her mother, from whom she was determined never to accept anything again, Felicia made a halter out of her cotton stockings and rode off bareback on her pony, carrying all her worldly goods—clothes and several hundred dollars saved out of her allowance—in two duffel bags, fore and aft.

When Cissy recovered from her rage, she dispatched Pearson in pursuit of the fugitive. Felicia's knowledge of the seventeen-mile trail to Jackson kept her well ahead of Drew. In Jackson she took the bus, which was still called the stage, to Victor, Idaho. There she bought a railroad ticket to Salt Lake City. Just as the train was pulling out of the station, Drew swung aboard, hurried through the cars and sat down beside her. She barely listened or spoke to him.

In Salt Lake City, Felicia decided to look for a job. Drew suggested marriage instead. She glared at him incredulously. "You bore me," she said, "and the more I see of you, the more bored I get." She walked away from him on the street.

Drew had no alternative but to return to the ranch and report his failure. As Felicia's suitor he disarmed Cal Carrington, the ranch foreman, who had a way of hazing male visitors, even Schlesinger, whom he suspected of admiring Cissy. Rose Crabtree, the Jackson innkeeper who was Cissy's closest Western friend, let it be known that Drew, in her opinion, looked very much like John Gilbert. In Woods Hole that summer and in Washington that fall, Cissy "consoled herself," according to her biographer, "with the company of Schlesinger and Young Drew Pearson."

Mrs. Patterson made no effort to aid her missing daughter. Felicia, she said, must be taught a lesson. According to her detectives, that glamorous young lady, who had been required at Foxcroft to take her turn waiting on table, found a job, not as a waitress, but as a dishwasher in a Greek restaurant. Her provocative appearance created difficulties. To escape the unwelcome attentions of her boss in Salt Lake City, she went to San Diego, where she lived at the YWCA under the name of Marian Martin.

Alarmed by the depletion of her funds, she moved to a $12.50-a-month rooming house, where the other girls, she discovered, catered to the Navy Yard trade. Through one of the girls she obtained a job as a waitress in a joint called the Sailors Hash House. That also became uncomfortable, so she found a better job as a waitress at a middle-class luncheon club called the Caya Maka. She located a more respectable rooming house.

During a period of joblessness Felicia tried selling door-to-door subscriptions to a local newspaper, without much success. Her chief problem was financial; she had never been taught the price of anything. Even after her savings vanished she could not learn to live on a small income. Cissy was disturbed by reports from her detectives. At Schlesinger's suggestion, she let Drew know how to reach Felicia on condition that he keep the source of his tip secret.

No knight-errant ever came more opportunely to the aid of a

damsel in distress. Felicia felt inordinately grateful for the initiative of her admirer, who was, he said in his letter, making $150 a week, an excellent newspaper salary in those days. Drew's solid qualities took on more ample dimensions in Felicia's mind.

"I always wanted to make my own way," she wrote proudly, having found another job as a waitress. "There are worse things than waiting on table. I don't mind telling you I've learned to sling a mean tray."

In a later note she enclosed some literary sketches, mostly local color, which she had written in longhand. She was saving her pennies, she wrote, for a typewriter to get some of her more colorful experiences down on paper. Pearson arranged to send a portable typewriter to Felicia. The unexpected gift won her heart; at least it induced assent to his renewed suggestion of marriage. He hurried to San Diego, and there they were married by a justice of the peace.

Mrs. Patterson, informed by wire of the event, issued an announcement in Washington. Felicia, she said, had been attending a business college in San Diego. Drew Pearson, a writer associated with the United Publishers Corporation who had been courting her for a year, had come to San Diego and persuaded her to give up her pursuit of a business career. Cissy added that she was "delighted at the outcome of a romance which from the first had my knowledge and approval."

Paul and Edna Pearson were more surprised by the news than Cissy. They had not realized the extent to which Drew's affections were engaged. In the annual diary which he kept in addition to a daily one, Dr. Pearson put the event as gently as he could: "Though it can hardly be said of Drew that he is slow yet he married nearly two years later than his brother who is two years younger. On Mar. 12, 1925, Felicia became a member of the family. We were all attracted to her and gave her a loving welcome. As the ceremony was in faroff California no members of the family attended."

Felicia did get a warm welcome in Swarthmore. She basked in the Pearson family solidarity, a quality largely lacking among the McCormicks and the Pattersons. Then the newlyweds went to New York City for an Easter dinner with Cissy and Schlesinger.

Cissy said she had never seen Felicia looking so well. The girl was radiant.

Taking advantage of the friendly atmosphere, Drew suggested that Cissy and Elmer seek the happiness achieved by him and Felicia. Schlesinger seconded the suggestion with enthusiasm. On the wings of impulse and persuasion, Cissy found herself carried off to City Hall in the morning and there married to her persistent suitor.

Pearson was the only witness. "Drew talked me into it," Cissy explained later to her incredulous friends in Washington.

CHAPTER V

Marriage

FELICIA PEARSON BLAMED her chronic uncertainty of mind on the fact that when she was growing up she never stayed long enough in one place to know who she was or where she belonged. Drew had the advantage, she said, of being reared in a single house.

Drew did not quibble over details: Evanston and Cambridge bulked small in his recollections, and the different Swarthmore houses merged into one. It was true he had never lived in an apartment, always a house. He knew who he was. He attributed his wife's complaint to some lack of affection or encouragement during childhood.

She was born in Blanski Castle in the Austro-Hungarian province of Moravia on September 3, 1905. Cissy's pregnancy had been marked by neurotic collapses and frantic sleighrides to Vienna hospitals. Her year-old marriage to Count Gizycki was virtually over. Gizy, as he was called, reacted to growing peasant unrest on his rundown estates by drinking and gambling more than ever at the Vienna Jockey Club. On rare visits home he disdained the baby girl since he had wanted a boy. Cissy also avoided the nursery.

When Felicia was two, Cissy fled with her and her Polish nurse to England. The Count called it a kidnaping. Secreting Felicia and the nurse in a suburban boardinghouse, Cissy embarked on a hectic social life in London until detectives employed by the Count located Felicia and took her by force to Austria. During the next two years Felicia was shifted from convent to convent to frustrate efforts by her mother's detectives to get her back. Hearst's *Herald and Examiner* in Chicago, always alert to discredit the family operating the rival *Tribune*, produced a feature story about Felicia as "the most-kidnaped girl in American history."

Flexing its political muscles, the Patterson-McCormick newspaper trust persuaded President Taft to appeal to "friend Nicky," as he called Czar Nicholas of Russia. The Czar forced Count Gizycki to return Felicia to her mother. Another eight years of litigation and negotiation between husband and wife were required before the Count acceded to a divorce in return for a final financial settlement. It was in this nonmarriageable limbo that Cissy learned to take men as she found them.

Having regained her daughter after this Homeric struggle, Cissy proceeded to ignore her. "Little children," she would explain, "are a nuisance." Felicia grew up in the shadow of a string of governesses. At times she had a bodyguard as well. When she played hide-and-seek with her cousins, the bodyguard hid with her.

Felicia put roots down nowhere. One summer she would be sequestered in a Southern resort, another in Newport, a third in Woods Hole. She attended seven exclusive and expensive boarding schools, including Foxcroft in Virginia, where she acquired a reputation for sophistication by writing a short story about a man who killed himself to allow his friend to marry his wife. "Mother hates me," she told classmates, with a fling of her blond hair, "because I look like my father."

While Cissy was in Paris writing two autobiographical novels, Felicia used to tell strangers that she was an orphan, which came close to the fact. Cissy wrote as Countess Eleanor Gizycka, finding the title useful for social and literary promotional purposes. Her first novel, *Glass Houses*, featured a rough-hewn admirer resembling her ranch foreman, Cal Carrington. He shoots somebody patterned on Senator Borah for trifling with the heroine's affections. Despite competition from a bitchy Washington hostess (Alice

Roosevelt Longworth), this noble deed clears the way for marriage between the heroine and a diplomat (Count von Bernstorff, with a few touches of Count Gizy).

Glass Houses first appeared in French in Europe. Since it portrayed Cissy's mother as an unspeakable vulgarian, the English version was delayed until the elder Mrs. Patterson died. Similarly, the second novel, a cruel account of life with Gizy entitled *Fall Flight*, did not appear until after his death.

When she returned to Washington from Paris, Cissy found her ugly-duckling daughter nubile and attractive. "Suddenly mother wanted me around all the time," Felicia told Drew during their wedding trip, "but by then I was always in a state of terror, laughter or rage in her presence."

Drew had been planning a journalistic excursion to the Far East, this time minus the lecturing. He had a syndicate lined up to distribute his stories and pledges of financial help from Uncle Drew, who was making more money than ever as the publisher of *Iron Age* and other trade magazines. Wedding gifts from relatives, including Cissy Patterson, transformed an adventure-on-a-shoe-string into a honeymoon "first-class, all expenses paid."

The newlyweds did travel first class across the Pacific on the S.S. *President Monroe*, on which Drew had worked as an ordinary seaman during his previous trip. Thereafter the quality of their accommodations varied. The troop train "full of fleas" from Mukden to Tientsin did not seem first class to Felicia, but she dutifully typed out notes and tried not to feel bored in the intervals when she was not stiff with fright.

Felicia and Drew had not known each other too well when they married. During the trip they found occasion for the exchange of confidences of the sort that are ordinarily made during courtship, but there were other times when their differences in background and temperament emerged. Felicia shivered when Drew told her tolerantly that it was "nice to be amused by one's wife on one's honeymoon." She realized she had been prattling.

Renting a car, the Pearsons traveled across the Gobi Desert in the company of Mary Waller, a Chicago friend of Cissy, and Helen Van Sant, a nurse from the Peking Hospital. They were stopped at the border between Inner and Outer Mongolia. The commissioner of police invited them into his round felt tent. After accepting presents of cigarettes, chocolate and blue-and-gold handkerchiefs he used a paintbrush to paint a large passport to the sacred capital of Urga for "Drew Pearson and his three wives."

In the remote area between Russia and China they witnessed the arrival of a motorcade of two hundred American automobiles carrying cases of rifles. The accompanying Russian soldiers stopped to torment a wounded eagle. Pretending, to Felicia's disgust, to enjoy the sport, Drew got close enough to snap pictures without being observed. As soon as he could, he filed the documented story because a covert imperialistic move by the Soviet Union outweighed any vague Marxist sympathies in his mind.

Pearson's account of what he had seen greatly interested the American military attaché in Peking. The story, however, did not excite U.S. editors in that isolationist era of speakeasies and Wall Street speculation. Only one newspaper, Hearst's New York *American*, printed Drew's exclusive about Russia's preliminary probe into Mongolia.

On the way home he stopped in India for another attempt to interview Gandhi. The Mahatma was out of jail by this time, but he may have resented Drew's article in the magazine *Asia*. He sent word that he was fasting and could not be disturbed. The new rebuff shook Drew. He accused himself of missing journalistic opportunities in an effort to keep Felicia amused. There would, he realized, be no string of great-man interviews to redeem his costly hybrid jaunt. At the end he would have an expensive wife to support, no job in sight, not even teaching. He had a ghastly prevision of utter professional and domestic failure, which Felicia somehow sensed and shared.

In New York things looked brighter. Cissy and Elmer Schlesinger were on hand to welcome them with competitive designs for the future. Cissy offered Felicia an astronomical allowance, but Felicia wanted no allowance at all. Her husband, she said, would support her. She would not even consider a loan to get Drew on his journalistic feet.

As if he had anticipated how Felicia would act, Elmer Schlesinger then advanced his own idea. Elmer was a black-knit-tie and stiff-white-collar man, austere in appearance but known for his daring flights of imagination as a lawyer. He had set aside $100,000 to establish Drew in the printing business in Philadelphia. He was wealthy enough in his own right to afford the gesture, he pointed out. Drew's business competence could not be questioned after his achievements in Serbia, Schlesinger argued, and if public life was Drew's goal, hadn't Ben Franklin started as a printer in Philadelphia?

Drew agonized over the decision, seeking advice from relatives and friends. Dr. Pearson, whose Swarthmore Chautauqua was reeling under increasing competition from radio and the movies, advocated acceptance of the offer. Edna Pearson noted that if her elder son worked in Philadelphia, he, like Leon, would be able to live near them again in Swarthmore. John T. Flynn, Drew's friend from Columbia University days, counseled rejection. "Do you want to be a Quaker," he demanded, "or do you want to make money? You can't have it both ways."

Drew decided not to become a printer. Almost immediately— so quickly, in fact, as to suggest that he may have glimpsed the new project before he said good-bye to the old one—he obtained the journalistic foothold in Washington of which he had been dreaming. He became foreign editor, no less, of David Lawrence's experimental but well-financed new *United States Daily*.

David Lawrence was an established Washington correspondent. Though his *United States Daily* evolved into a weekly magazine known as *U.S. News & World Report*, it began as a repository for documents of governmental importance. It was being broadened in scope to include diplomatic material. Drew would receive only a moderate salary as foreign editor, but he would be permitted to cover international conferences on a free-lance basis, at his own expense, using his connection with the paper for purposes of accreditation. The arrangement seemed tailored to his convenience.

The offer, Drew explained to Felicia, came through Uncle Drew. This seemed plausible. He had extended himself frequently to be helpful to his nephew and namesake. Actually, Cissy was responsible. She had encouraged Lawrence and put money in his new project during conferences at the Dupont Circle. Interviewed forty years later, Lawrence confirmed that Cissy had asked him to help her son-in-law on a confidential basis so as not to hurt her daughter's pride. With the passage of time he saw no further need for secrecy.

"I was not taken then or later with Drew Pearson," said David Lawrence dryly, "and I had no contact with the man you refer to as Uncle Drew."

2

Cissy made another generous gesture for which nobody gave her credit. She established residence in New York, partly to please her husband and partly, perhaps, to leave the young couple a clear field in Washington.

Schlesinger was glad to resume practice with his old New York law firm of Chadbourne, Stanchfield & Levy, though he would have remained in Washington if his wife had wished. Cissy rented an enormous apartment on Fifth Avenue accessible to the law office. For social purposes she purchased the fifty-seven-acre Vincent Astor estate in Sands Point, Long Island. When she expressed admiration for the meals produced by Clementine, the Vanderbilts' French cook, Elmer stole Clementine by offering her more money.

Despite his devotion, Schlesinger never felt sure of Cissy. During their wedding cruise on a private yacht through the Mediterranean she had written friends in Washington that her marriage might not work out but that Felicia, at least, would be happy—"for she has a lovely boy." As an endorsement of marriage, that ranked with Tallulah Bankhead's appraisal of her vows to John Emery as "a slip of the tongue."

In Cissy's absence Felicia could hardly object to making temporary use of the third-floor suite at The Dupont Circle reserved for distinguished guests. Grace and Calvin Coolidge occupied that suite the following spring when the White House was being renovated, and Colonel Charles A. Lindbergh stayed there when he reached Washington after his exciting solo flight across the Atlantic to Paris.

On the theory that they had to learn to live on Drew's salary, Felicia and Drew moved from The Dupont Circle to a small rented house in Bethesda, Maryland, in the summer of 1926. The change was too abrupt. They knew nobody among the neighbors. Suburban existence itself disgusted them. In the fall they shifted back to the District of Columbia.

In what later became a major housing trend, a number of young white couples known to Felicia were buying up and restoring old crackerboxes in Georgetown, then a black slum. The Pearson house, however, was a large, beautiful structure dating back to the Federal period. "We scraped our money together to buy it," explained Felicia, but her friends understood that it was a gift from Cissy Patterson. The place was so large it required a minimal staff of two servants. The mere upkeep strained Drew's finances.

Once established socially by the house, Felicia began to go to four or five parties a week. Drew's journalistic friends, who were on the lean, intellectual side, wondered how he could work in such a frivolous atmosphere. They viewed Felicia as an undisciplined, irresponsible young woman.

Sensing her disadvantage, Felicia began to review movies for the Washington *Post*. She wrote less vigorously but with more style than her mother. Having intrigued boldly for the job through Evalyn Walsh McLean, owner of the Hope Diamond, hostess of Friendship House and wife of Ned McLean, publisher of the *Post*, she felt obliged to plug away at it, though it proved more arduous than she had expected. It got in the way of the novel she wanted to write, it did not reconcile Drew's friends to her and it did not add much to the family income.

Drew insisted on a close watch over expenses, but Felicia had nobody to explain domestic economy to her. Out in Bethesda, she told friends indignantly, Drew had wanted her to press his pants. Among these friends she promptly became a martyr to a highly unsuitable marriage. Imagine a countess, or the daughter of a countess, pressing pants!

From the beginning, Drew had been an outsider in his wife's crowd. One of her disappointed suitors invariably referred to him as "that Chautauqua lecturer from Pennsylvania." The adjectives used were "cheap" and "lousy." Others tagged Drew as a fortune hunter who had so disgusted Cissy that she moved to New York to get away from him.

Early in 1927 Felicia paid a hurried visit to The Dupont Circle. President Coolidge's personal possessions were being moved in. Noticing forty-eight stacked pairs of black cotton socks, she gleefully abstracted one pair as a souvenir for Drew. A distorted report spread among her friends that Drew had been wearing one of Cal's cast-off suits.

Drew did not worry over his lack of popularity with Felicia's playmates. This was the era of wonderful nonsense in Washington as well as elsewhere. The socially active young-marrieds concentrated on gossip about adultery and the excessive consumption of bootleg liquor. Drew had other interests. Unless somebody touched on them he tended to be a drag in social conversation. He could be sarcastic and cutting, but he lacked any gift for banter. Felicia knew that her friends brushed him off as a bore or worse.

As the months rolled by, Felicia accumulated grievances. Drew cherished her in some ways, she told intimates, but he did not consider her important as a person. In the morning she could not get to him through his newspaper. In the evening she had learned not to chatter about the events of her day. If she had made a literary discovery, Baudelaire or Villon, for example, he would talk about immoral Frenchmen. He had a thing about Frenchmen.

Drew did not give her enough of his time, his mind or his body, Felicia concluded. He did not love her, she said; he had married her "for other reasons." She drank more than she should in an effort to determine who she was, where she belonged and what she wanted to do. Though he restrained comment on Felicia's domestic shortcomings and her persistent flitting about, Drew bore down on her drinking. On one occasion he reminded her that she had been tipsy three times in two weeks. She promptly offered him a divorce. "You are my wife," he replied stiffly, "and I shall try to be a good husband always."

3

Drew and Cissy kept in contact. When she came down to The Dupont Circle on visits, they exchanged comment on the political and social developments uppermost in their minds. Invariably Cissy had new ideas for helping her daughter, but Felicia cherished what was left of her independence. Some things could be arranged through Drew, who made occasional trips to New York.

In her customary flamboyant style Cissy was reaching out for social prominence in Manhattan. One evening Drew arrived unexpectedly at the Schlesinger apartment on Fifth Avenue after the invited guests had assembled for a dinner party at which topless quadroon girls from Harlem danced the black bottom. Cissy may not have relished an extra man at that particular party or the butler may have made a mistake. He told Drew that Mrs. Schlesinger was not available. Drew left with no display of irritation. Coming by a week later, he was warmly welcomed.

Drew realized that he was making no impression on Washington. He conscientiously edited and turned in State Department releases and documents for the *United States Daily*, but he did little writing and his byline was less familiar around town than his wife's. Deciding on a social splash, he threw a large party in Georgetown with the help of Cissy's guest list, using his extensive and beautiful rear garden to supplement the space within the house.

The guests included many of Washington's top politicians. Some of them did not know the host, but they came anyway, including one Supreme Court Justice, the cherry on the social fruit cup. There were starched shirts, white ties and formal dresses, masses of flowers, a free-flowing bar and an eight-piece orchestra.

Arriving late and alone from New York in Russian sables and diamonds, Cissy was greeted at the door by an impeccably dressed Drew with an effusive kiss and a booming "It's a wonderful party, Mother." So it was. The newspaper society reporters gave it extensive coverage. Traffic outside was tied up from 8 P.M. to 4 o'clock the next morning. Everybody seemed impressed except Felicia's friends. To them it was stuffy.

Felicia had news for Drew and her mother: she was pregnant. Drew was touched. He took his wife to the movies—the first time they had been out alone together for months. After the show they strolled to a place on Wisconsin Avenue for a snack and a talk in which they reached desperately toward understanding, since they were both still in love.

The domestic atmosphere changed. Felicia dropped movie-reviewing and most of her party-going. Drew was profuse in small attentions. Cissy Patterson came down more often from New York with presents which Felicia was willing to accept as her due. Drew took Felicia to Swarthmore for a visit, exposing her again to the comforting affection that existed among his mother and father, his sisters and brother and their families.

New York seemed to be losing its appeal for Cissy. With the death of the elder Mrs. Patterson, her first novel had appeared in the United States. Though chintzy in conception and clumsy in execution, it gave her entree to the Algonquin Round Table of creative back-scratchers in Manhattan, including Herbert Bayard Swope, her croquet-playing neighbor in Sands Point; Neysa Mc-Mein, Heywood Broun, Dorothy Parker, Alexander Woollcott and others.

Cissy's association with this literary group was primarily social. She had stopped writing. Glamorous but somewhat faded, she would appear at Round Table gatherings with an entourage of two or three attentive young men, since Elmer Schlesinger was usually too absorbed in his legal work to accompany her. Their marriage was reported to be unraveling.

Cissy pounced on Washington when she heard that Ned Mc-Lean, on the verge of a nervous breakdown from overdrinking, wanted to dispose of the Washington *Post*. Cissy had money enough to outbid any prospective rival for that newspaper. What should she do? Knowing the intensity of her journalistic craving, Drew urged her to do what she wanted, but her brother Joe came down from New York to argue vehemently against taking over a losing operation in a town known as a graveyard for publishers. In the end Cissy followed Captain Patterson's advice and let Eugene Meyer pick up the *Post* at a bargain price.

4

Reporters tend to identify with those they encounter on a beat. Thus a man covering police headquarters begins to sound like the cops and robbers he writes about, a sportswriter takes on the attitudes of athletes and a political reporter adopts the manipulative habits of politicians. As a diplomatic correspondent Drew Pearson looked without humility upon Presidents and Secretaries of State. He did not esteem them in general: American foreign policy since World War I, in his opinion, had been shortsighted, money-grubbing, isolationist and mean.

To survive in Washington Pearson needed to enlarge his journalistic beachhead. He kept his eye open for other reporters who would sympathize with his views enough to steer him eventually into a position with some major newspaper or news service.

Most of the regulars in the State Department press room were as dapper, discreet and conservative as their diplomatic counterparts. Not so Robert S. Allen, the young Washington Bureau chief of the *Christian Science Monitor*. When Drew first noticed this doughty little man, he was waving a pejorative finger at Secretary of State Frank B. Kellogg and demanding to know why Marines had been sent to Nicaragua, why Mexico had been "attacked" and why other countries south of the border were being "picked on." Kellogg protested to the *Monitor*, which rebuked its correspondent for impertinence. Overnight Drew Pearson and the smoldering Bob Allen became friends.

Allen was a native of Kentucky who got into the Army in World War I by adding a couple of years to his age. He lost a toe in combat. He had worked on newspapers before, during and after his student days at the University of Wisconsin. He joined the Ku Klux Klan to expose it. He covered a closed conference of the Non-Partisan League from a hiding place in the rafters over the auditorium and heard enough for a national exclusive even though he fell to the stage in the middle of the proceedings.

Bob Allen had a way of stumbling into news. He was taking postgraduate work at the University of Munich when Adolf Hitler tried his beerhall putsch. Allen became an impromptu foreign correspondent. In the wake of that success he had worked all around the globe on special assignments for the *Monitor* before he was assigned to Washington.

Another Pearson friend was Ludwell Denny, a tall gaunt man who had been a Unitarian minister and a free-lance correspondent before he took to writing left-of-center editorials for the Scripps-Howard chain of newspapers out of Washington. Drew became a frequent visitor to Denny's home and a favorite with his wife, Josephine, a fresh-faced, plump woman known as "Peter," and their two children.

A different kind of associate was George Abell, the son of Charles Shepherdson Abell, publisher of the Baltimore *Sun*. George was a jovial, warmhearted fellow who went through life with the insouciance bred of large trust funds. Through his uncle, Francis T. Homer of Baltimore, who acted as financial adviser to Ned McLean, he obtained a reportorial job on the Washington *Post*. Assigned to the night trick at police headquarters, he showed up in fur coat, bowler and cane. He drove to stabbings and murders in the slums in his own blue electric automobile.

Dixie Tighe, a rival reporter, made the mistake one evening of calling George a snob. George, who had been drinking, left the press room with dignity. Returning with a large pair of shears, he cut off half of Dixie's glorious bronze tresses, a mutilation and humiliation for which she never forgave him.

Drew had been cultivating Latin-American diplomats whom he met originally the The Dupont Circle. Inasmuch as they were ignored by most Washington correspondents, they appreciated a little attention. Every once in a while they came up with something they wanted to see in print. Drew could not use their tips in the *United States Daily*, but he could pass them along to George, an apolitical fellow who enjoyed stirring up excitement for the fun of it.

Copies of some letters from Lawrence Dennis, a State Department official in Panama, giving details of American corruption in the Canal Zone, had been turned over to Pearson. He gave them to Abell. George kept the name of the letter writer out of his stories, but the information was traced to Dennis, who lost his job. Dennis emerged later as an intellectual leader of the pre-World War II isolationists.

Another Pearson-Abell exclusive involved Gustave Pabst, scion of the Milwaukee brewing family and newly appointed First Secretary of the U.S. Embassy in Lima, Peru. Traveling by train to his post, Pabst got into a quarrel with an overbearing stranger. He knocked the man down. Later he learned to his dismay that the stranger was President Leguía, the dictator of Peru.

The American Ambassador, when informed of the incident, apologized abjectly to the dictator. Nothing about the quarrel appeared in the Peruvian press. Disclosure in Washington created such a ruckus that the State Department felt obliged to deny it. A formal demand was made that the Washington *Post* fire Abell. The *Post* confirmed the facts through an independent investigation and gave George a substantial raise in salary.

Drew covered the Geneva Disarmament Conference in 1927 as a stringer for several American newspapers. He returned a week before the end of the conference, early in July, in order to be with Felicia when she had her child. Before he left Geneva Drew knew that the conference had been frustrated by William B. Shearer, a fake reporter with credentials from the New York *Daily News*. Drew's reports led to a Senate investigation. Shearer, it was confirmed, had been paid $250,000 by several U.S. naval shipbuilding companies. He had earned his money by spreading false reports which fomented disagreement between the U.S. and British delegations to the conference.

Felicia bore a six-pound daughter, the sweetest, prettiest, most affectionate baby imaginable. She was named Ellen Cameron after her stern Methodist great-grandmother on the Pearson side, but her red hair obviously came from Grandma Cissy on the Patterson side. Cissy and Drew were fascinated by Ellen. He began doing more of his work at home. When he concentrated on a job, he could be as oblivious as a capo-regime of a woman in the house, or, for that matter, a baby, but if and when he wanted to look at or talk to Ellen, as he often did, there she was.

Audacity was the order of Drew's journalistic day. Hearing that President Coolidge intended to go by battleship to Havana for the sixth International Conference of American States, he wired the White House for permission to go along. The President granted his request.

The attitude of the Latin-American nations at this time was fraught with suspicion because of the dispatch of American Marines to Nicaragua. After President Coolidge's vaguely conciliatory speech on January 6, 1928, a State Department spokesman said pointedly that the United States reserved the right to use military force at any time anywhere in the Western Hemisphere to protect the lives and property of its citizens. The best the conference could do was postpone for another two years any discussion of the periodic forcible intervention of the United States in the domestic affairs of its neighbors.

After Drew's savage reports on this imperialistic lapse appeared in several newspapers, President Coolidge wrote to Andrew Cameron Pearson in New York. He had been deceived, the President complained. He had offered accommodations on his battleship to an old friend who contributed to his campaigns and who came down to Washington every so often to lobby for lower postal rates on magazines. Lo and behold! in his place had come a younger Drew Pearson, from Washington, who had betrayed his hospitality.

Uncle Drew was not an undiluted admirer of Calvin Coolidge. He liked to tell about the time the President pulled out a box of choice Havana cigars in front of a visiting delegation, selected one and lit it, then returned the box to a drawer without offering it to anyone. After a talk with his nephew he conceded that Cal had known the difference between the two Drews right along.

That ended the incident, except for a letter from Uncle Drew to his brother Paul in Swarthmore. Dr. Pearson was relieved to hear of his son's innocence. He wished, however, he said in a return letter, that, instead of causing so much turmoil, Drew would try the dignified kind of editorial writing produced by Walter Lippmann.

Drew worried chiefly over Felicia's reaction. He explained nervously that he had more than covered expenses on the Cuban trip. He had added two Havana newspapers—*El Mundo* and *Nación*—to the string of publications which he serviced with Washington items at space rates. To his relief, she gave him an admiring glance. She had a good mind, she said, to throw out that dirty old pair of Cal's black socks which they had been saving as a souvenir!

Drew was working at home on a campaign for an international agreement to outlaw war as an instrument of national policy. This idea, which provided the sole occasion for U.S. cooperation with Europe during the 1920s, came from Salmon O.

Levinson, a sincere if somewhat ingenuous Chicago lawyer. Levinson carried the idea to Senator Borah, Borah went to Secretary Kellogg and Kellogg approached Aristide Briand, the canny French Premier, who was receptive on the theory that it might pave the way for his own pet project of European union.

More active than Pearson in drumming up public support for outlawing war was Dorothy Detzer, an intense, busy little woman with auburn hair who for twenty years lobbied in Washington for Ski Hull's mother's old outfit, the Women's International League for Peace and Freedom. She and Drew had been introduced by Ludwell Denny one day when Miss Detzer came to the State Department for a personal interview with Secretary Kellogg.

"Not the Saint of the Serbian Mountains!" exclaimed Dorothy Detzer with mock reverence when she met Drew. Having worked with the American Friends Service Committee in Vienna in 1920–1922, she had heard quite a bit about his reputation for austerity and hard work at Peć. They became friends on sight. In addition to their common experiences abroad, they were about the same age and had a similar attitude toward most of the questions of the day.

By spring Drew's domestic situation had deteriorated. He and Felicia engaged in open quarrels in which he usually gave way. She was drinking again and going about socially with companions of whom he disapproved. The situation became so strained that he moved out. Ludwell and Josephine Denny and Dorothy Detzer took him on picnics to cheer him up, but he was a poor companion, unable to credit his own unhappiness.

Representatives of the world powers gathered in Paris in the early summer of 1928 to exorcise the specter of war forever with a few strokes of the pen. Since the American media found it convenient to assign their European correspondents to the ceremonial signing, Drew turned out to be the only reporter traveling to France with Secretary Kellogg. They became well acquainted during the leisurely voyage across the Atlantic.

At ceremonial functions in Europe people wondered about the identity of the sober young man in formal clothes who almost invariably appeared at Secretary Kellogg's side. It was Drew

Pearson. A few days before the Paris ceremony, an enterprising American journalist, Harold Horan, unearthed and published a secret memorandum between France and Britain which seemed to rely on the old system of alliances to avert war.

Indignantly, President Coolidge instructed Secretary Kellogg to cancel his plan to visit London after the signing and, instead, pay an anti-British call on President William T. Cosgrave of the Irish Free State. Pearson accompanied Kellogg to Dublin and again was the sole reportorial escort of the Secretary of State on board ship headed for home.

Drew was in the radio shack of the liner one morning when a news item arrived to the effect that Herbert Hoover, already campaigning for President since Coolidge did not choose to run again, was listing the Kellogg-Briand Pact as a Republican achievement. Pearson was disturbed. If the pact became an issue in the presidential campaign, its ratification by the Senate would be doubtful.

Persuading the radio operator to shelve the item, Drew sent a wireless message to the *New York Times*, with which he had a free-lance arrangement, asking that they query Kellogg as to whether he was going to permit his pact to "become a football of politics." When the query was placed before him, Kellogg predictably denounced partisanship. His statement landed on the front page of the *Times* and forced a vastly embarrassed Hoover to change his tune. Pearson produced an exclusive follow-up for the United Press, with which he also had an arrangement. The result was quick and overwhelming ratification of the pact by the Senate.

Drew was acquiring the kind of journalistic clout which at one time might have impressed Felicia's friends and even Felicia. It was too late. While he was in Europe, Felicia had made up her mind. She had gone to Reno, leaving Ellen in the care of a housekeeper. Long-distance appeals from Drew and Cissy to Felicia went unanswered. Descending in a State Department elevator one afternoon in mid-August, 1928, Drew glimpsed in another man's newspaper a headline announcing his divorce. It was, he always said, the greatest failure of his life.

He sustained a second setback of a family nature. Andrew

Cameron Pearson had been displeased by the appearance of a feature article on Drew Pearson as an outstanding critic of Herbert Hoover. Coolidge was one thing and Hoover another. The ardent Republican publisher literally worshiped Herbert Hoover. To avoid further confusion, he announced to the family, he was dropping the name of Drew. Henceforth, he said, he would be known by his initials, A.C., which were already used at his office.

Except for the impact of the news on Paul and Edna Pearson, to whom family solidarity was sacred, Drew was not unduly disturbed. A. C. Pearson would not discuss his decision with Drew. From then on the two men did not speak to each other.

The divorce arrangement between Drew and Felicia divided custody of Ellen between them, for six-month periods. Increasingly, Felicia felt that she could not bear to give up her daughter. One day before the expiration of her custody period she departed by ship for Europe with Ellen, leaving a message for Cissy that she would place herself under the protection of Polish relatives of Count Gizycki, with whom she had been secretly in periodic touch since her father's death in 1926.

Nothing could have enraged Cissy more. Her granddaughter had been kidnaped by her daughter, she said hysterically, dispatching Drew in pursuit by the next available ship. He left in such a hurry that he had to wireless back from the mid-Atlantic asking the family's black maid, Izetta, to forward his favorite black sweater, which he had forgotten.

Pressure was put on the State Department to pick up Felicia's passport in Poland as a way of forcing her return to the United States. Felicia eluded the trap by going to Paris, where she found a job writing corset ads for the European office of *Harper's Bazaar*. In letters to friends in Washington she confided that she hoped in time to emulate her mother's literary career.

Month after month the messy maneuvering over Ellen's tiny body continued. On both sides it seemed to be an almost compulsive repetition of the earlier struggle over Felicia. This time the family had one consolation: the story did not get into the newspapers.

CHAPTER VI

Desperate Years

DURING HIS TRAVELS ABROAD Drew Pearson tried to make contacts which would be of future use. He first met Michael MacWhite, a wide-smiling Irishman, at the 1927 Geneva Naval Disarmament Conference. As a member of the British delegation to that conference, MacWhite did not conceal his subversive sentiments from the Yankee reporters. He was such an Anglophobe that at the League of Nations, where he was also accredited, he spoke in French—knowing no Gaelic—lest somebody think he was English. When he showed up subsequently in Washington as Ireland's representative, Drew knew where to go for anti-British policy on any diplomatic issue.

Two friends of MacWhite approached Drew in Dublin during his 1928 trip with Secretary of State Kellogg. The three had dinner together. Richard James Duggan and Joseph McGrath studied the thirty-year-old American with care. They saw a tight-lipped journalist, independent, apparently tough and, to judge from his frugal style, in need of some cash. He held an editorship on what seemed to be a semigovernmental newspaper in Washington; he had good social and political contacts there and a special knowledge of Latin-American affairs. Duggan and McGrath were satisfied; he matched MacWhite's description per-

fectly. If their plans worked out, they said, seeking no commitment in advance, he would hear from them.

Earlier in Ireland's brief history as a free state several small
hospital lotteries had flourished and died. Duggan and McGrath
projected a continuing mammoth lottery in which tickets sold
around the world—including the United States, England and
other countries where such sales were illegal—would be drawn
on horses in a famous steeplechase for maximum dramatic effect.

Arguing that it would help balance the Irish budget, the pro-
moters had prepared a Public Charitable Hospitals bill in which
20 percent of the take would be earmarked for various public
and private hospitals and 7 percent for themselves as managers
of the enterprise. A year later, when the Dail passed the bill,
Drew received through diplomatic channels an offer of a five-year
contract, starting in 1930, as Western Hemisphere director of the
Irish Hospitals Sweepstake, at $30,000 a year, a chauffeur-driven
Lincoln Continental (a shrewd touch, that, for Drew!), plus legal
and other expenses.

The Irish Sweep posed a problem of conscience for many
Americans, particularly Drew. Lotteries had been popular during
colonial times—many early American newspapers would not have
been born or survived after birth without lottery advertisements
—but the Puritan tradition gradually asserted itself. By 1800 only
one governmental lottery, in Louisiana, was left; by the 1920s
the proliferation of lotteries had been discouraged by being
banned from the mails.

Not everybody condemned gambling for a worthy purpose.
Some said it was no worse than taking a drink. The predom-
inantly Irish hierarchy of the Catholic Church in America permitted raffles. Other religions hedged on the issue over the years.
Only the Society of Friends consistently and completely opposed
commercial games of chance.

Handling the Sweep would require Drew to repudiate part
of his Quaker heritage. Since much of his religious belief had
already been displaced by a composite political philosophy, this
presented no obstacle. The Friends would probably never know
about it. Here was an opportunity to earn a great deal of money
quickly for what could be construed as a technical violation of law.

However, it involved some risk of exposure, disgrace, even imprisonment.

He accepted the offer. Why did he do so? Lacking any explanation from Drew—this was one thing he never talked about—it may be surmised that he remembered the genteel poverty of his youth. Having tasted the delights of unlimited money and unchallengeable social status during his three-year marriage to Cissy Patterson's daughter, he was determined to live in the great world on his own terms.

He rented a desk in the ratty-looking office of a Dutch lawyer named David Babp in the Evans Building on New York Avenue not far from the White House and hired a former prohibition undercover man as his assistant. Nearby desks were devoted to similarly devious purposes, one to agitation in the Virgin Islands, another to revolution against Machado, the Cuban dictator.

An RCA cable would come to Drew's assistant saying that $500 or $1,000 had been lodged that day in a Swiss bank. Later Drew would turn over $500 or $1,000 in large bills to the assistant to meet expenses. The assistant was never told how Drew obtained the money from Switzerland, but he got the impression that the Algonquin Hotel in New York City was used as a drop.

Information on those who had drawn horses in the three big races every year would reach Babp's. Multiple copies would be made at Drew's house for distribution by Western Union to the newspapers. Packages of tickets arrived at Babp's. Special communications from Douglas Stewart Ltd. in London, a bookkeeping firm owned by Joseph Freeman and his son Sidney, who had arrangements with Duggan-McGrath's Irish Hospitals Trust, also flowed across the desk at Babp's, but Drew himself never appeared there, only his assistant.

Thus it came about that Drew introduced modern mass gambling to North and South America. He never claimed credit for this—on the contrary, he went to extraordinary lengths later to cover his tracks—but the secret job enabled him to coast through the desperate years after his divorce.

Some hint of internal stress could be detected in his social life during this period. He allowed George Abell to tutor him in drinking and Senator Millard Tydings, a carefree young bachelor from Baltimore, to instruct him in evasive tactics with women. He had moved around the corner from N Street to an odd, smaller structure at 1218 Thirtieth Street which was sandwiched in between two buildings on a steep hill. With its dormer windows and long, protruding eaves, his "woodland retreat," as George called it, was a romantic advertisement for a bachelor who was accessible but not anxious for feminine company.

To those who asked about his impressive car and uniformed chauffeur, Drew said he was doing public-relations work of a confidential nature. His companions considered him a man of mystery. That had one small advantage: it cloaked his continuing lack of effervescence in ordinary conversation.

For the fun of driving his fancy car, Drew soon assigned his chauffeur to other duties. After dinner one evening on a Maryland estate when he had drunk more than usual, he ran into an iron gate, damaging the car badly and landing in bed with painful though not serious injuries. Thereafter he used his chauffeur or kept his alcoholic consumption within limits when he drove.

In the company of Cissy Patterson, who relished a blend of brilliance and wickedness in a man, Drew threw out hints of dangerous endeavor. She pretended to be mystified, but she made it her business to discover what he was doing and she did not consider it heinous. They were on better terms than ever. She blamed Felicia not only for kidnaping Ellen but also for the breakup of the marriage with Drew. Very little news came from Felicia, though she did accept some money from her mother for Ellen's upkeep.

Cissy was maneuvering with considerable intensity and skill for control of one of Hearst's two Washington newspapers. She spent less and less time with Elmer Schlesinger in New York. Late in January, 1929, she informed her husband that she wanted a divorce. A week later, he had a heart attack on a golf course at Aiken, South Carolina, where he was visiting a friend, and died.

Frantic with remorse, Cissy left with Drew in her three-room private railroad car to bring back the body to Washington. Drew handled all the arrangements for an impressive funeral service at The Dupont Circle. The honorary pallbearers included the Speaker of the House, the British Ambassador, cabinet members, Congressmen and industrialists.

Soon after Schlesinger's body had been interred on Long Island in a mausoleum designed by his widow, Drew's journalistic ship made port. He was named diplomatic correspondent in Washington for the Baltimore *Sun*. Though he had long wanted something like this, he saw no reason to abandon the *United States Daily*, which meant prestige, particularly abroad, or the Irish Sweepstakes, to which he was contractually bound.

Conditions in the United States had been favorable to penetration by the Duggan-McGrath transmogrified gamble. Irish immigrants and others clamored for a chance to sell and buy tickets. The hospital benefit cast a philanthropic veil over promotional profits. The drumbeat of ballyhoo from Dublin kept global interest alive between draws.

Postmaster General Walter F. Brown, President Hoover's political mentor, had the responsibility for enforcing the U.S. antilottery statute. For a while he was preoccupied with the negotiation of contracts for flying the mail across country at fat subsidies. By the time he noticed the Irish Sweep, an American had emerged as a large prizewinner and an enthusiastic clientele was being serviced by strings of agents who kept two free tickets for themselves out of every book of twelve they sold.

All Sweep tickets were printed in Ireland. The Postmaster General ordered the seizure of those which entered the country in unsealed envelopes. Duggan-McGrath promptly sealed the envelopes. When suspicious-looking sealed envelopes from Ireland were opened anyway, the envelopes were routed via Canada and Mexico. When even those were opened, tickets moved into the country in other containers, including hollowed-out religious books.

Efforts to pounce on individual ticket sellers were met by the formation of "clubs" of lottery clients.

Periodic revision of lottery rules and tactics kept sales rising. Arrangements were made in Dublin for every horse to be drawn twenty times instead of once, thereby assuring twenty manageable first prizes instead of a monstrous single one. (Nobody thought of the more modern wrinkle of breaking down a huge prize into an annual lifetime income.) In the United States, Drew learned to direct his publicity not at the stuffy city desks, which handled general news, but at the freewheeling sports departments, where a few writers were always glad to peddle tickets on the side.

The Post Office Department Solicitor, Horace J. Donnelly, threatened to bar newspapers from the mails for printing stories about big wins, which heated the public imagination. Somebody—presumably Drew—induced publishers to howl "Censorship!" Donnelly soon had to concede that a score in the world's largest and most spectacular lottery was legitimate news.

A borderline situation involved stories telling how large winners spent their loot. Some newspapers steered clear of these as dangerous, while others took a chance in hope of building circulation. A safe compromise worked out by Pearson eliminated lottery news from editions which went through the mails and let things rip in editions sold from newsstands.

Pearson's greatest coup as a gambling underboss was a Samuel Goldwyn moving picture called *The Winning Ticket* about a Brooklyn scrubwoman who won a half-million dollars on the Irish Hospitals Sweepstake. After all arrangements had been made, Drew hired a former Washington *Post* reporter, later on *Time*, to go to Hollywood at $250 a week to watch that the provided script —including one scene showing Irish cops selling the illicit lottery tickets—was not changed at the studio.

Despite all legal obstacles and moral objections, the Irish Sweep grew from year to year. British Prime Minister Ramsay Mac-Donald said its popularity in England demonstrated "the crumbling of civilization." The crumbling continued; before the expiration of Drew's five-year contract more tickets were being sold in New York City than in Ireland itself.

2

Drew was achieving through George Abell what he had failed to accomplish during his marriage to Felicia: a base in Washington society among those who wanted to keep their names out of the newspapers—the young set, the intellectuals, the poker-players, the Don Juans and the heavy drinkers. He went to the right parties with George, who had entree everywhere; he drank and flirted enough to get by. At the same time he kept one foot in Cissy's half of society—the Congressional pushers, cabinet members, military brass, professional entertainers and others who did want their names in the newspapers. It may or may not have occurred to him that sociability provided an excellent cover for his gambling operations.

A little like a Mafia counselor buying a Manhattan skyscraper with quarters from a Harlem numbers racket, Drew put some of his hot dollars into a confidential news service run by Wilfred Fleisher, a *New York Times* correspondent. The news service circulated pretty well in Washington, though not so well elsewhere. It gave Drew an outlet for an uninhibited analysis of diplomatic maneuvers. Not a few American politicians and foreign diplomats, other correspondents and local editors learned to watch for his news service articles, which supplemented his more routine dispatches to the Baltimore *Sun*.

The *Sun* was then a gentlemanly, if not a conservative, Democratic newspaper. Particularly during the predepression portion of the Hoover administration, it shrank from going as far in exposing American foreign policy as its diplomatic correspondent wanted. It proved more receptive to the smaller sensations he generated out of his continuing contacts with Latin-American diplomats like Carlos Dávila, the scholarly Chilean Ambassador who had been a revolutionary in his youth, a newspaperman and later (at Drew's suggestion) a lecturer on the Swarthmore Chautauqua.

Perhaps the most reverberating exclusive broken by Drew for the Baltimore *Sun* concerned the social war between Dolly Curtis Gann and Alice Roosevelt Longworth. Dolly, as the half-sister and official hostess of Vice President Charles Curtis, felt entitled to go in to Washington dinners ahead of any other woman except Mrs. Herbert Hoover. So did Alice, the wife of Speaker Nicholas Longworth. Their jockeying for social precedence began at Carlos Dávila's home. Drew heard about it from Dávila but, to protect his source, did not write the story until the struggle flared up again at Eugene Meyer's home.

The Vice President and the Speaker backed their ladies. The chambers of Congress over which they respectively presided became involved. From party to party the table tempest rose. The 220-pound Dolly, dressed like an Indian in full regalia, was a perfect Middle American foil for the slim, sophisticated Alice. Dolly's dull little husband, Edward Everett Gann, became a folk hero in some quarters for standing firm when President Hoover subtly supported the Longworths.

Drew tried to remain neutral. The House was "closer to the people" than the Senate, he wrote; that favored Alice's husband and therefore Alice. On the other hand, the Speaker had serious legislative duties. Maybe Curtis, as a mere figurehead in the Senate, was a more logical choice as "chief administration diner-out"? That in a way favored Dolly.

Meanwhile, Drew was entangled in a quarrel of his own. He first criticized Sir Esme Howard, the British Ambassador, at that disarmament conference where he met Michael MacWhite. Sir Esme was vacationing on Long Island, Drew noted, when he should have been in Geneva helping to avert a split between the U.S. and British delegations. The British Ambassador retaliated by severing diplomatic relations with the foreign editor of the *United States Daily*.

Drew returned to the attack some time later when Sir Esme, responding to an appeal from an American dry, issued a pious news release promising to respect American prohibition by not importing any more liquor for his embassy in Washington. Mac-White had a friend inside the embassy. Drew was able, therefore, to detail in print a variety and quantity of intoxicants already in storage there vastly exceeding any possible requirements of hospitality during the Ambassador's lifetime.

Sir Esme, by far the most influential diplomat in Washington, deplored this story in an unsporting letter to the Baltimore *Sun*. Drew evened up the account through the State Department Correspondents Association, which he had organized with himself as its first president.

In planning the organization's first annual dinner, he chose to honor Manuel C. Telles, the Mexican Ambassador, who in defense of President Calles and the Mexican Revolution had won every diplomatic joust with the United States since 1923. He arranged a special tribute to the Haitian Minister, who was ordinarily ignored at such affairs because of the smallness of his country and the color of his skin, and he "forgot" entirely to invite the British Ambassador, who was also dean of the diplomatic corps.

In a story for the *Sun*, which was not, unfortunately, cleared with J. Fred Essary, chief of its Washington Bureau, Drew described the Ambassador as "peeved" over the "snub" by the State Department reporters. He did not mention his rigging of the invitations or his connection with the association.

J. Fred, a tall, austere Tennessean who had covered the Wright Brothers' flight at Kitty Hawk, was appalled. An old hand in the Gridiron Club, Essary made a practice of never offending a news source, and he happened to be a particularly close friend of the British Ambassador. He had not been consulted originally about the addition of Drew to his staff. Confirmed in his suspicion that the recruit was a loner, incapable of working in harness or with discretion, he did all he could, short of risking his own position, to undermine Drew in Baltimore. The thrust against the Ambassador, he contended, damaged the newspaper's prestige.

Fortunately, George was available. As the great-grandson of the founder of the paper, he knew the predilections and habits of *Sun* executives. More important, he had influence with their wives. Even so, it was a close call; Drew almost lost his job. The Secretary of State, the French Ambassador and some other officials felt obliged, out of sympathy for Sir Esme, to boycott the first annual State Department Correspondents Association dinner, but the "parade of the diplomatic underdogs"—as somebody dubbed it—attracted a fair crowd.

The covenant of friendship between Drew and George held that Drew was the doer and George the writer. Drew disclaimed any ability to produce copy in the graceful style of which George was capable. All George needed to achieve literary distinction, he said, was the steady application of his pants seat to a typewriter chair. George accepted the homage without becoming less playful.

Drew gave heavily alcoholic, catered dinners, even occasional lunches, at his house. There were usually three at table besides himself, occasionally five, never more than seven. Less frequently, he splurged with large buffet suppers on the sweep of lawn behind the house. During one soul-searching evening drinking session with two colleagues, he succumbed to an impulse to get some papers from his attic office, stumbled on the steep stairs, fell and broke an arm. The session was not repeated.

At mixed social affairs Drew's specialty was an extradry double martini with a hint of vermouth and hardly any ice. At George's suggestion, these drinks were called Titanics because they were so large and went down so easily. Swishing this concoction in a silver shaker until the outside frosted, Drew would inform guests learnedly that too much ice "bruised" the gin.

The trouble with Titanics, opined Sir Willmott Lewis, veteran correspondent of the London *Times* who owned an abutting house, was that "One is not enough, two is not enough and three is much too much." An alternative beverage favored on warm summer evenings was a mint julep served Maryland fashion by crushing the mint. Under its influence, women hinted at love affairs and public officials blurted out secrets, to the amusement of the host, who, in Cissy's tradition, felt obliged to remain relatively sober.

It being *de rigueur* during the prohibition era to brag about one's cellar, Drew learned to display deceptively packaged liquor acquired through his lottery assistant, who still had access to bootleg supplies. George introduced him to the diplomatic-booze racket. Foreign liquor came by ocean freight to Baltimore, then by truck under convoy to the Washington embassies and legations.

A truckload of rare wines assigned to the Siamese Legation had been seized by capital police early in the Hoover administration. Once the State Department straightened that out, it became possible for wealthy Washingtonians to place orders for particular brands through their diplomatic friends, particularly at Christmas time.

As a reward for having taken a German diplomat named Emil Wiehl to Baltimore to visit his Uncle Homer, an influential pro-German American, George received several cases of Rhine and Moselle wine from the German Embassy. Since he had no storage space at his boardinghouse on Eye Street, George left the treasure at Drew's house.

"Why transport it any farther?" said Drew when his advice was sought on getting the wine to Baltimore. "We can use some good wine at our own parties."

"How can we do that?" demanded George. "My uncle expects the wine."

"I'll show you," said Drew. He led the way downstairs to the cellar closet where the wine had been stored. Wrenching a plank off the top case, he smashed a couple of bottles with a hammer.

"Good God," said George. "What are you doing?"

Drew smiled. The consignment must have arrived in poor condition, with many bottles smashed, he said. "Write your German friend about it, give two or three bottles to your uncle and we'll keep the rest. Nobody will ever know."

That's what was done and nobody ever knew. The successful stratagem inspired Drew to augment his supplies through his Latin-American friends.

Romance temporarily deprived Drew of George's social services. Several years earlier George's horse had dropped dead on New Hampshire Avenue while pulling a sleigh after an uncharacteristically heavy snowfall. He went to the nearest house to ask permission to use a telephone. The door was opened by a tall, cool girl of seventeen—Luvie Butler Moore—to whom he was attracted at first sight. She was living there with her grandmother, Mrs. Alben J. Butler.

Luvie's mother, Luvean, was dead. Her father, Colonel Dan Tyler Moore, modernizer of the U.S. Field Artillery and boon companion of President Theodore Roosevelt, had taken a South American woman as his second wife. Feeling uncomfortable with their stepmother, the three children by the first marriage went to live with their wealthy grandmother in a Washington house which was a replica of the Palazzo Caleone in Vicenza, Italy.

After acquiring polish at Miss Porter's School in Farmington, Connecticut, Luvie made her debut in Washington in 1928. She became a member of the Virginia horsy set, playing tennis, flirting, drinking mint juleps and riding to the hounds. Mrs. Butler tried to discourage George Abell's persistent attentions on the ground that he was not what family tradition required in a husband: a military man or a diplomat. Early in the summer of 1929, George appeared unexpectedly on the deck of the S.S. *Minnewaska* as the liner was about to leave its New York pier for Europe, with Mrs. Butler and Luvie among the passengers. "I think the visitors' gong sounded," said Mrs. Butler.

George smiled infuriatingly. "I'm going with you," he revealed. He had thrown up his newspaper job and booked passage.

Mrs. Butler managed to shed her granddaughter's suitor in Europe. George returned to Washington after visiting a friend in Brittany. From Lausanne he received a wire from Luvie, a girl who knew her own mind: "Come on over, let's get married."

After a honeymoon in the Swiss Alps, the couple returned to New York so George could look for employment. Jobs were scarce. Drew came to the rescue with a phone call from Washington: there was an opening with Lowell Mellett of the Scripps-Howard newspapers. George hurried down, applied and was accepted for work very much to his liking on a new gossip column called "Capital Capers."

George and Luvie stayed with Drew while they hunted for Washington quarters of their own. To Drew, Luvie seemed delightfully straight and witty. She was impressed by his crisp assurance. The three lived amicably together until George found, purchased and fixed up a small house not far away at 3140 Dumbarton Avenue. Naturally, the first Washington dinner party of the George Abells was in honor of their closest friend, Drew Pearson. In turn, the Abells came to one of Drew's small dinner parties.

Drew followed Cissy's formula for stimulating conversation by mixing up the guests. On a given evening he might seat a labor leader across from an industrialist, or Mrs. Ernest Simpson, a sophisticated woman from Baltimore whose name was not yet associated with the Prince of Wales, at the same table with Mrs. Jacob Leander Loose, a well-meaning Washington hostess whose late husband had owned the Loose-Wiles Biscuit Company.

Later, George regaled some of his more rowdy companions with an imitation of the mousy squeaks given by Mrs. Loose just after she sat down to dinner. She had felt a man's hand fumbling at her venerable thigh. Drew apologized profusely for not having mentioned his Quaker custom—which the other guests knew—of holding hands briefly under the table in a silent grace before starting a meal. Mrs. Loose subsequently sent her host a tin of Loose-Wiles biscuits as a token of forgiveness.

Drew played the social game on a more pragmatic level than George. He did not waste time, Drew said, on women who were not socially or professionally useful, or physically approachable. He scorned the H.B.V.s (High-Bosomed Virgins), as the debutantes were generally referred to in public. Let the British attachés handle them!

He often left parties early, with a remark to George that he was going to visit one of his girls but would be back home by midnight. If George came by at midnight and saw a light in the garret where Drew sat before a typewriter in his old Bessarabian dressing gown, he would go in to describe what happened at the party after Drew left. He suspected that his friend invented conquests to conceal an excessive devotion to work.

If George came by at 4 A.M., the light might still be visible in Drew's garret. On one such occasion Drew complained about the regular 5 A.M. jangle of a milk wagon on the Georgetown cobblestones. "Why can't the bastard make less of a racket?" he demanded, revealing passion by the uncharacteristic epithet. "All he ever thinks about is milk!" He made up for the sleep he lost at night by taking catnaps during the day, he told George.

Drew was seen most often in public in the company of Dorothy Detzer, the left-wing lobbyist for peace, and Cornelia Mayo, a real estate agent. Miss Detzer knew everybody and everything in Washington and was excellent company as well as an excellent source of stories. Drew's intentions seem to have been entirely honorable. He went to considerable trouble to bring Miss Detzer's parents from the Midwest to meet his parents in Washington, thus avoiding any possible repetition of the unannounced matrimonial plunge with Felicia.

However, DD—as Drew called Miss Detzer—was involved emotionally at the time with a member of the British House of Commons. Her overseas romance kept the relationship with Drew on a platonic level. They remained friends until his death.

Mrs. Mayo, a well-to-do merry widow with glossy black hair and snapping black eyes, was trying to round up property which would serve Drew as a combined office-home. This provided an excuse for frequent consultation, but his invitations for lunch or dinner or rides in his car became so numerous as to take on the semblance of courtship. At a large party in Alexandria one evening, Cornelia and Drew appeared to be quarreling. Drew endured the festivities until 11 o'clock, when he offered to drive Cornelia home.

"I can manage by myself," she said distinctly. Drew turned and left. A half-hour later she departed with another escort.

The widow, who was several years older than Drew, although her bouncy, sexy manner made her seem younger, lived in Georgetown about four blocks from Pearson's house. When she turned on the light in her second-story rear bedroom some time after midnight, she saw Drew standing there with a grin on his face.

An umbrella which Cornelia had thought of taking to the party but had discarded at the last minute lay across a chair. Grabbing it, she swung furiously at the intruder. Shielding his head with his hands, he retreated toward an open window. They were panting with exertion and excitement as she tried wordlessly to punish him and he tried wordlessly to escape. Backing through the window, he clung to the sill with his hands, well above the ground.

"I hit his face with one hand," Cornelia told George Abell when he came to see her later. "I must have scratched him, but it wasn't until I beat his hands with the umbrella that he dropped into the box hedge in the garden. He couldn't have been hurt much because he ran around the house and disappeared when I yelled 'stop thief!' from the window."

With his Boswellian curiosity about people, George felt obliged to hear the other side of the story. He found his friend in bed, swathed in bandages, both eyes blackened, one finger broken. The interview was brief and stilted. George did not mention Cornelia. For once inhospitable, Drew did not discuss his injuries.

Cornelia's version of virtue triumphant which she provided at parties indicated she had swung a tennis racket rather than an umbrella. This creative touch permitted amusing interjections about the score: 15–love, 30–love and so forth. All the points were scored against Pearson. He seemed to have lost the game at love.

3

Drew wrote a will in Washington on September 14, 1930. It was really his first will since previous farewell letters to his family did not dispose of any property. In the will he left all he possessed to his father and mother, with a request that they use it "for their own best interests and happiness and for that of my daughter, my brother and his family, and my sisters." The rest of the document focused on his daughter, Ellen, then three years old and living with her mother, Felicia, in Paris:

> I ask my parents to save that part of my personal belongings, my papers and my furniture which they think might help to make my daughter better acquainted with her father and give them to her when she is of sufficient age.
>
> I ask that my brother take charge of my personal correspondence and destroy those letters which he thinks should be destroyed, except only that he is to save for my daughter all letters exchanged between her mother and me. I know that my former wife will not only continue to be the thoughtful mother she always has been but will try to make up for what little I have been able to contribute to the baby's life. I hope that she [Ellen] may go to college and I would caution against too much money and too much attention from nurses and governesses.

Drew, then thirty-two, with forty years of active life ahead of him, ended on a note of self-contempt: "As I grow older I become more shallow. . . . I am not worth very much concern or very much regret and I hope there will be none."

Cissy Patterson, who considered herself cynical, cried when she read that will. On impulse—or was it at Drew's suggestion?—she sent a copy of the will to Felicia in Paris. It was her thought—or was it Drew's?—that the will might induce Felicia to consider seriously the idea of returning Ellen to Washington, where she could be reared in surroundings more suitable for the only granddaughter and heir of one of America's wealthiest women.

4

The Swarthmore Chautauqua broke down as a vehicle of educational uplift during the summer of 1929. For several years its revenues had been lagging behind expenses in one circuit after another along the Eastern seaboard. Extra assessments on sponsoring businessmen at the end of one season reduced their enthusiasm for the next. Drew's father tried to forget about the tightening inner spiral by making loud cheerful noises. His rodomontade disturbed James A. Michener, a sensitive recent graduate of Swarthmore College who was working as a tent boy that summer.

"There was something doing every day in a seven-day circuit,"

Michener recalled years later when he had become well known as a writer. "Paul Martin Pearson could handle any one of the twelve programs except maybe blow the tuba. . . . On Wednesday there would be a play which the local people had rehearsed a week; on Friday a speech by the president or somebody equally formidable and on Sunday a joint religious service as climax.

"Dr. Pearson's daughter Barbara drove him around the circuit and sometimes starred in a local play. Barbara was a glorious girl about my age, but the good doctor, that stocky sanctimonious man with white hair, sticks in my mind as an amiable fraud, a theological Paul McNutt, a megalomaniac. . . ."

One weekend in the fall of 1929 Paul Pearson appeared humbly at his son's Washington residence, in flight from disaster and his wife's tongue. Since Chautauqua earnings during the good years were always plowed back into ambitious new programs, there had been no cushion of family savings when the whole nonprofit enterprise collapsed.

Overnight, Dr. Pearson had become a pitiable figure. He looked smaller physically. His blue eyes watered behind steel-rimmed glasses. He had focused so steadily on Chautauqua that he found it difficult to talk about anything else.

"Not a single tent in any of the circuits blew down during the last six years," the bankrupt president of the Swarthmore Chautauqua reminded his son again and again. "Isn't that remarkable?"

Drew agreed it was remarkable. Since his father seemed to be on the verge of a nervous collapse or a heart attack, he paid up the old man's life insurance in full to protect Edna against any contingency. He persuaded Dr. Pearson to remain a while in Washington, sightseeing, resting and reading. When Edna came down to see how her husband was, Drew invited George and Luvie Abell to join them in a dinner without alcoholic refreshments.

Though he found Dr. Pearson a "bore" and his wife a "chatterer," George returned the social compliment after Edna went back to Swarthmore. An hour before the scheduled dinner Drew appeared at Abell's house. "Father can't stand the sight of liquor," he reminded George. "I thought we might have a snort now."

George frowned. "There will be other guests," he pointed out.

Luvie suggested that the other guests be taken aside one by one as they arrived and given what they wanted; that way the table would remain teetotal.

"No," decided George. "I will not serve anybody in secret just to fool your father." He turned on his friend in indignation. "I wish he could see some of your parties!"

Drew's concern proved groundless. Everybody drank except Luvie, who was being tactful; Drew, who declined his customary dry martini; and Dr. Pearson, who accepted a root beer with an unconscious disapproving glance at the less abstemious ones. The evening passed pleasantly.

Since social contacts seemed to have a healing effect, Drew arranged for distinguished local Quakers to pay their respects to his father. George was on hand one day when a visiting Friend asked Drew: "Does thee not care for alcohol?" The latter's reply —"No, I only like grapejuice and buttermilk"—drove George into a fit of coughing.

When Edna came down again to Washington, Cissy invited her and Paul to dinner with Drew. The only other guests were the Carlos Dávilas. Coffee, tea and milk were served. Cissy displayed the consideration of an Eleanor Roosevelt in the presence of somebody who was blind or deaf.

Afterward the senior Pearsons could not say enough in praise of the distinguished hostess, but they were puzzled by the difference between her gentleness in private and her contentiousness in public. William Randolph Hearst had finally gambled on the chance that Cissy might put some life into his moribund Washington *Herald*. His sole condition in hiring her as editor at $10,000 a year—a pittance compared with her loans to him— was that she discard Schlesinger from her name and resume being Cissy Patterson.

Within a week after her first languorous stroll through the *Herald* city room trailed by two poodles which were allowed to bite people, Cissy had turned the newspaper and the town upside down. Her maiden issue bore a front-page sketch of herself by Neysa McMein, along with signed tributes to herself as a famous writer from other members of the Algonquin Hotel Round Table. A few days later, she renewed her half-forgotten feud with

Alice Roosevelt Longworth, who had just presumed to pose as political campaign manager for the widow of Cissy's first cousin, U.S. Senator Medill McCormick. The boxed front-page declaration of hostilities went as follows:

INTERESTING BUT NOT TRUE

Reports that Mrs. Alice Roosevelt Longworth will manage the Senate campaign of Mrs. Ruth Hanna McCormick are interesting but not true.

Mrs. McCormick takes no advice, political or otherwise, from Mrs. Longworth.

Mrs. Longworth could not possibly manage anyone's campaign, being too lofty to newsmen and too aristocratic for public speaking.

Mrs. Longworth gives no interviews to the press.

Mrs. Longworth cannot utter in public.

Her assistance, therefore, will evolve itself as usual into posing for photographs.

ELEANOR MEDILL PATTERSON *(Signed)*

"How amusing" was Alice's reply for publication. "Disgusting," said Cissy's brother, Joe. "Scrapping with Alice is all very well," wrote Arthur Brisbane, "but you must keep the high Joseph Medill level." Hearst chortled with long-distance delight. The *Herald's* circulation had gone up slightly.

Cissy bewildered, frightened and annoyed members of her newspaper staff. Were it not for the depression, many would have quit. She dropped one managing editor who had bad breath. Reporters who seemed idle at their typewriters when she passed by were in danger of being written off as drones or drunks. She pensioned some old hands and fired others. Her once-spare newspaper office had been redecorated to exhibit antique furniture and family portraits, including a forbidding one of Joseph Medill. In the presence of the founder of the Chicago *Tribune*, district men were brought in separately and told that they were responsible for a scoop a day.

Strangest of all was Cissy's preference for women in the largely male precincts of newspaperdom. Her galaxy of newly hired young chicks, beautiful but untrained, went flying around town on impossible assignments. Those girls who showed talent as reporters were likely to receive expensive items of clothing and other marks of esteem from the grateful editor, but one by one, sooner or later, they would be ferociously rebuked, perhaps fired, for their inevitable and invisible fault: none was, in fact, the successor to the departed daughter whom Cissy sought unceasingly.

Cissy experimented with personal journalism. Under the alias of Maude Martin, a variation of the name Felicia had used in Salt Lake City and San Diego when she ran away from home, the millionaire editor pretended to be a penniless woman in search of a meal and a place to sleep. She contrasted the hardships into which she blundered with the apricot silk sheets and other luxuries at The Dupont Circle.

The applause she received for these exhibitionistic articles induced Cissy to order a series on poverty in Appalachia, which she had glimpsed from a touring automobile. She assigned the job to Frank Waldrop, a young reporter from Tennessee, with explicit instructions on photographing the mountain people for maximum tear-jerking effect. The articles appeared under her byline.

Cissy also tried Drew's specialty—great-man interviews. Her subjects ranged from Al Capone, the Chicago mobster living in guarded exile in Florida, to Albert Einstein, the mathematician of the universe, whom she had caught naked, sunbathing on a blanket on the edge of a desert near Palm Springs, California. The interviews bore no relation to her conclusions—that one man was sexy and the other a mental giant—but they were good for circulation. They amused her son-in-law.

Drew's mode of living was transformed by Josephine Denny's discovery of two small old three-story buildings of faded yellow brick at the southeast corner of Dumbarton Avenue and Twenty-ninth Street. The price was reported to be $6,000 for property which, with a great deal of modernization, was eventually worth $80,000. By combining the buildings, Drew could work there and have plenty of room for his daughter and a couple of servants.

By adding a new wing at the juncture of the buildings, extending like the stem of a T into the rear gardens, he added facilities for guests.

Ellen had been sent back from Europe by her mother on the sensible ground that an American heiress, nearing school age, would be better off in Washington. Other factors contributed to Felicia's decision: the difficulty of caring for a delicate little girl in a Parisian whirlpool of party-going and drinking; Cissy's offer of an allowance on condition that Felicia be reasonable about custody; and perhaps the copy of Drew's humble will which had been sent to her.

With the help of her mother's money, Felicia rented a palace in Geneva. Her social behavior had become eccentric, Dorothy Detzer reported after a visit. Invited to dinner at 8, she and the other guests left at 9:30 because their hostess had not appeared and the servants had not even been expecting them. Undiscouraged, Miss Detzer invited Felicia to dinner. Her guest arrived at 9:30, an hour and a half late, wearing riding pants!

The presence of a charming blond granddaughter in Washington pulled Paul and Edna Pearson more frequently to Drew's home. They had adjusted gradually to their reduced status. Dr. Pearson did a little lecturing and writing, but as a man not yet sixty and in fair health, his wife thought he should be looking for a larger role. He agreed in principle: he hoped to land something in moving pictures, with which he had experimented during the closing days of Chautauqua.

Irritated by promises without action, Edna harried Paul one day until he shouted: "Woman, will thee shut up!" and stalked off. Cissy happened to be there to take Ellen for a walk. She mentioned that President Hoover was looking for a suitable appointee as Governor of the Virgin Islands, which were no longer useful as a naval base and were soon to be transferred to civilian rule.

Because the poverty-stricken population of the islands was 93 percent black, the President had asked Herbert D. Brown, head of a special Bureau of Efficiency in the White House, to suggest a properly qualified Quaker who could be relied upon for religious reasons to be color-blind and sympathetic to poor people.

The presidential troubleshooter was already canvassing prospects for the job. When he reached Swarthmore, an Eastern locus of Quakerism, several leaders of the Society of Friends warmly recommended Dr. Pearson. The good doctor himself, when interviewed, found it necessary to confess that he was a Democrat who read *The Nation*. He had voted, he said in an incredible display of candor, for La Follette for President in 1924 and for Al Smith in 1928!

Dorothy Detzer had been active in the effort to get the Navy out of the Virgin Islands. After an evening at the home of the Herbert Browns she reported by telephone to Drew at midnight that his father was still under consideration despite his tactlessness.

"Drew was deliriously excited," Miss Detzer reminisced years later. "He insisted I go at once for a drive with him; he'd pick me up and we would drive around so I could tell him all the details. After he dropped me, he telephoned his father in the early hours of the morning."

Dorothy Detzer and Cissy Patterson brought direct pressure on the White House. Drew kept out of sight since he had been *persona non grata* with Mr. Hoover since he disclosed the extent of press censorship on the battleship *Utah* during a presidential trip.

Morris L. Ernst, a New York lawyer who had won presidential respect through his mailed suggestions for meeting the depression, was induced by Miss Detzer to recommend Dr. Pearson as a choice which would have a favorable political impact. Others with access to the presidential ear made similar representations, avoiding, of course, any suggestion of ulterior interest.

In the end, Paul Pearson was appointed on nonpartisan grounds of reputation, achievement and religion. President Hoover was not ignorant of his relationship to Drew. Was he trying indirectly, as enemies of Drew contended later, to soften his diplomatic critic? No evidence can be found to support such a theory. Certainly Drew continued to write as sharply as ever about American foreign policy.

CHAPTER VII

Merry-Go-Round

R<small>OBERT</small> S. A<small>LLEN</small> <small>CHAFED</small> under the sedate restrictions of correspondence for the *Christian Science Monitor*. He had broken loose in 1929 to the extent of contributing two signed Washington columns to *The Nation* on President Hoover's goodwill trip to South America, only to be warned by his newspaper against any further writing on the side. He did not intend to risk his job, yet he could not conceal his delight over a letter from Henry L. Mencken, the literary power of the day, praising *The Nation* articles and inviting him to Baltimore for a talk.

The two men lunched in an Italian speakeasy in the heart of town. Mencken wanted cutthroat sketches of Washington public nuisances for his big green monthly, *The American Mercury*, which was then required reading for intellectuals and dissenters. Bob Allen agreed to furnish the articles if his identity was concealed. He started with Vice President Charles Curtis, called "Egg Charley" in honor of his invariable campaign anecdote before farm audiences in 1928. Sinister interests, it seemed, had asked the Kansas Senator to join in removing the duty on foreign eggs, whereupon he reared back and roared: "You have come to the wrong Sen-a-toah!" This and later portraits etched in acid were so well received that they gave Allen the idea for a book.

Bob had married Ruth Finney, a Scripps-Howard regional reporter from California whom he met in the Senate press gallery and courted on President Hoover's campaign train in 1928. They lived quietly in Georgetown, rarely giving or going to a party. Ruth handled domestic chores on top of her newspaper work, while her husband banged away at his typewriter every night in the basement. She produced numerous insights and factual details for the book.

Early in 1930, Boni & Liveright, the New York publishers, dispatched editorial assistant Tom Smith to Washington with proofs of several chapters by Allen and a suggestion which was hard to refuse: why not find a collaborator to write social and diplomatic chatter which would lighten the tone of the book and enhance its appeal?

Allen accepted the idea. "I have just the man for you," he said. He phoned Drew Pearson, who agreed to join in the anonymous literary effort. However, Drew left almost immediately to cover the London Naval Disarmament Conference for the Baltimore *Sun*. A subsequent visit to Havana further delayed production of his share of copy. The latter trip, arranged by his friend the Cuban Ambassador, Orestes Ferrara, was part diplomatic coverage, part journalistic fence-building and junket.

Before the Spanish-American War, Ferrara had been a bomb-throwing teen-aged anarchist. Since then he had become rich and fat as a sugar grower and newspaper proprietor. He was an authority on Machiavelli—he demonstrated his mastery of cynical doctrine by sponsoring the 1928 Pan American Conference in Havana to the embarrassment of the United States without losing the goodwill on which his boss, the dictator Machado, relied for survival—and, as Drew liked to point out, he was "the best judge of wine in Washington."

Free transportation for two having been proffered by Ferrara, Drew asked George Abell if he cared to go to Havana. George could not get away, so Luvie, who had been ailing, went in his stead. Some of George's social associates raised their eyebrows over this, but George maintained he could trust his wife and his best friend and there was no indication that his confidence was misplaced. Luvie's health improved during the trip.

Newspapermen generally find difficulty in meeting the distant deadlines of a book. Drew's immediate obligations were many. "It's like pulling teeth to get anything out of you," complained Allen. Drew tried harder; he was not able to evade his various jobs, so he cut down on gallivanting and drinking. Along with Paul Pearson and, to be sure, little Ellen, Bob Allen could claim credit for drawing Drew out of his postmarital slough of despondency and dissipation.

Once he focused on the new task, Pearson proved invaluable to Allen. Their experiences and opinions meshed. They wanted to expose "the welter of hypocrisy, demagoguery, cowardice and reaction that pervades Washington" and "the whole horrible failure of the capitalistic industrial system so starkly revealed," but they had to struggle against the sugary influence of the publisher's new formula.

They wrote separately—Bob in his basement, Drew in a new ground-floor study, which long ago had been slave quarters. As soon as one finished a chapter, he turned it over to the other for emendations, corrections and inserts. They rekindled each other's enthusiasm. The modified product was rushed piece by piece to Tom Smith, who had taken up residence in the Mayflower Hotel for quick editing. Toward the end they did not bother to revise each other's output.

Tentative titles for the book included "On the Potomac" and "Under the Capitol Dome." Neither had any particular oomph. During a meeting with Pearson and Smith, Allen mentioned seeing a British moving picture called *Carrousel*. An idea seized him. "How about 'Washington Carrousel'?"

"I think you have it," exclaimed Smith. " 'Washington Merry-Go-Round'!"

Demolishing Herbert Hoover was the single most important political purpose of the book, yet Smith placed a chapter on the President behind an opening chapter on Washington society and another on the social mishaps of diplomats, not ignoring sex, gambling, drinking and drugs. Allen led off the assault on Hoover by telling how Herbert as a boy burned down his father's barbed-wire factory in Iowa. It was not until forty years later that Herbert told about his experiment in arson; he had wanted to see what would happen if he tossed a flaming stick into a caldron of tar!

Hoover never was a Great Humanitarian, a Great Administrator, a Great Engineer or a great anything, according to Allen; he was a promoter full of vanity, timidity and ineptitude. As President, he did not permit photographic close-ups because his face was flabby; he never said one flat word as to whether he was a wet or a dry and he tried to cure a national depression by concealing it.

Pearson contributed a charge—with Yugoslavia in mind—that Hoover had used his European food-relief mission not merely for humanitarian purposes but to balk uprisings by "oppressed masses against the masters who precipitated the catastrophic world war." He recalled a Baltimore *Sun* exclusive about the rigging of airmail contracts by Postmaster General Brown so that only one company—which employed Herbert Hoover, Jr.—could bid on certain Western routes.

Allen blamed the depression primarily on Andrew W. Mellon, Secretary of the Treasury under three Republican Presidents. Mellon's tax favors to plutocrats, he said, triggered an orgy of speculation which caused the crash. Mellon "blew up the stock market bubble and breathed new life into it every time it showed signs of deflation." After thus draping national disaster around Mellon's frail shoulders, Allen revealed the Secretary's behavior toward his wife, Nora, in such a way as to encourage the formation of a lynch mob.

Allen's chapter on the House of Representatives was originally called "The House of Mutes." Smith changed it to "The Monkey House" to exploit a sentence describing the membership as "a cross between a troop of monkeys and a herd of sheep." This followed the theory of "talking points," which Lord Northcliffe, apostle of a new journalism which had spread from England into the American tabloids, said were the key to mass readership. Northcliffe's title for the House of Commons had been the Upas Tree—a tree in Java fabled to be so poisonous it destroyed everything within miles of it. Allen wrote:

> The 435 members [in the House] with a few exceptions are the lowest common denominators of the ignorance, prejudice and in-

hibitions of their districts. . . . The House is one of the most debasing influences in government. . . . For the most part it is the willing instrument of partisan and predatory interests. . . . It has approved colossal tariff steals, voted for tax cuts to big incomes and huge estates and approved billions of dollars for local pork-barrel projects.

In his assigned social role, Drew revealed that the outstanding bachelor in Congress was newly elected Senator Millard Tydings of Baltimore. Millard played footsie under the table with Georgetown ladies and "held the Senate heart-throb record," according to the writer, who had reason to know. "He has caused more capital beauties to dream of hooking a Senatorial husband than any member of that body for years. One of them even took a trip to Reno with that in mind. . . . The thought of him clad in purple dressing gown, painting hunting scenes in his attic studio at midnight, is enough to bring out the sacrifice complex in any woman."

Allen and Pearson never revealed who wrote what in the book, but there was a detectable, if slight, difference in their styles, which united uneasily like the vinegar and oil in salad dressing. For the most part, Allen used traditional muckraking lingo, whereas Pearson displayed an uninflected kind of murderous candor.

Allen rewrote his *Nation* exposé of Vice President Curtis for one chapter under the same title, "Egg Charley." It wound up with a fresh snatch of dialogue overheard as the bachelor half-brother of Dolly Gann left the home of Mrs. Ruth Hanna Mc-Cormick Sims after a pleasant social evening.

"Come again, Charley," the hostess called to her old friend.

"Where do you get that Charley stuff?" he replied. "Don't you know I'm Vice President now?"

Much later, when the identity of the authors had become known, Mrs. Sims remembered telling about the Vice President's pomposity at a party where the guests included Drew Pearson. She crossed Drew off her guest list.

"If Drew promised Jesus Christ he wouldn't tell a soul about a second coming because he had heard it in a social context," an irreverent friend of Pearson remarked in those days, "he'd tell it just the same. More than anyone else I know, he has the journalist's defenselessness in face of a large exclusive."

Though Allen and Pearson had recurrent doubts about the publisher's formula, *Washington Merry-Go-Round* proved commercially successful. It caused a furor when it appeared in the spring of 1931. People oppressed by the cruelties of the depression rose to the political incitement of the book. More dispassionate souls focused on the social chapters, which provided a multitude of the talking points so highly esteemed by Lord Northcliffe.

Boni & Liveright's compilation did not quite achieve literary distinction. Its semiseriousness was indicated by the lack of any index. Its hurried collaboration had caused confusion and duplication. (Speaker Longworth, who died while it was in preparation, was described as both quick and dead.) There were instances of downright silliness: labeling Dwight Morrow as "Little Nemo" and brushing off the German Ambassador, Friedrich Wilhelm von Prittwitz und Gaffron as "von Nittwitz." Even so, this was a watershed volume.

Long ago Washingtonians had gasped and snorted over columns in the Alexandria (Virginia) *Gazette* by a lady in reduced circumstances named Ann Royal. When John Quincy Adams, the sixth President of the United States, refused to be interviewed, Ann tracked him through the marshes south of the White House, where he used to swim in the nude. She sat on his clothes until he told her what she wanted to know. In her column she repeated a favorite jingle—"Hail Virginia/ Old and crazy/ Her people poor/ Proud and lazy"—often enough to get ducked in the Potomac as a common scold.

The *Washington Merry-Go-Round*, its successor and the column flowing from these books restored to the capital the pejorative journalism missing since Ann Royal. The vigor and irreverence of the column made existing Washington columns by such competent reporters as Paul Mallon and Ray Tucker look anemic. From a biographical point of view, the first *Merry-Go-Round* book is particularly valuable. It shows the development of Drew's adversary relationship to people and events; it discloses his feelings at the time toward friends other than Tydings, female companions, his mother-in-law and himself.

In contrast to his gruffness toward great-power diplomats, Drew presented verbal bouquets to his friends among the representatives of small, weak or unpopular states. Though the Latin Americans generally deserved an "AA rating for phlegmatic inertia," he grouped Messrs. Telles, Dávila and Ferrara as men of exceptional ability and charm.

At Irish-American affairs no more eloquent or popular speaker could be found, he wrote, than that engaging individual, that credit and glory to the Irish Free State—Michael MacWhite! (You could almost visualize the wide-smiling Michael rising, with a glass of Irish whiskey in one hand and a pack of Sweepstake tickets in the other, to take a bow!) Boris E. Skvirsky, unofficial representative of the Soviet Union, was a "success" to the extent of having survived a decade in Washington despite the failure of the United States to recognize Russia. Dr. C. C. Wu, the Chinese Ambassador, kept active "because the limelight brightens his soul as sunlight builds bonny babies"—the last phrase having been borrowed without credit from Ellen's Scottish nurse.

In his opening chapter, which, according to the title—"Boiled Bosoms"—dealt with female drunks, Drew traced the feud between Cissy Patterson and Alice Roosevelt Longworth backward from its recent revival by Cissy on the front page of her Washington *Herald*. The editor herself was described as a smart woman who "pretended to enjoy coarse newspaper revelries at which she tried hard to be one of the gang" and in other ways "dissipated her gifts on trivialities."

Mrs. Longworth—"brilliant if not gifted who through the prestige of her position [he meant former position as wife of the Speaker] and the vitriol of her tongue dominates Washington's ultra-fashionable group more than any other"—had been a rival of Cissy, he pointed out, since they were both debutantes competing for the same eligible males. Cissy married and eventually divorced her Polish Count, while Alice married Nicholas Longworth. Around 1920 the two "social whipcrackers," as Drew called the two ladies, contracted a competitive fondness for the person of Senator Borah, who was, of course, married.

Cissy's intemperate praise for the lion-maned Senator in a Hearst newspaper article embarrassed him sufficiently to give

Alice a temporary triumph. Cissy evened the score by portraying their relationship in an unenviable way in one of her novels. Even so, the quarrel gradually faded. Cissy was invited to a gathering at Alice's house. In an upstairs library after dinner Cissy monopolized—Drew's word—the young nobleman who had sat at Alice's right during dinner. Next day, Cissy received a waspish note from Alice reading: "Upon sweeping up the library this morning the maid found several hairpins which I thought you might need and which I am returning."

"Dear Alice," responded Cissy in a return note, "Many thanks for the hairpins. If you had looked on the chandelier you might also have sent back my shoes and chewing gum." (Cissy's private version of the story substituted "panties" for "chewing gum.")

In reporting on the Longworths' agreement on freedom of movement within the marital bond, Drew named three swingers who had been referred to as "Nick's girls." Cornelia Mayo was the only one of them, he added, who went so far as to seek the Speaker's intervention to "get an invitation to a costume ball." Whatever that meant, it gave Drew an additional reason to maintain anonymity.

Dorothy Detzer was mentioned in a chapter on Secretary of State Henry L. Stimson, entitled "Wrong-Horse Harry." The Secretary apparently made mistakes, but he had one good deed to his credit: the granting of a passport to Miss Detzer despite protests from patriotic groups over her refusal "to take an oath swearing to defend the Constitution with traditional rifle and pitchfork."

Ludwell Denny won praise in a final chapter, on the press. So did Lowell Mellett, the Scripps-Howard executive who gave George Abell his job at Drew's request; William Hard, who had introduced Drew to Cissy; and Lawrence Todd, the Washington representative of Tass, the Soviet news agency.

Most of the local reporters were brushed off as indifferent, ignorant, provincial, smug, sycophantic and timid. Their bosses were ridiculed as knee-benders to authority. The Senate and House press galleries, it was noted, excluded legitimate Negro journalists. The Gridiron Club, consisting of fifty trained seals, had an unwritten rule barring Jews, which had been broken to admit Charles Michelson, publicist for the Democratic National Committee, but which still kept out David Lawrence, publisher of the *United States Daily*, and Frederic William Wile, CBS newsman and former Chautauqua lecturer.

Since Drew and Bob rated at greater or lesser length virtually every reporter of any magnitude in the capital, Allen felt obliged to insert a deserved plug for his wife, Ruth Finney, as "a talented writer . . . an authority on water power and social problems." His appraisal of his own newspaper and himself was terse and honest:

> The Christian Science Monitor has one of the larger Washington bureaus. It is manned by competent and conscientious reporters who are held down by the conservative views and many prohibitions of their organization. Robert S. Allen, head of the staff, is the youngest large bureau chief in the capital. Despite his youth he has had important newspaper experience in the United States and abroad.

The Baltimore *Sun* was praised as an example of "that now practically extinct spectacle in American journalism of honest and independent reporters working for honorable and brilliant newspapers." J. Fred Essary, chief of the *Sun*'s morning bureau in Washington, was described as "that most laudable of newspaper executives, a staunch and loyal defender of his reporters." There was another man on the *Sun* for whom the book expressed a regard equally high but perhaps more sincere:

> The Sun's expert on foreign affairs has the reputation of knowing more about the State Department than most of the people who run it and to a considerable extent this is true. He has been a fixture at the State Department for so many years that few people realize he was once a sailor, circus hand and vagabond journalist working his way around the odd corners of the world. . . .
>
> Pearson takes cynical delight in lampooning some of the diplomats who once high-hatted him when he enjoyed less fortuitous circumstances. He is the State Department's severest critic yet because its members either fear him or value his opinion, he is taken into their confidence on many important international moves. Because of his independence he is either loved or hated; there is no middle ground of affection where Pearson is concerned.

2

On the publication date of *Washington Merry-Go-Round,* Drew was in the Virgin Islands trying to help his father out of difficulties caused largely by the good doctor's political naïveté. President Hoover had complicated matters by making a last-minute appearance at the island inaugural. If the President's purpose was to burnish his fading public image, it failed.

When his battleship anchored off Charlotte Amalie, Paul Pearson rode out in a launch to welcome him, forgetting to bring along Herbert D. Brown, the White House troubleshooter, who was on hand to smooth the transition to civilian rule. Brown, whose report on Dr. Pearson had been weighed by the President when he made the appointment, was upset by this slight. At a subsequent reception he spoke loudly and rudely to the Governor within the President's hearing. Summoning his dignity, Paul Pearson squelched his heckler in Chautauqua style. Brown and his wife spent the next few years looking for revenge.

The Virgin Islands had been sequestered from the world during the naval occupation. At sight of the Chief Executive of the United States, an almost godlike figure in their minds, the ragged residents gaped instead of cheered. Misinterpreting awe as hostility, the President grumbled to reporters about the islands being "an effective poorhouse." The resulting controversy helped neither him nor his civilian Governor.

Governor Pearson chose the best-equipped men he knew for his cabinet, including Andy Simpson, the "family engineer" who had worked with Drew in Yugoslavia, as Commissioner of Public Works; Harry Taylor, a retired trade-magazine publisher recommended by A. C. (no longer "Drew") Pearson, as Commissioner of Industry; and experts in other fields known to him from Chautauqua days.

Republicans in and out of the islands had anticipated picking the twenty-five political plums at the disposition of the Governor. Prodded by Brown, they charged these had all gone to "cronies" of Dr. Pearson. He was summoned to the White House to explain, which he did satisfactorily.

Mrs. Pearson had dispatched thirty trunks full of old Chautauqua costumes, scenery and things like bells and drums so her husband could organize "rhythm bands," teach handicrafts and produce plays for the natives. Brown exploded over the hiring of an old Chautauquan hand at $4,800 a year to stage free Gilbert and Sullivan operettas for the bewildered populace. Again he was overruled by President Hoover.

In accordance with his racial-equality mandate, Dr. Pearson invited blacks to a reception at Government House. The upper fringe of educated wealthy whites who had run the islands without much interference while the Navy was in charge could hardly believe their eyes. They spread scurrilous stories about the Governor.

Because Edna insisted on staying in Swarthmore until she could dispose of the house and its contents, Paul had brought down his unmarried niece Dorothy, the elder daughter of A. C. Pearson, as his official hostess. Rumors were circulated that she was the Governor's mistress. When her sister Josephine, who had been married and divorced, came down later to help her uncle, she also was labeled a mistress until she met and married a local school principal.

The primitive Virgin Islanders had the notion that having a civil governor would mean a job and a vote for everybody. However, the voting prerequisite of $300 in yearly income kept all but a few from the polls. Jobs were not plentiful. Even virgins were scarce.

When he learned about this, the Quaker at the head of government issued a tactless release deploring the 65 percent of all insular births which were illegitimate. With hostility added to the natural credulity of the natives, Drew did not see that much could be done about the gossip which worried his father.

The islands' underlying problem being their extreme poverty, Drew suggested an appeal to Congress. Dr. Pearson liked the idea. He and Boyd Brown, a Swarthmore College graduate and friend of the family who held the important post of Government Secretary, went to Washington. With help from Drew, they buttonholed enough Congressmen to win assurances of a million-dollar appropriation for relief.

When Dr. Pearson talked carelessly in the islands about his achievement, the clique hostile to him noted that he had brought back no money. Where was it? they asked slyly out of his hearing; had the Governor put it in his pocket? By the time the money arrived, the implied embezzlement had been accepted by many as a fact.

Worried over his picture of Paul as an honest man in a den of thieves, Drew made another trip to the islands, this time accompanied by Luvie. Though they occupied separate rooms at the home of Lieutenant Governor Lawrence W. Cramer and behaved with circumspection, their traveling together aroused debate between Drew's cousins, Dorothy and Josephine.

Dorothy, a liberal in politics, agreed with Drew's mother, Edna, that he could do no wrong. As a Republican sharing her father's political distrust of Drew, Josephine argued that his unconventional behavior might cause still more gossip about the family.

During their visit Drew found his father standing on his own feet. The canards about Dr. Pearson's mistresses having evaporated with the delayed arrival of Edna, the Governor's critics were peddling new lies that he was impotent and suffering from paresis. Somehow he had heard about the slanders. He would show them, the good doctor said calmly; despite all their underhand tricks, he would make the Virgin Islands self-supporting and happy by attracting new industries and tourists.

Not being needed, Drew returned with Luvie to Washington. There he heard that President Hoover had asked the Division of Investigation (later the FBI) to find out who wrote *Washington Merry-Go-Round*. The remarkable thing was that the book's anonymity lasted as long as it did. Bob Allen went on an NBC radio show and criticized the Washington press in the identical terms used in the book. Ruby Black, a local newspaper girl, promptly accused him of authorship. Drew told Dorothy Detzer of his role, and maybe one or two others. As a result, Pearson and Allen were kept busy denying rumors they had helped to start.

During his social rounds Drew quietly absorbed reactions to the book. Secretary of War Patrick J. Hurley was said to be infuriated by the assertion that when he first came to Washington, he and his wife Ruth "rehearsed their entrances and exits, their conversation and their bows before every big party."

John Franklin Carter, a former editorial writer for the *New*

York Times, complained he had lost his job with the State Department as a result of a *Merry-Go-Round* statement that he wrote inaccurate but amusing articles under a pseudonym. His threats of mayhem against the unknown author led some Washingtonians to suspect him of having written the book. Others blamed a Georgetown group of liberal correspondents who met irregularly at each other's houses to gripe about the standpattism of the Hoover administration. The group included Bill Hard, Henry Suydam of the Brooklyn *Eagle* and, interestingly enough, Bob Allen. Suydam suspected Allen but kept his mouth shut.

Drew was relieved to discover that Cissy was not disturbed about the hairpin anecdote; she considered she had fared rather well in the account of her feud with Alice. Besides, she had been well buttered up elsewhere in the book by references to her genius as a publisher and the bizarre brilliance of her parties.

Cissy was creating controversy and circulation for the *Herald* with various be-kind-to-animal promotions. To the delight of Luvie and other antivivisectionists, she published gruesome pictures of medical-school experiments on dogs.

Next Cissy tried to save the ducks in Rock Creek Park, which were starving because they could not break the ice to get food. Unfortunately, the put-put planes hired to drop containers of food hit close-gathered ducks and killed some of them. The enterprising editor rushed an oxygen tank to the park zoo when N'Gno, the popular gorilla, contracted pneumonia, but the ungrateful beast died in Cissy's tent.

From the moment the Pearson-and-Allen collaboration hit the best-seller list—it eventually sold 180,000 copies in various editions—they were committed by Tom Smith to a second volume. Speed was essential if the sequel was to make a dent on the 1932 presidential election. Bob grumbled over his partner's trips and tardiness in typing, and once again Drew's performance improved.

Inevitably, the Department of Justice uncovered the writers of *Washington Merry-Go-Round.* President Hoover's reaction on learning their names was to make a vow—which he kept—never to speak to Pearson again. His feelings were more mixed about Allen, whom he had come to like during the 1928 campaign. Nevertheless, he sent his press secretary to the *Monitor* as well as the *Sun* to ask if they took responsibility for the foul things their correspondents had been writing about the President of the United States.

Managing Editor Walter Harrison of the *Monitor* informed Allen by registered mail that "information had been received" that he was involved in the book. Allen conceded he had "contributed" to it. He was then fired with two weeks' severance pay, which he boosted to a month by threatening suit.

After being out of work for several months, Bob was offered a job with Hearst's International News Service. At first he did staff work at the Capitol, then a column called "Under the Dome." Secretary of Labor William Nuckles Doak proved to be his nemesis. One of Allen's *Nation* profiles, subsequently revised for use in the second *Merry-Go-Round* book, described "Greasy Bill" as a not-too-literate former railroad yardman living pretentiously on a Virginia estate called "Notre Nid."

Doak, who had an excellent memory, reminded Hearst by letter that the publisher had just asked him, as a favor, to throw a certain Georgian prince out of the country. Impressed by the logic of this reminder, Hearst fired Allen. Greasy Bill then deported the prince.

The *Sun*'s position was different from that of the *Monitor*. It had no desire to negate the book's paean of praise to its honor. With J. Fred Essary proving that he supported one of his men in time of trouble, Drew was allowed to stay on the staff. Since neither the President, the editors nor Allen disclosed these maneuvers, the anonymity of the forthcoming sequel was preserved.

President Hoover could have punished Drew by removing his father as Governor of the Virgin Islands. Pat Hurley recommended this form of retaliation. However, Paul Pearson was asking Congress for more money to build low-rent houses and set up a government company to finance new industries. Removing a fellow Quaker under such circumstances might have been embarrassing and controversial, so the President permitted Dr. Pearson to push an economic and cultural program in the islands which bore some resemblance to the later New Deal on the mainland.

3

The George and Luvie Abell matrimonial situation got so tangled at times that their friends despaired of ironing it out. Luvie could not or would not keep up with George's rollicking. He required gossip for his gossip column, he argued. He conceded he might be drinking too much and staying out too late, but he found the reforms advocated by his companions difficult to achieve since they did not practice the restraint they preached.

A disarmingly frank man, George considered it appropriate to tell Luvie that he had strayed sexually with one of her friends. Taking one of their two poodles as a fair division of family goods, she went to Tulsa to visit her uncle, Alben Butler, Jr., while she weighed a course of action. George followed her to Oklahoma and won a reconciliation with promises of more chaste behavior. After their return to Washington, word spread that Luvie was pregnant. Her son was born on August 9, 1932.

More Merry-Go-Round, which appeared early that fall, indicated in the most indirect possible way how Drew felt about the up-and-down developments in the Abell household. Relying on his invisibility as an author, Pearson revealed that his friend George had printed a damaging story about Cissy Patterson in his column. Without checking, George had used an item from a New York newspaper to the effect that Cissy would spend the winter social season at her Sands Point, Long Island, estate.

Since this insinuated neglect of her editorial function, Cissy buckled on her armor and invaded the plant of the rival newspaper. She strode into the sanctum of Ralph Palmer, managing editor of the *News,* demanding: "Where is that hairy ass, George Abell?" The book omitted the descriptive phrase for Abell. It asserted, however, that Cissy, turning on Palmer in the absence of Abell, "used language that would have brought blushes from a stevedore."

Luvie named her son Tyler after her genealogical connection with the late President Tyler. The boy was a tiny replica of his father, which properly pleased George. Several weeks later, however, Bob and Ruth Allen came to dinner at Drew's house. To their surprise, they found Luvie and the baby there as house guests. George was visiting his sister in Baltimore, it was explained, and the heating plant at his house had failed.

The temperature outdoors was not sufficiently low to make the second reason plausible. The Allens got the impression that some new seismic disturbance in the Abell household had forced Luvie to seek refuge in the home of her husband's friend. Not long afterward, the Abells were reunited, seemingly harmonious. Relations between George and Drew improved, though they no longer made the social rounds together.

4

More Merry-Go-Round was a fatter, flabbier work than its predecessor. It also carried no index. It lacked political punch, though it may have had a mild effect on the 1932 presidential campaign.

Inasmuch as Herbert Hoover could not be eviscerated twice and Treasury Secretary Mellon had been kicked upstairs into the ambassadorship to Great Britain, the sequel provided lesser scapegoats for the depression, ranging from Secretary of War Hurley to the members of the U.S. Supreme Court. Pat Hurley was blown up as a menace: the "Cotillion Leader" who kept Washington society dancing callously while groups of jobless, homeless and half-starving Americans besieged the capital for help.

The Supreme Court chapter, called "Nine Old Men," proved to be the kernel from which grew a later Pearson-Allen book with the same title. Drew Pearson subsequently took credit for originating the phrase, but Allen always said it came to them from Edward Pritchard, secretary to Felix Frankfurter.

General Douglas MacArthur was held up to particular ridicule for his efficient, if heartless, execution of orders from Secretary Hurley to evict the bonus-seeking veterans. However accurate, the account was sufficiently barbed to register the hidden author of the book in the General's war-oriented consciousness as a desirable object for future hostilities.

A prohibition chapter ranked high for politically tinged diversion. It revealed the arrest of Bertha Huddleston, wife of Representative George Huddleston, an ardent Alabama dry, for driving while intoxicated; the tampering with a shipment of champagne for the Italian Embassy, as a result of which Ambassador Giacomo de Martino found himself toasting Mussolini in seawater; and the names and achievements of local bootleggers. This last contribution came from Drew's lottery assistant, who in a previous job had worked for the Anti-Saloon League.

There were the usual personal references to friends, including Dorothy Detzer. By effective lobbying against armament, Drew reported, Miss Detzer had caused the Army and the Navy "more headaches than any other civilian, and the patriots have responded by endeavoring to prevent her from renting offices near the State, War and Navy building." She was credited with persuading President Hoover to appoint the able Mary E. Woolley as an American delegate to a disarmament conference.

Most intimate of all was an account of further contact between Ralph Palmer and Cissy Patterson. The Washington *News* executive had been impressed by his fellow editor's passion of language and appearance when she came ahunting for Abell. This was not surprising; though almost fifty, Cissy remained a most provocative woman.

Palmer began to dream of sharing the embroidered peach crepe de Chine sheets which Cissy was said to be currently using. When he phoned to express his dishonorable intention, he was invited to a dinner party. Drew did not mention Cissy's imperial habit of choosing an occasional one-night partner. Palmer must have known this. Palmer must also have realized that if he ingratiated himself with her, he might have a professional future in view of the heavy turnover at the *Herald*.

Except for those omissions, Drew followed a factual line: Palmer arrived at The Dupont Circle with cerise silk pajamas under his formal clothes. At one point he pulled his pants leg up sufficiently to give his hostess a glimpse of his nether costume.

"Mr. Palmer has come to sleep with me," shrilled Cissy. She called over Senator Arthur Capper to view the cerise pajamas. The Senator had just opened a boxed present from Mrs. Patterson consisting of diaphanous black-lace panties with a card inscribed "To Rose Douras Nano." Rose was the wife of the Rumanian Chargé d'Affaires, a sister of Marion Davies and the acknowledged beauty of the diplomatic corps. Unable to adjust to the double shock, the elderly Senator asked for his hat and went home.

Palmer did not get between Cissy's sheets that evening. He tried again several nights later. When he reached the marble palace around 9:30, Cissy had not yet returned from a dinner party. With journalistic resource, Palmer cultivated the butler, with whom he chatted on homely topics while consuming four or five highballs. After the butler retired, the managing editor wandered upstairs in a confused state. Locating a bed with green, not peach, embroidered crepe de Chine sheets, he pulled off his clothes, slid under the covers and fell asleep.

He was awakened by voices. "He's in Felicia's room," one of them said. Cissy's daughter was in Paris, but her room was, as ever, kept spotlessly clean and ready for her improbable arrival.

"Get him out!" said a feminine voice. Two burly footmen helped Palmer get dressed. "The embroidered crepe de Chine sheets, both peach and green," trumpeted *More Merry-Go-Round*, "retained their pristine purity." Well, as Lord Northcliffe might have said, it was a talking point.

Pearson was enveloped by enemies. J. Fred Essary, who suspected Drew of gunning for his job as bureau chief, reminded Pat Hurley's wife, Ruth, that she was the sister of the *Sun*'s business manager. Ruth went to Baltimore. Drew received a summons from there: Managing Editor William H. (Big Bill) Moore wished to converse with him.

Rumbling as though he were Mount Etna on the verge of an eruption, Big Bill opened the discussion by mentioning Bertha Huddleston, who seemed to be a relative or close friend. (He never mentioned Ruth Hurley.) He echoed Bertha's displeasure over the fact that the book not only recorded her arrest for drunken driving —she the wife of a dry Congressman!—but went on to mention a subsequent suit for alienation of affections filed by the wife of a much younger salesman with whom she had been riding when arrested.

Big Bill produced a letter from former Secretary of War Newton D. Baker, denying a Pearson dispatch to the *Sun* that he had been rebuffed when he sought to see Pat Hurley. (That in itself was probably ground for discharge.) Finally, the managing editor reviewed the soiling of Cissy's sheets. "The Sun is *not* a keyhole paper," he shouted. He gave Pearson a month's pay and the choice of resigning or being fired.

Drew, who had learned about Essary's maneuver through Ulric Bell, Washington correspondent for the Louisville *Courier*, accused the Secretary of contriving his discharge out of annoyance at being portrayed as a socially ambitious fop who had ordered the clearing of the Anacostia Flats without a pause in his fripperies as the town's "Cotillion Leader."

Hurley denied complaining to the *Sun*, but his denial was lost in the national excitement over the newly revealed identity of the authors of the *Merry-Go-Round* books. The story was played as a combination of the Peter Zenger freedom-of-the-press case and the Dred Scott Decision. One side effect was to implant the notion that the prime mover in the books was Pearson, though the idea, the title and four-fifths of the work had been contributed by Allen.

In the wake of the hurly-burly, Drew was dropped quietly by the *United States Daily*. He still had the lottery as a backstay, plus papers all over the world which he serviced with Washington news, the latest being the Latin-American clients of the Havas News Agency in Paris.

Cissy read *More Merry-Go-Round* on a train running from Chicago to Washington. "Mad as a snake," she began to compose in her mind a front-page box denouncing her son-in-law. At the office, Arthur Brisbane was waiting for her by appointment on another matter. The voice of the grand old man of the Hearst organization quivered with apprehension when he heard of her plan to air a family squabble in her own newspaper. Gradually, he talked her out of it. Given a breathing space, Drew argued there was nothing discreditable to Cissy or Felicia in the Palmer episode. He agreed to expunge the anecdote from later editions, but the unexpected bankruptcy of Boni & Liveright saved him from that necessity.

Bob Allen was back in harness. After a further period on the beach he had proposed to the Philadelphia *Record*, the Raleigh *News & Observer* and the Sacramento *Bee* that they pay him $50 a week each for alternate coverage of the campaign trains of Herbert Hoover and Franklin D. Roosevelt. All three accepted the idea. Black-sheeting—that is, sending identical stories to his clients—he gradually took on additional work for the *Record*.

Realizing that to many editors he and Drew looked like lepers,

Bob asked his friend Bill Evjue of the Madison, Wisconsin, *Capital Times* to sponsor a joint column capitalizing on the *Merry-Go-Round* books. Evjue could not swing it, so Allen tried various syndicates. He was at a ranch in Arizona, still on the campaign trail, when Drew phoned excitedly from Washington: United Features, the Scripps-Howard syndicate, wanted them both immediately in New York to discuss a sample column which Bob had written and sent to Karl Bickel, the United Press president.

"Well, go up there," said Allen impatiently. He could not afford to come East. They were comrades in arms who trusted each other. Drew went to New York, made the deal and signed the contract. Since it did not seem important at the time and Allen did not dissent, the column was offered to newspapers across the country under the byline of Drew Pearson and Robert S. Allen, in that order. Allen had begun to lose control of his brainchild before it was born. The first column appeared on Drew's birthday in 1932.

Cissy Patterson discovered that the notoriety of her sheets amused her sophisticated friends. The public had not complained; *Herald* circulation was up. She and Drew returned to their old relationship. Some junior executives at the paper were concerned lest Drew's growing influence prejudice their own standing. One of them tried to warn that her son-in-law was no more trustworthy than ever.

"Drew may be the bastard of the world," replied Cissy, in the muted profanity she considered suitable for newspapermen, "but he has been father and mother to Ellen. I'll never forget that." She was the first editor to subscribe to the "Washington Merry-Go-Round" column. She told Pearson and Allen to turn in their copy to Frank Waldrop. Privately, she asked Frank to "keep those crazy sons-of-bitches out of trouble—if you can."

CHAPTER VIII

The General's Mistress

Drew Pearson's artistic, physically handicapped younger brother, Leon, felt harried and unhappy. He had followed the family blueprint for success without getting anywhere. He had qualified as a teacher with an M.A. from Harvard, as prescribed by his father. He had married his Chautauqua assistant, Anna Mary Brown, as recommended by his mother. He had taught temporarily at the University of Pennsylvania before moving into a more secure niche as a teacher of oral English at the Haverford School for Boys in Pennsylvania, where a friend of his father was the headmaster.

What was the result of all his docility and hard work? A frustrating job with no future, three sons and a daughter to rear on a meager preparatory-school salary! Ben Franklin said beaten paths were for beaten men. Leon wondered if this applied to him. He thought of Drew, who, though only a year and a half older, had always been the venturer and problem-solver during their childhood on the basis of a sturdier physique and greater daring. He wrote to Drew, who was starting a syndicated newspaper column with Robert S. Allen, asking if there was anything he could do in Washington, anything at all, which would pay a living wage.

Drew, it developed, had something in mind which was important and remunerative but highly confidential. Leon went down to hear about it. He was shocked when he learned what it was. His brother's five-year secret contract as Western Hemisphere director of the Irish Hospitals Sweepstake had one more year to run. By this time the work was pretty well standardized, but Drew needed somebody he could trust to take over his duties while he concentrated on his main chance in the field of political journalism.

As the most devout of the four Quaker children of Paul and Edna Pearson, Leon did not want to violate any law, and particularly not a law against gambling. The Society of Friends disapproved of gambling. The violation would be technical, Drew assured him; officially, Leon would be writing for the "Washington Merry-Go-Round."

Though the column was only making $25 a week for each of the partners at that time, it was gaining subscribers. Leon, it was suggested, could prepare himself for eventual work as a column assistant by contributing occasional items. That would have the advantage of improving his cover. Meanwhile, he would be paid for his work on the lottery. Drew did not disclose his own $30,000-a-year salary from the Irish Sweep or allot more than a fraction of that sum to his inexperienced substitute.

Leon hated to deceive people, particularly his wife, Anna Mary, but he went along with the proposal on the theory that whatever Drew did must be all right. Comforted by the additional thought, stressed by Drew, that he would be responsible for his brother's reputation, Leon brought his family to Washington and reported to the hidden headquarters in the Evans Building to learn the arcana of international gambling. He had the help of Drew's assistant, the former prohibition undercover man, and that of Drew when he needed it.

Since he and Bob Allen were pets of the incoming Roosevelt administration, Drew gave some thought to gaining political tolerance for the Sweep. The two *Merry-Go-Round* books had classed as campaign documents. Allen had even ground out a third pro-Roosevelt opus entitled *Why Hoover Faces Defeat*. Drew had joined Sumner Welles in drafting the Good Neighbor foreign-policy plank in the Democratic campaign platform in 1932.

Before the inauguration Drew had gone down to Warm

Springs, Georgia, at the invitation of the President-elect. FDR had asked for advice on, among other things, dealing with the Washington press. "Don't worry about the publishers," counseled Drew. "Make friends with the fellows who cover the White House. They're on the firing line. They fire five thousand words a day compared to the one editorial a day written for the publishers." President Roosevelt took the advice.

Postmaster General James A. Farley, the political mechanic of the new administration, appreciated Drew's preferred position with his chief. He was an amiable New York Catholic, almost a professional Irishman, a moralist in most matters who saw no peril to his soul in playing Bingo or getting a small bet down on the horses. As the man responsible for enforcing the national anti-lottery statute, he agreed to see a delegation of prominent Irish-Americans assembled by Drew.

Farley sympathized with the views of his visitors. He told Drew so in a private talk. He found a public occasion to say that he did not intend to bar newspapers from the mails for printing stories about winners in an international lottery for charitable purposes. "If it is going to impair our morals to know what is going on in the world," he said obliquely, "that is a problem for our pastors, not the Post Office." In plain Gaelic that meant the Irish Sweep would be exempt from federal harassment. Thereafter Leon slept sounder at night.

A. C. Pearson, Drew's trade-magazine publisher uncle, died in the spring of 1933. Drew accompanied Leon to New York for their uncle's funeral. He wept openly during the services. "Touching," said his Cousin Dorothy, remembering how her father had wrapped the burning little Santa Claus in a rug and saved his life at Christmas time when they were all children together in Evanston.

Drew's evidence of sorrow seemed hypocritical to her sister Josephine. She cited her father's refusal to speak to Drew after their estrangement and his comment during his final illness: "Drew outraged me. He had the most ability of anybody in the family and he abused it."

Dorothy and Josephine were perfectly companionable—they shared an apartment in New York later in their lives—but on that one subject of Drew the sisters could never agree. Drew's assertion that no middle ground existed where he was concerned and that people tended to love him or hate him was being verified within the family.

On the train returning to Washington after the funeral, Drew brought up the subject of lecturing. In his father's Chautauqua tradition, he had been accepting quite a few of the requests for appearances that flowed in on the tide of *Merry-Go-Round* notoriety. It had come to his attention that Leon was lecturing at a private school in Washington to defray the tuition of two of his sons. He hoped Leon would not expand in this field, Drew said. *He* was now the Pearson family lecturer; competition between two of them with the same name might confuse the public. After an incredulous look, Leon agreed not to confuse the public.

A one-sentence entry in the diary of Secretary of the Interior Harold L. Ickes two months after Franklin D. Roosevelt's inauguration in March, 1933, hinted at a new family involvement. It read: "Drew Pearson in, in the interests of the retention of his father as Governor of the Virgin Islands." Several weeks later the Secretary met Dr. Pearson at a buffet supper at Drew's house. He enjoyed the Governor's cheerful anecdotes about the Swarthmore Chautauqua, and his analysis of current problems and prospects in the Virgin Islands. As a progressive Republican in a Democratic administration, he found himself sympathizing with the plight of a progressive Democratic holdover from a Republican administration.

Drew gradually widened his covert campaign of support to include Assistant Secretary of Agriculture Rexford Guy Tugwell, like him a child of Chautauqua; Gardner (Pat) Jackson, the millionaire defender of Sacco-Vanzetti; Heywood Broun, the columnist; Eleanor Roosevelt and others who might influence the President. He learned of his father's impending reappointment during a picnic at Hyde Park to which he had been invited by Mrs. Roosevelt. She confided that she had enjoyed his strictures against General Douglas MacArthur in the *Merry-Go-Round* books. The General had pushed in alongside her in the rudest way imaginable at the inauguration ceremonies, she said, in order to get himself into group pictures which were being taken by photographers.

The restless energy of the President's wife led her to make an inspection of the Virgin Islands early the next year. She reported to Ickes, and no doubt to her husband, that Governor Pearson was doing well, though she doubted he had "always been the right kind of Governor in the past." She liked the Governor's idea of making the islands into a tourist resort for middle-class folk who could not afford the Bahamas. Firming of support on the highest levels in Washington, Drew felt, would enable Governor Pearson to fend off efforts of machine politicians, no less determined in a Democratic national administration than in a Republican one, to slip drones and incompetents onto his staff.

Drew Pearson never dreamed that President Roosevelt would try to destroy him. He considered himself a supporter, on the whole, of the New Deal. When harsh things had to be said, he said them, including the fact that during his first year in office the President initiated a new period of American economic and diplomatic isolation in world affairs. He had heard, and believed, that FDR was sensitive to personal criticism, but he did not adequately gauge the weight of grievance piling up in the White House.

Though Pearson and Allen spoke of their column in orthodox terms as a collection of items ahead of the news, they were committed to audacity by the preceding *Merry-Go-Round* books. Some of their punching bags had vanished with the advent of the Roosevelt administration, but others remained that were too tantalizing to be ignored. They included John Carter, the former State Department writer who had founded an American Fascist Party; conservative Congressmen from both major parties; overage reactionaries on the U.S. Supreme Court; and, above all, the Army Chief of Staff, General MacArthur, who to Drew personified militarism.

Drew and Bob continued to write separately, one in his Georgetown home, the other in a newly acquired twelfth-floor office in the National Press Building. They exchanged and criticized each other's contributions to the column. Drew concentrated on the diplomats, the departments of State, War, Navy and Justice, while Bob covered politics, Congress, the Supreme Court, agriculture and the labor movement. They picked up information where they found it, from society hostesses and ambassadors, cabinet members and clerks, newspapermen who passed along stories too sharp for insertion in their own papers, Senators, even the President himself.

Spadework for new books helped to fertilize the column. Drew had begun collaborating with Constantine Brown, diplomatic correspondent for the Washington *Star*, on an up-to-date review of foreign policy to be called *The American Diplomatic Game*. In 1933 they discovered that President Roosevelt, a big-Navy man ever since his service as Assistant Secretary of Navy under President Wilson, was planning to divert funds from a public-works program in order to build battleships. The news was too hot for Constantine Brown's reflective essays in the *Star*, so Drew borrowed it for the column. Its appearance there led an overwhelmingly Democratic Congress to vote its first public rebuke of the new Democratic President.

Bob Allen and Drew were working on a book-length expansion of the "Nine Old Men" chapter in *More Merry-Go-Round*. From this research, Allen contributed a column item that Justice Willis Van Devanter, an antediluvian from Wyoming, would create the first vacancy in the High Court. The prediction appeared on a Monday morning. White House confirmation at noon placed it among the classic exclusives which have been confirmed within forty-eight hours.

When a Senate investigation into the American munitions industry began largely as a result of prodding from Drew's friend, peace lobbyist Dorothy Detzer, Pearson and Allen testified about the actions of War Secretary Patrick J. Hurley and General Mac-Arthur during the Hoover administration. The General did not reply, but Hurley, who had become an oil lobbyist, charged in rebuttal that the columnists were "muckrakers." He considered that an insult, but his targets pretended to enjoy the appellation.

Pearson and Allen put in nineteen-hour working days during this period. Drew usually kept busy from 6 A.M. to 1 A.M., whereas Bob's official schedule ran from 8 A.M. to 3 A.M. Bob was chief of the Washington Bureau of the Philadelphia *Record*, a full-time job in itself. Drew delivered lectures and wrote articles under his own name and four or five pen names for a variety of magazines. If these articles were prevailingly critical of the New Deal, that was because people were less interested in civic virtue than in governmental misbehavior.

As a cripple and an artist at the head of the state, Franklin

Roosevelt employed techniques which were insufficiently understood at the time. People thought of him as two-faced because he
listened to visitors so intently, nodding and saying "Yes" when all
the "Yes" meant was that he got the message—without necessarily
agreeing with it. He used all sorts of people, including his wife,
Eleanor, as his eyes and ears. He sought always to keep his channels
of information open. He encouraged differences of opinion among
his advisers, played cabinet members off against each other, delayed
decisions to the last possible moment and followed each faint
shift of public opinion in the newspapers.

The "Washington Merry-Go-Round" offended him in many
ways. It intervened periodically in favor of its informants and
friends like Secretary Ickes and Under Secretary of State Sumner
Welles against conservatives in the administration. It provided
garbled accounts of private debates of governmental significance.
It went so far as to predict presidential appointments before the
President was ready to announce them, sometimes before he had
made up his mind.

Revealing an unannounced jurisdictional victory for Ickes, for
example, over Presidential Adviser Harry Hopkins in the handling
of public-works projects, Drew wrote: "For Ickes, canals; for Hopkins, ditches; for Ickes, highways; for Hopkins, sidewalks; for
Ickes, water systems; for Hopkins, reservoirs; for Ickes, public
buildings; for Hopkins, landscaping; for Ickes, big dams; for
Hopkins, little dams."

The humiliated Hopkins sneered that Pearson was up to his
usual stunt of describing "fights in a harem," but that was not the
opinion of President Roosevelt. To him, these were real fissures in
the New Deal power structure which Pearson opened from day to
day. White House instructions on secrecy to cabinet members induced Secretary of State Cordell Hull to start a staff conference
with the indignant query: "Is this for the room or for Drew
Pearson?" The remark was repeated in the "Merry-Go-Round," as
were written instructions against leaks distributed confidentially
by several other Secretaries.

President Roosevelt flirted with the idea of taking legal action
to drive the column out of business as a menace to his processes
of government. Advisers were unanimous in their objections; it
probably would not work, they said, and it would certainly be dis-

astrous from a public-relations viewpoint because of the specter of attempted censorship it would raise.

With a Machiavellianism unsuspected by Pearson and Allen, President Roosevelt then invited General MacArthur to the White House. He knew MacArthur wanted reappointment for another four years as Chief of Staff in order to finish projects he had already begun. He was aware that the General's *amour-propre* was punctured at intervals in the "Merry-Go-Round" as the medal-happy brass hat who had routed bonus-seeking veterans from the Anacostia Flats.

After sympathizing with the General over the unfair and cruel attacks made on him, FDR noted that the column was also embarrassing the White House. His hands were tied, he said, but anybody with an actionable grievance would do the country a service and recommend himself for special consideration if he took the logical steps to eliminate the "Washington Merry-Go-Round." MacArthur obeyed the veiled command of his Commander-in-Chief. At a time when Pearson and Allen were earning very little from syndication, he filed a staggering $1,750,000 suit against them and the United Features Syndicate. One reason for the suit, he told friends, was that the column had written disrespectfully about his mother, with whom he still lived at Fort Myer. Whatever the motive, it looked like curtains for the column.

Louise Brooks Cromwell, an impetuous Philadelphia society lady who had married MacArthur, divorced him in the Philippines and later married Lionel Atwill, the actor, was a regular guest at Drew's buffet suppers. On one occasion she was squired by Allen W. Gullion, Provost General of the Army. When Gullion delayed leaving in order to explain military strategy at length to Elizabeth Altemus Whitney, Louise floored him with a roundhouse right, yelling: "Don't give yourself airs! I've knocked down four-star generals!"

In softer moods, Louise did takeoffs of her former four-star husband preparing for war in front of a mirror. Hearing about his suit against Drew, she mentioned a Eurasian girl who was supposedly in financial straits in Washington because MacArthur had cast her adrift. Drew spread word through his network that he was prepared to help the girl if she got in touch with him.

The first tip came from Representative Ross Collins of Mississippi, head of the House Appropriations Subcommittee for the War Department. He knew a woman who lived on the same floor at the Hotel Chastleton with a standoffish Chinese girl who was often visited by General MacArthur. However, the Chinese girl had recently left the Chastleton. Collins had requested his friend to pass the word, if she saw the Chinese girl again, that the columnist was prepared to become her new protector.

Dorothy Detzer was having dinner at Drew's house one evening when the phone rang. He returned from taking the call in uncharacteristic excitement. It was a woman, he said, who had something he might want to buy; she would be there in half an hour. Afraid of a trick of some kind, Drew asked Miss Detzer to remain. If the visitor insisted on secrecy, as he suspected she might, Dorothy was to go and sit on the stairway leading up to his second-floor office, and listen.

"When Drew's Negro manservant ushered the lady in," Miss Detzer recalled years later, "I thought I had never seen anything so exotic and exquisite. She was wearing a lovely, obviously expensive chiffon tea gown, and she looked as if she were carved from the most delicate opaline. She had her hair in braids down her back.

"We were dawdling downstairs over our coffee. It was soon obvious that the visitor was not going to open up while I was there. I excused myself and went out and established myself on the staircase. The girl then produced three letters, which Drew read. He asked if he could 'rent' them overnight. He raced up to his office, got $50, typed a receipt in my name, which he got me to give her. Then he called a cab, paid for it and sent her to the rooming house where she had taken refuge.

"He phoned Morris Ernst, his lawyer in New York, and asked Morris to come to Washington the next day. Then I went with Drew until he found an all-night photo company (this was before Xeroxing) to copy the letters."

Helen Robinson, a former chorus girl in Singapore, was the daughter of a Chinese woman and a Scottish businessman living in Manila. What she had to sell was a packet of letters tracing in detail her liaison with General MacArthur. At Drew's request, Miss Detzer took Helen to lunch once or twice at a place where they were not likely to be noticed. Dorothy bought the Eurasian girl a dress or two for street wear since virtually all her clothes were tea gowns, which she wore over the laciest of underpinnings. Meanwhile, by lavish use of cash and promises, Ernst was working out an agreement for possible use of the amatory documents.

The first six letters were written by the General late in September, 1930, as he traveled from Hong Kong and Shanghai to Yokohama and Kobe before sailing from Japan to assume new duties in the United States. The letters included expressions of affection and instructions for Helen's separate trip to the States.

It was only nine days, the General recalled, since they had said good-bye on a pier in Manila, but it seemed like an eternity to him. Their five months together had been the happiest of his life, he declared. He recalled intimate incidents during their relationship in that period and asked her to take care of herself and remember his parting words of advice.

A later letter told of going to a gambling casino and watching fat elderly gamblers picking up beautiful young Chinese girls. This distressed him, making him remember difficulties which Helen had faced in Singapore and surmounted with his help. He reminded her that she would sail in less than a month and closed with extravagant and explicit pledges of his love.

From Shanghai the General wrote that he had gone to a nightclub and been disgusted by the sights he saw there. He had bought his mistress a fur coat, he revealed, promising to think of her continually until she arrived in the United States to claim it.

From Japan MacArthur wrote a four-page letter pledging unlimited devotion so long as he lived and after his death. He would die, he declared, if she did not return to him.

The writer of these letters was no gawky adolescent, but a seasoned man of the world, fifty years old, soon to become the virtual dictator of the American armies. Despite his torrential expressions of sentiment, Helen became hesitant at the last minute. She sailed from the Philippines only after an anguished telegram from San Francisco, signed "Daddy," assured her that disturbing reports she had heard were untrue.

Helen was installed in a comfortable apartment on Seventeenth Street in the Northwest section of Washington, then in a suite at the Chastleton Hotel on the Sixteenth Street hill overlooking the city. As Mrs. Robinson she had a fur coat and a car and chauffeur at her disposal, a poodle and the continued devotion of a General who on trips of international importance did not forget to send her postcards. From places like Paris and Vienna he mentioned the honors paid to him, assuring her that he thought only and un-interruptedly of her.

As time passed and Helen became aware of the freedom of movement possible for a young, pretty and well-to-do American matron with time on her hands, the aging General who paid her bills began to display signs of uncertainty and jealousy. When she made a trip to Havana, he wrote from the United States liner *Leviathan* that he hoped she found everything dull without him, but he did not sound at all sure.

Then abruptly, in an envelope postmarked September 11, 1934, a chilling dismissal with a small severance in the form of tickets by train to the West Coast and thence by ship to the Philippines. Though in a preceding letter MacArthur had refused her request that he find a job for her brother, that did not seem to be sufficient cause for the otherwise unexplained break. That he was emotionally upset was indicated by the torn newspaper column of "Help Wanted" ads inserted in the envelope and an unsigned note advising her to look for any future help to her father or brother.

Helen had no intention of going back where she came from. She had moved from the hotel into the rooming house and was considering a search for a job when she heard about Pearson.

Pretrial testimony was already being taken in the MacArthur libel suit. Newton D. Baker represented United Features and Morris Ernst sat in as Drew's personal lawyer. At the end of a session, Baker mentioned casually that he would like to question a Miss Helen Robinson when they reconvened. Frank Hogan, representing MacArthur, had an immediate premonition of trouble.

General MacArthur took the news calmly. He instructed his aide, Major Dwight D. Eisenhower, to find Helen Robinson. Word reached Drew that Army investigators were scurrying around town on the trail of a mysterious Chinese girl. Anticipating this move, Drew had already assigned Leon, his ever-dutiful, trustworthy younger brother, as Helen's guardian.

Family Idyll: Edna Pearson sketches her husband, Dr. Paul Martin Pearson, their elder son, Drew, 11 *(left)*, and Leon, 9, on the lawn outside their Swarthmore home in 1909.

Drew Pearson as a senior at Swarthmore College in 1919, when he had accomplished everything within reach and was looking for new worlds to conquer.
Andy Simpson

The Young Lion: Drew Pearson, 26, in a publicity photo used in 1924 to advertise Chautauqua lectures on his global adventures.

Andrew Cameron Pearson (*center*), presiding at a New York dinner meeting of his executives in what became the United Publishers Corporation, which issued *The Iron Age* and other influential trade publications. Pearson, a close friend of President Hoover, played a big role in the early career of his nephew Drew, until they quarreled so violently over politics that he asked other members of the family to refer to him no longer as "Drew," but as "A.C."

Drew Pearson and his first wife, Felicia Gizycka, shortly after their marriage by a justice of the peace in San Diego, in 1925. Her mother was Eleanor Medill (Cissy) Patterson, newspaper publisher and one of the country's wealthiest women. Relatives from neither family were present at the marriage, which dissolved in divorce three years later. *New York Daily News Photo*

Countess Felicia Gizycka poses for the press in her New York apartment upon the publication in 1939 of her autobiographical novel, *Flower of Smoke,* in which she described her former husband, Drew, as "a mean careerist and poor lover named Lion." *New York Daily News Photo*

Mrs. Eleanor Medill (Cissy) Patterson, most successful woman newspaper publisher of her day, pictured soulfully with her poodles, which she allowed to bite
reporters who came too close as she walked them through the city room of her
Washington *Times-Herald*. In her capacity as mother-in-law and employer Cissy
played the stormiest role in Drew Pearson's career. *New York Daily News Photo*

Drew and Luvie Pearson, pictured triumphantly aboard transatlantic liner as they arrived in New York with her son, Tyler, after they "rekidnaped" the boy from his father, George Abell, on the English Channel island of Sark. *New York Daily News Photo*

Drew Pearson *(left)*, Bob Allen *(right)*, and their guest, Postmaster General James A. Farley, toward the start of their sensationally successful weekly radio program out of Washington. The fourth person in the picture is an unidentified radio station official.

Colonel Robert S. Allen, pictured before he lost his right arm in combat with General Patton's armored forces in Europe during World War II.

Jack Anderson, at the time he took over the "Washington Merry-Go-Round" after Drew Pearson's death. *Mel Chamowitz Photo*

Following up the greatest newsbreak of his career, the revelation that a Soviet spy ring working out of Canada had captured U.S. atomic secrets, Drew Pearson interviews the defecting Soviet code clerk, Igor Gouzenko, on TV. The purpose of the cloth over Gouzenko's head was to prevent his identification and possible assassination. *Wide World Photos*

Drew Pearson working in his study at home in 1948, with timely assistance from Cinders (Cindy), his cat. *Thomas McAvoy, Life Magazine,* © *1972 Time, Inc.*

Members of Drew Pearson's staff work self-consciously for the camera in his office-home in 1948. Confidential Secretary and Office Manager Marian Canty is at left, with secretaries Joyce St. Peter and Hilda Langwasser; legman Fred Blumenthal at rear. *Thomas McAvoy, Time Magazine,* © *1972 Time, Inc.*

Drew Pearson, patriarch, at annual family Thanksgiving reunion in 1948 at the Swarthmore home of his sister Ellen (Mrs. Lockwood Fogg, Jr.). *Seated (left to right):* his sister Barbara (Mrs. Gordon Lange), Drew, Josephine Lange (niece), Lockwood Fogg III (nephew), Drew's wife Luvie, Barbara Fogg (niece). *Standing (left to right):* Paul M. Pearson II (nephew, son of Drew's absent brother, Leon), Lockwood Fogg, Jr. (brother-in-law), Drew's sister Ellen, Gordon Lange (brother-in-law), Julie Lange (niece), Tyler Abell (Drew's stepson), Betty Anne Fogg (niece), Anne Pearson (niece), and Jonathan Lange (nephew). The dog belongs to the Foggs. *Jules Schick Photo*

Drew Pearson leaves court in blissful mood in 1951 after winning his most troublesome libel suit, brought by former California Attorney General F. Napoleon Howser, whom he had described as the tool of a gambling ring. The winner is flanked by his daughter, Ellen (*left*), his wife, Luvie (*right*), and his lawyer, William P. Rogers, who in the Nixon administration became Secretary of State. *Wide World Photos*

Actress Anne Pearson, Drew's niece, in January, 1969. She became involved in a tragic occurrence toward the close of his career. She was acquitted on a charge of murdering her fiancé in Annapolis, Maryland, after the Mayor of that town, other politicians and prominent businessmen appeared to testify to her good character and veracity. *New York Daily News Photo*

Moment of Triumph: Drew Pearson at a private celebration of his seventieth birthday at the Federal City Club in Washington on December 13, 1967. Two hundred specially selected prominent residents of the national capital, ranging from Vice President Hubert Humphrey to Soviet Ambassador Anatoly Dobrynin, turned out for the occasion. *J. Wayne Higgs Photo*

Averell Harriman chatting with Drew Pearson in 1967. They were close friends, and Averell always claimed that Luvie Pearson was the best bridge player in Washington. *J. Wayne Higgs Photo*

Frank Sinatra chats with Drew Pearson in the latter's colonial garden in May, 1968, the afternoon before Drew took the actor-singer unexpectedly to the White House in the middle of the night to say hello to President and Mrs. Johnson. *J. Wayne Higgs Photo*

Drew Pearson gets a warm welcome from his seven-year-old granddaughter, Felicia Arnold, who was named after her grandmother, Countess Felicia Gizycka. *Leonard McCombe, Life Magazine,* © *1972 Time, Inc.*

Farmer Drew Pearson, at the age of 71, directing work on his Potomac farm, with some of his beloved cows and his home in the background. *Leonard McCombe, Life Magazine, © 1972 Time, Inc.*

Since her rooming house was only a few blocks from the State, War and Navy Building, Leon begged the Eurasian beauty to stay indoors. He brought her food and flowers, listened to her small confidences and ran her errands, however bizarre, but she was getting restive, he told Drew. She might even be slipping out at night. Drew went around to warn her personally that General MacArthur's "gunmen" had instructions to kill her. There was no evidence of this. Perhaps the worst they would have done if they had found her would have been to offer her a bribe. Nevertheless, Drew mentioned his continuing concern about Helen to his friend George Abell one evening. The girl was so distinctive in appearance, he pointed out, that she would attract attention anywhere. He wondered out loud what the Army investigators would do if they found her and she refused a bribe. Would they have the nerve to kidnap her? Could they deport her?

By this time, the lottery contract having expired, Leon was an actual assistant on the "Washington Merry-Go-Round." Having gained a couple of hundred subscribers during the first year, the column could afford to pay him a modest salary. As a thoughtful, sensitive man, Leon did well as a reporter. He dressed well and had pleasing manners. By cultivating officials he admired, he was able to produce important exclusive stories.

Drew had also recommended for column service the former prohibition agent who had helped with the lottery. Bob Allen blackballed him after an interview during which the investigator bragged about his exploits. "I never heard such a confusing story in my life," said Allen. His choice for assistant fell on Tom McNamara, a reporter with Capitol Hill experience.

The former prohibition agent, whom Drew kept on his private payroll for part-time work, had a habit of sticking his ear into matters which did not concern him. According to his story, George Abell, at Drew's suggestion, had taken Helen to a hideout in Baltimore, which would be safer than her Washington rooming house. Pausing outside the hideout one day, he reported to Drew and Luvie, he heard sounds of laughter and clinking glasses from within. The rest of his story, which George Abell denied, was that detectives who broke down the door found Helen and George *in medias res.*

According to George, he and Luvie were separated again, for

the second or third time. To distract Helen, he said, Drew had suggested that they take her to an Eddie Dowling show in Philadelphia. After the show, Drew noted that the girl seemed to like George and might be willing to stay overnight with him in Philadelphia. George rejected the idea and returned by early-morning train to Washington because, he said, "I was beginning to get leery of Drew and his schemes."

Without public explanation, compensation or apology from the "Merry-Go-Round," General MacArthur withdrew his suit. He defrayed $16,000 in legal defense fees. His representative handed over an additional $15,000 in $100 bills to Drew's agent during a Christmas Eve meeting on the mezzanine of the Willard Hotel.

Several sets of copies of the letters were kept by Pearson and Allen as protection against any resumption of legal warfare by the General. The originals were turned over to MacArthur with a promise that the copies would not be used during his lifetime. Helen signed a receipt for the $15,000 as payment in full for all claims. She was escorted by Leon to a Midwestern city and set up as the proprietor of a profitable beauty parlor.

Fleet Admiral William D. Leahy heard about MacArthur's capitulation from the General himself. "He could have won the suit," he told friends. "He was a bachelor at the time. All he had to do was look everybody in the face and say: 'So what? Cunt can make you look awfully silly at times!' You know why he didn't do it? It was that old woman he lived with in Fort Myer. He didn't want his *mother* to learn about the Eurasian girl!"

CHAPTER IX

Family Matters

DURING THE LATEST SEPARATION of George and Luvie Abell, Luvie took her son, Tyler, by then three, to her uncle's home in Tulsa. Once again George turned up at intervals to see his boy and rewoo his wife. Though puzzled and not a little concerned over reports of visits by his quondam friend, Drew Pearson, George felt that his wife loved him and would eventually take him back. His personal qualities, he believed, outweighed the other man's growing public reputation.

Drew wrote another short will, on the Western Union sheets he used ordinarily for column copy. "In case of a crash" by the airplane on which he was leaving for a trip, he informed his family, virtually all he owned should go to his eight-year-old daughter Ellen, with the reservation of one of his Washington houses for his parents in case they returned from the Virgin Islands.

After asking Bob Allen, his partner, and Morris Ernst, his lawyer, to arrange "future benefits" for his brother, Leon, from the column and the radio show he had begun with Allen—a vague bequest rather difficult to carry out—Drew left $5,000 for Tyler, "to be put in the custody of his uncle Dan Moore and given to him at such time that in the opinion of Dan it will be most useful."

Dan had more influence over his sister Luvie than anybody else in the Moore family. Getting his permission for this arrangement assured Drew that news of his kindly intentions toward Tyler would reach Luvie. Was this a contrivance in courtship, a demonstration that he cared enough for another man's son to bring him up, if things could be worked out, as his own?

Despite the will, which was dated December 17, 1935, Luvie could not make up her mind. It was not until the following summer that she complied with the six weeks' residency requirement in Reno for an uncontested divorce. Instead of returning East, she took Tyler to the Pejauque Ranch outside Santa Fe, New Mexico, where friends were staying.

Throwing his career into the balance, George gave up his job in Washington and purchased the Santa Fe *Sun*. Operating a marginal newspaper in a strange town was designed to prove to Luvie that he had turned over a new leaf. She was not sure, she said, that she wanted to be married again, to him or to anybody else. He redoubled his attentions; by the time he left for New York on a business trip he thought he had a commitment from her on reconciliation.

Not long after George's departure, Luvie hurried to Washington. There she met Drew and traveled with him to Europe. George could scarcely believe the reports that his former wife and his former best friend had gotten married in Venice. How long, George wondered, had they acted out a charade for his benefit? Drew, he concluded, must have tried to compromise him with that Chinese chorus girl in Washington! Luvie must have sweet-talked him out West to avoid any challenge to her custody of Tyler.

George wanted revenge on his own terms. He bided his time until Tyler came to him for a brief period the following summer under a court-approved arrangement. He and Tyler promptly dropped out of sight. Luvie could find no trace of them anywhere; she became frantic. Since George had sold his newspaper, she suspected he might have gone abroad. She remembered a nursery rhyme he used to recite about the English Channel islands of Jersey, Guernsey, Alderney and Sark. With money from one of his recurrent family bequests he had bought an estate on Sark.

Drew selected friends and enemies on the basis of broad political principle, but he could adjust in an emergency. He did not wish to flounder around again as he had when Felicia walked

off with Ellen. Despite his columnar tirades against J. Edgar
Hoover as a nightclub kind of cop who never made a personal
arrest, he felt obliged to relay word of his predicament privately to
the FBI chief. Hoover was delighted to get the annoying journalistic critic off his back.

George and Tyler had fled to Canada by way of New England,
the FBI network established. In Montreal they had boarded the
S.S. *Montcalm* for the British Isles. Drew and Luvie hurried to
London. There they were informed by Scotland Yard, in whose
hands the considerate Mr. Hoover had placed them, that the Abells
had gone island-hopping from Jersey to Guernsey to Sark.

At the head of a contingent of police and private investigators,
the Pearsons invaded Sark. They caught Tyler on an outing with
his nurse. The good-natured five-year-old had been enjoying himself with his father, but he saw no objection to rejoining his
mother. Told about the kidnaping by an hysterical nurse, George
tried vainly to arouse island police in time to prevent the escape of
the raiders.

When the deprived father reached London, Drew obtained
an injunction restraining him from interfering with Luvie's
custody pending a court determination of parental rights. Luvie
and Drew left surreptitiously with Tyler on a liner for the United
States without waiting for the hearing. An English judge denounced them for leaving, but that was about all he could do.

"I'll follow them to the ends of the earth to get back my child,"
George Abell told reporters in London. "When I meet Pearson,
I will know how to use my fists!"

"I'll be glad to meet him anyplace any time," said Drew Pearson, with equal long-distance bellicosity, in New York.

On legal advice, Luvie went to Reno. The judge who had
presided over the divorce gave her sole custody of Tyler on the
ground that George had violated a signed agreement that neither
parent would take the child out of the country without the other's
permission.

Unable to face the loss of Tyler, George brought a new suit,
in the District of Columbia, for custody of his son. He denied
Luvie's charges of infidelity, and she denied that she had taken
him back once and promised to take him back a second time.

"You are unfit parents," said Justice Daniel W. O'Donoghue.

"Your minds are poisoned with selfishness to such an extent that you are using the child to satisfy your ill will and hatred of one another."

The judge's refusal to change the Nevada decision wounded George's already black-and-blued spirit. In the presence of his drinking companions he made violent threats.

"George says he is going to shoot you," friends warned Drew.

The columnist thought of getting a judge to bind George over to peaceful behavior, but he gave up that notion because it involved a public hearing. He had no intention of spreading the quarrel over the front pages of the newspapers.

Drew applied to the police for a gun permit. A detective, having checked with George about Drew's charges, discovered that the ex-husband owned no gun. Withdrawing his application, Drew hired his former lottery assistant and now part-time investigator, who always carried a gun, as a bodyguard for Tyler on trips to and from school just in case George was inspired to try a re-kidnaping.

As time passed and George—as they say in the Westerns—failed to make his move, the Pearsons relaxed. During the great American political division over Spain in the mid-1930s, George Abell gave lively pro-Franco parties in Washington, usually with a poster of Stalin as doormat. Drew intrigued and wrote in a futile effort to stimulate a flow of munitions to the outnumbered and outgunned Loyalists.

George took an isolationist stance toward the European threat created by Hitler, whereas Drew swung behind FDR's collective-security program, to the distress of Dorothy Detzer and others who had relied upon him as a pacifist. On these and other issues, Luvie stood with her new husband.

George Abell served in the Navy during World War II. After some postwar occupation work in Europe he returned to Washington. It was, perhaps, poetic justice that he fell in love with and married Luvie's best friend, Jane Kendall, whom Mrs. Calvin Coolidge once described as "the most beautiful girl ever to enter the White House."

Luvie attended Jane's engagement party. Tyler witnessed his father's second marriage in Paoli, Pennsylvania, at a ceremony marred slightly by the disappearance of $22,000 worth of Jane's jewelry, including a platinum bracelet bearing charms from such admirers as the Duke of Kent and the Duke of Windsor. The FBI was called in, but was unable to solve the case.

2

Cissy Patterson had consolidated her newspaper position in Washington by leasing the afternoon Hearst newspaper, the *Times*, in addition to the morning *Herald*, then buying both papers and merging them in one ten-edition round-the-clock operation. She had put the imprimatur of approval on Drew's second marriage by hiring his new wife, Luvie, to do movie reviews for the combined Washington *Times-Herald*. She added Leon Pearson to the staff as a columnist on Latin-American affairs.

Leon qualified as an expert on the countries south of the border through his secret hemispheric work for the lottery and his later servicing of Drew's Latin-American clients for the Havas News Agency. He had been complaining that his column salary no longer sufficed for a large family with children approaching college age. Cissy's beneficence enabled Drew to avoid giving his brother a raise.

A year after Drew's marriage to Luvie, Cissy Patterson presented her granddaughter Ellen a 285-acre farm near Potomac, Maryland, as a tenth-birthday gift. She had owned this valuable property for years but had neglected it for a more convenient estate called Dower House, near Marlboro, Maryland, which had once been owned by Lord Baltimore. Drew, whom she designated to manage the farm as trustee since Ellen was under age, promptly built a modern stone house on the property to accommodate winter visits by the family, in which he included Cissy.

Though Ellen lived with Drew and Luvie during the school year, she was required to go to Paris each summer in care of a governess to see her mother, Felicia. One summer Ludwell Denny noticed the child standing alone by the rail of a luxury liner in the mid-Atlantic. "She was the most forlorn-looking little girl I ever saw before I spoke to her," he reported to Dorothy Detzer. "She just about broke my heart."

Ellen could not bridge the gap between her grandmother and her mother. During a visit to London Felicia had impulsively married a young British broker whom Cissy never met and whose name (Edward Delevigne) she said she could never remember. That marriage ending quickly in divorce, Felicia wrote for a while in Sicily before returning to Paris.

Cissy met Felicia briefly in New York when the latter's cruel novel about her parents, entitled *The House of Violence*, was published by Scribner's in 1935. "Haven't you done enough?" Cissy murmured. Felicia shook her head; she was already working on another family novel, she said. Back in Washington, Cissy hurled dishes at Felicia's portrait, screaming: "You're a terrible girl!" Asked by her friend Adela St. John why she did it, she burst into tears and retired to her room. Her real family, she wrote tactlessly to her brother Joe, had come to consist of Ellen, Tyler, Drew and Luvie.

"It's a sand family," scoffed Joe. "It will dissolve in the first storm."

Her brother might be right, Cissy told friends, but for the time being she felt most at home in the Pearson household. Her relationship with Drew was not one-sided; he served willingly and without pay as her journalistic adviser. Though disturbed by the "alphabet soup" of New Deal agencies, FDR's Court-packing plan and other programs, Cissy supported Roosevelt as late as the 1940 election—largely because of Drew's influence—long after the Chicago *Tribune* of her cousin, Colonel Robert R. McCormick, was howling against the administration.

Cissy was capable of barbaric gestures. Becoming enraged at Eugene Meyer for asserting the Washington *Post*'s legal claim to certain syndicated *Daily News* comics which she thought belonged to her by right of blood, she dispatched a pound of raw beefsteak to Meyer under flowers in a box with a note: "So as not disappoint you." References to her Shylock pound-of-flesh gift crept into the news magazines.

Eugene and Agnes Meyer were deeply offended. Drew convinced Cissy that she had gone too far and should apologize. He persuaded his friend Sumner Welles to give a "reconciliation party" for Cissy, the Meyers and himself. Cissy apologized. For one evening she and Mr. and Mrs. Meyer spoke courteously to each other, but they never returned to their former intimacy.

Though Ellen and Tyler were brought up on equal terms in Drew's house, it was natural for Luvie to be more interested in her son. When Ellen was twelve and Tyler seven, they attended their first White House party, an affair given by Eleanor Roosevelt in honor of Diana Hopkins, the daughter of Presidential Adviser Harry Hopkins.

Tyler was the center of attention at the party. After all the fuss over his kidnaping and counterkidnaping he had become a kind of child celebrity. All Drew remembered of the occasion was that Luvie "seemed more anxious than usual that Tyler have his hat on straight."

Ellen was too pretty to be a wallflower at Miss Shippen's exclusive dancing school, but she was less popular than Tyler. In Drew's tradition of putting a bagged skunk behind a school radiator, his stepson brought field mice from the Potomac farm to class in a box under his coat. Release of the mice among the girls during a sedate fox trot, according to one of Luvie's favorite anecdotes, "started the trend toward the frug and the monkey."

While Tyler went to St. Albans School in Washington, Ellen was soon attending a series of exclusive and expensive boarding schools, starting with Miss Gill's in Bernardsville, New Jersey. A withdrawn, sensitive girl, she sometimes had the sensation, when she returned to the Georgetown house from school, of being invisible in her own home. This applied even to the farm of which she was in theory the owner.

One Christmas Felicia decided in her impulsive fashion to spend the holidays with her mother at The Dupont Circle. When she arrived from Geneva, where she had been writing in preference to Paris, Drew suggested a special family dinner, including himself, Luvie and Tyler, Felicia and Ellen. Cissy accepted the idea and issued the invitations. Drew played the patriarch at the dinner. Something about the occasion and the memories it stimulated upset Felicia and she left the table in distraction before dessert was served. Cissy was as pro-Drew as ever, but on this occasion she had to sympathize with her daughter.

"Drew sat there like a pouter pigeon," she confided later to one of her friends. "He had his present and former wives and each wife's child—not to mention me, his mother-in-law—all looking up to him, the cock of the walk, the goddamned boss of the barnyard!"

Felicia had the last word. In a transparently autobiographical novel about marriage called *The Flower of Smoke*, published in the spring of 1939, when she returned to live permanently in the United States after eleven years abroad, she portrayed Drew as a mean careerist and a poor lover named Lion.

3

The situation of Governor Paul Pearson in the Virgin Islands deteriorated under constant demands for local political patronage from the Democratic boss of the islands, a man named Paiewonsky, whose son became a later Governor. Paiewonsky reportedly had the backing of Senator Millard Tydings, the influential Democratic chairman of the Senate Insular Affairs Committee.

In a left-handed effort to be diplomatic, Governor Pearson sent word to Tydings that he would consider a few qualified Democrats for his staff. Not hearing immediately from the Senator, he named Eli Bauer, a Baltimore Democrat, as government attorney, on a report that Bauer was Tydings' protégé. It turned out that the two men had quarreled and become temporary enemies.

Seeking to smooth over this misunderstanding, Drew appeared at Tydings' office. He was not helped by the embarrassing references to the Senator's hard-boiled behavior as a bachelor which had appeared in the first *Merry-Go-Round* book, especially since Tydings was now courting the daughter of Joseph E. Davies, a millionaire lawyer who became Ambassador to Russia.

"Look, Millard," said Drew, breaking through the constraint between them, "I've always protected you. If you don't treat my father right, I'm going after you!"

Tydings ignored the ultimatum. The pair parted on polite terms. Later the Senator told a Democratic colleague: "Hell, we're old friends. If he had said, 'My old man's in trouble,' I'd help him, but I can't let him threaten me."

Tydings decided to go fishing in the Virgin Islands. He announced he was sending down Senator Robert Reynolds, a North Carolina Democrat, as chairman of an Insular Affairs Subcommittee to hear complaints against Governor Pearson. Drew immediately got in touch with his friend, O. Max Gardner, former Democratic Governor of North Carolina and still a power in that state. He provided Gardner with his version of events; Gardner relayed it to Senator Reynolds, and Reynolds promised privately that the hearings would be fair.

Millions of dollars in federal funds had been poured into the islands. Tons of free food had been distributed. Some three hundred formerly destitute families had been relocated in neat little cottages on farms equipped with plows, tractors and bulls from Uncle Sam. The Virgin Islands Company, dreamed up by Paul Pearson and financed by Congress, was running sugar cane plantations, sugar factories, rum distilleries, even a tourist hotel known as Bluebeard's Castle.

The gratitude which might have been anticipated locally had not developed. Bankers and businessmen grumbled about government competition. Many poor families which had not obtained homesteads and bulls for their cows were jealous of the lucky few that had. Mobs formed outside the office of Welfare Commissioner Alonzo Moron to shout that he was holding back supplies of food, which he did not in fact possess.

Most of the witnesses against Governor Pearson wilted under questioning. One complaint was sustained; to obtain spare parts for a broken refrigerator, the Governor had traded $12 worth of lumber from Government House. Since the transaction did not reach the General Accounting Office books, it constituted a technical but not unduly serious offense, Chairman Reynolds noted in his report.

Though they did not convict the Governor of malfeasance, the hearings verified that the islands had become a snarling, spitting cage of political tomcats. On the ground that fresh charges had been filed by Paul C. Yates, a former reporter serving on the Governor's staff, Senator Tydings called hearings before his full committee. Yates, an unstable fellow who had been out of work when Robert S. Allen recommended him for the job, was among those brought to Washington to testify at government expense. He encountered Allen in a corridor of the Senate Office Building prior to his scheduled appearance as lead-off witness on the morning of April 2, 1935.

"Double-crosser," said Allen, intently.

"Why, you son-of-a-bitch . . . " blustered Yates.

The smaller Allen knocked the other man down with a single punch. Yates arose, only to be decked again in a flurry of blows which cut his lip and closed one eye. Senate Office Building police intervened. Yates went to a hospital for repairs. Allen won release from detention as soon as he could put through a telephone call to his friend, Senator James F. Byrnes of South Carolina, chairman of the Senate Office Building Committee.

Senator Tydings smiled benignly as Judge T. Webber Wilson in a folksy Southern manner related vile rumors about Governor Pearson. Senator Tydings publicly congratulated Eli Bauer after his on-and-off follower contributed another measure of slander.

Senators on the committee avoided excessive questioning lest they annoy the chairman. A request that Department of Interior lawyers be allowed to cross-examine witnesses was denied by Tydings. "This is not a trial," said the Senator. He went so far as to introduce a rambling unsupported affidavit from an Episcopal clergyman calling Paul Pearson a liar, a crook, a bastard and a son-of-a-bitch.

Harold L. Ickes, not known as the Old Curmudgeon for nothing, stung Tydings in news releases and denounced him at cabinet meetings. The President agreed that the hearings were outrageously unfair. He twitted Tydings in private, but he shrank from intervening publicly in a feud which seemed to be aligning Congress against the executive branch.

Senate Majority Leader Joseph T. Robinson, Senator Pat Harrison and other Southern stalwarts had already been to the White House to back Tydings. Vice President John N. Garner grumped that the President's legislative program was being jeopardized by failure to drop a Republican holdover. Drew Pearson tried to redress the balance by sending a personal warning to the President resembling his earlier warning to Tydings: "Be fair to my father—or I will cease to support you!"

Ever since the mysterious termination of the MacArthur suit, the President had gone out of his way to conciliate the column.

He turned his magnetic charm on Drew periodically in private meetings at the White House. He slipped tips to Drew for exclusive stories in areas of the latter's special interest, such as his intention to recognize Russia. He nodded emphatically and said "Good man!" when Drew urged Morris Ernst as Counselor to the State Department or somebody else for some other position, though he did not usually make the suggested appointments.

Pearson and Allen's *Nine Old Men* appeared in 1936 only a few weeks before President Roosevelt unveiled his plan to increase the membership on the Supreme Court and force the retirement of sitting Justices at seventy. The book was a journalistic tour de force. It included President Lincoln's historic comment that the Court, in a similar situation, had got the doctrine of democratic government down "as thin as the homeopathic soup made by boiling the shadow of a pigeon that had starved to death." Pearson and Allen amplified their warning with another: *Nine Old Men at the Crossroads.*

Enemies of FDR called the "Washington Merry-Go-Round" a propaganda organ for the President. Roosevelt himself harbored no such illusion. The column had just revealed that the New Deal made a secret arrangement with twenty-five Louisiana politicians convicted for crookedness, letting them off with token fines to assure Huey Long's support in the 1936 election. Under the circumstances the President was not disposed to take political risks for Drew Pearson's father.

During a weekend of yachting, drinking and card-playing on an excursion to Jefferson Island in Chesapeake Bay, with Senator Tydings acting as host, FDR instructed Ickes to secure a letter from Dr. Pearson requesting transfer to another government agency. Dr. Pearson declined to write the letter. No real evidence against him had been produced at extremely one-sided hearings, he pointed out. Ickes reminded him that the Governor of the Virgin Islands served solely at the pleasure of the President of the United States.

The President could remove him, Dr. Pearson conceded, but he would not write the letter. The most he would agree to do, after prolonged discussion, was to talk to Roosevelt if Ickes secured an appointment for him at the White House.

"My respect for Pearson went way up," wrote Ickes in his

diary. "He is a mild-mannered man, even to the point of gentleness, but his Quaker stability of character showed when the test came. Quakers have real moral courage and that is the highest form of courage. He is not willing to retire under a cloud and for that I respect him."

At the White House Dr. Pearson conceded nothing despite the fabulous persuasiveness of the President. Later he agreed to accept a position as head of the public housing section of the Public Works Administration if Ickes was permitted to appear in his behalf before the Insular Affairs Committee to answer publicly all the charges against him.

Tydings, who was under increasing pressure in his own committee, accepted the settlement with alacrity. In the course of a peace parley, he and Ickes decided to drop their personal quarrel. He asked Ickes to suggest to Pearson that the columnist also bury the hatchet. Drew listened to the suggestion without comment or facial expression.

Tydings had to run for re-election in 1938. By 1937 Drew had purchased a newspaper in Maryland and was servicing it and a dozen others with a free new column, called "The Maryland Merry-Go-Round," devoted to the Senator's political destruction. He lined up Ickes and other politicians of influence in Washington behind Representative Davie Lewis as a contender in the Maryland senatorial primary. He helped to persuade President Roosevelt to add the Maryland Senator to his list of Democratic disloyalists marked for purge at the polls.

As campaign manager for Davie Lewis, Drew raised $30,000, of which $17,000 came from himself and a coterie of Washington friends who could not afford to be listed as contributors. In cheerful disregard of the Corrupt Practices Act, he listed these contributions in the names of his married sisters living in Swarthmore, Mrs. Gordon C. Lange and Mrs. Lockwood Fogg, Jr. The good Quaker ladies were appalled to find themselves lawbreakers, but, like their brother Leon before them, they reasoned that whatever Drew did must be all right.

It was an uphill contest from the beginning, partly because Drew's former newspaper, the Baltimore *Sun*, and his mother-in-law's newspaper, the Washington *Times-Herald*, stood firmly in

Tydings' corner. Drew induced Mayor Howard Jackson of Baltimore to defy Tydings. He got Eugene Casey, a bright young politician in nearby Gaithersburg, to chair a Labor Day rally on the Eastern Shore addressed by President Roosevelt by promising that, however the election turned out, Casey would become a presidential assistant in the White House.

Roosevelt honored that and similar promises made by Pearson. Before the campaign ended the journalist found himself dispensing all Democratic federal patronage in Maryland. Using a $150,000 campaign fund to stimulate local annoyance over what was termed presidential interference in a state matter, Tydings won renomination easily and coasted to victory in the general election. Drew remained state patronage boss until Bob Allen forcefully pointed out that he had put the column in an embarrassingly partisan position. Drew then resigned. He never plunged so deeply into politics again.

Of all FDR's attempts to purge Democratic obstructionists, involving such states as South Carolina and Georgia as well as Maryland, only one in New York City against Representative John J. O'Connor, who took a particular lathering in the "Washington Merry-Go-Round," succeeded. The general effort did separate the Democratic sheep from the goats prior to the 1940 presidential campaign. It brought many waverers into line with the administration program.

Something similar happened with FDR's clamorously criticized Court-packing bill. Congress refused to pass it, but from the moment Supreme Court Justice Owen Roberts changed his vote on a crucial labor issue it became clear that the existing majority on the High Court was reluctantly adjusting itself to the New Deal.

Dr. Pearson did a competent job for the Public Works Administration. Despite failing health, he completed in Chicago the first integrated public housing project in the country. The work may have seemed to him a retreat from the twin peaks in his life, the presidency of the Swarthmore Chautauqua and the governorship of the Virgin Islands. He died in 1938, his heart broken, Drew always claimed, by those incomprehensibly cruel hearings before the Senate Insular Affairs Committee.

The death of his mother, following closely that of his father, put Drew's life in a new perspective. Pausing in Council Bluffs, Iowa, on October 13, 1938, during a lecture tour, he composed a properly witnessed will—unlike the preceding unwitnessed wills, which seemed to be impulsive gestures—leaving everything to Luvie except for $10,000 to Ellen and $5,000 to Tyler from insurance policies.

Dan Moore should handle the cash for Tyler, and Ellen should use her money for a college education, Drew specified, adding:

> I give all of my personal files and papers to my daughter Ellen, except for the index file to the Washington Merry-Go-Round which I give to my partner Robert S. Allen, and except for such files and papers which he or my brother Leon shall require.
>
> I give my old trench wrist watch to Tyler, my school medals to Ellen and my books to Ellen, except for such boyhood books as may be of interest to Tyler. I ask that Luvie give consideration to the use by Ellen of the small house at 2822 Dumbarton Avenue, in order that she may always have a home; this, of course, depending upon Ellen's own circumstances and those of Luvie.
>
> I ask that, if possible and practical, Leon continue my work with the Washington Merry-Go-Round during the five-year optional period specified by United Features. I ask that my good friends Morris Ernst and Bob Allen act as my executors.

CHAPTER X

At War

RADIO HAD COME INTO ITS OWN during the 1929–1933 depression. Millions of Americans with little money and much time to spend remained glued to their sets at home instead of seeking outside entertainment. Parties were rare, movies deserted, Chautauqua abandoned. Even as he deplored what was happening, Herbert Hoover let private interests take over the public air. When economic conditions improved under the New Deal, sponsors saw tremendous profits in hiring commentators with something to say about the puzzling forms of government emerging in Washington. From the start Pearson hungered for this kind of role.

Robert S. Allen, Pearson's partner in the "Washington Merry-Go-Round," shied away somewhat from nonjournalistic effort. He was mildly dismayed by the income-producing projects already draped around the column. Franchises had been awarded for the sale of a "Merry-Go-Round" game and "Merry-Go-Round" toys. "Hap Hopper," a comic-strip version of Pearson as crusading newspaperman, was being syndicated in competition with Dick Tracy, the lantern-jawed detective.

Drew argued that they needed radio to counter attempts at censorship by their newspaper syndicate. United Features had

balked at some of their stories. One involved Postmaster General
Farley's rejection of a $100,000-job offer from William Randolph
Hearst; a second attacked Pan American Airways as a monopoly
foisted upon South America by the U.S. State Department; a third
criticized Reconstruction Finance Corporation Chairman Jesse
Jones for giving money to political fat cats rather than to deserving
citizens. Farley did not deny the Hearst story, Drew pointed out.
The history of Pan American Airways, he said impatiently, had
been amply documented in the first *Merry-Go-Round* book.

Bob Allen, unlike Drew, had learned discipline under city
editors. He was usually prepared to accept a "kill" on a story and
proceed to the next order of business. He did not expect a syndicate
manager to judge a column item by background material in a book
or to spit in Hearst's eye when he was trying to peddle other
features to the Hearst chain of newspapers. Above all, he worried
over the Jones charge as possible provocation for another huge libel
suit like the MacArthur one.

Eventually, Pearson had his way on all three stories. He accused his syndicate manager of being friendly to Jesse Jones, which
happened to be true. That put over the Reconstruction Finance
Corporation story. However, Cissy Patterson, another friend of
Jones, felt obliged to apologize in the Washington *Times-Herald*
for allowing the item to slip into print. Jones did not sue.

Bob and Drew made their radio debut in Cincinnati. Talking
back and forth in informal fashion, they created enough of a
stir to be booked by NBC on a national hookup out of Washington for a half-hour on Sunday evenings. Their announcer always
specified how many newspapers subscribed to the "Washington
Merry-Go-Round." Since that seemed to be the aerial yardstick
for a commentator, Pearson began to call up individual publishers
and editors with offers of the column at a cut rate just to expand
the list of subscribers. It sounded good on the air.

Since his voice lacked the natural warmth of Bob Allen's,
Drew speeded up his delivery in imitation of Walter Winchell, the
pioneer among radio commentators. He could not duplicate
Winchell's verbal frenzy, his throaty chuckle over the imagined
discomfiture of enemies or the clacking telegraph key and buzzer
which the vaudevillian-turned-Broadway-columnist used as props.

In an effort to match the excitement generated by Winchell, Drew reserved the final segment of his weekly broadcast for "Predictions of Things to Come." This was gaudy stuff, packaged for sensation.

The Pearson and Allen batting average for correct guessing on the air was declared to be high. Such ratings could always be raised by predicting that Tuesday would follow Monday. An alternative method was to reveal something Sunday night from a news release which was not supposed to be used until Monday or Tuesday.

Many important and legitimate exclusives were aired by the columnists. In expectation of prevailingly favorable treatment, the President would slip the partners an occasional item of special interest, such as his program to pack the Supreme Court. On the other hand, they annoyed him by reporting prematurely his decisive deal with Winston Churchill to exchange American destroyers for British bases in the Western Hemisphere. In the *Times-Herald* Cissy Patterson chided the column for its mistake after the White House issued an indignant denial, but the story was confirmed two weeks later.

Nobody could surpass Winchell for sexy gossip in show-biz patois, but Pearson competed in the style natural to him. He grew an extra layer of epidermis to simulate the callousness of Winchell on the air. Winchell, meanwhile, was raising his sights from the narrow vistas of Broadway and Hollywood and Vine to ape the national and international revelations of the "Merry-Go-Round" pair.

During the struggle over President Roosevelt's guarded two-year effort to prepare the nation for war, Pearson and Winchell shared major news sources, including the FBI, British intelligence and the Anti-Defamation League of B'nai B'rith, which had extensive confidential files. The difference between them was that Pearson and Allen evaluated their tips whereas Winchell swallowed them whole, relying on his known capacity for terrible retaliation against anybody who gave him a bum steer.

When Winchell came to Washington, he made a point of visiting Pearson. They seemed fascinated with each other. One had emerged from a horrendous boyhood, paralyzed emotionally, without principles or friends but with an inspired news-handling capacity. The other operated from a solid family base and a Quaker–Chautauqua–Marxist–New Deal set of progressivist principles which could be sacrificed occasionally in the interests of expediency or friendship.

Winchell and Pearson had one quality in common. Despite the fact that after they got going on radio they were wealthy men, making thousands of dollars a week, they were both notoriously stingy. WW, as he was known, frequently displayed his bankbooks to prove to himself as well as others that he was a success. Drew would tell how he got away with paying his butler, Rudolph Gaull, a mere $150 a month by permitting Gaull to cater Georgetown parties on the side. Winchell and Pearson usually lunched in the Presidential Room at the Hotel Mayflower. If they could not lure some New Deal official with an expense account, such as Leon Henderson, into joining them, their outfumbling each other to avoid getting stuck with the check provided one of the better shows in town.

The only twentieth-century American journalist with a comparable trail-breaking capacity was Westbrook Pegler, a grouch who, from instinct and imagined grievance, was working out in his mind a blueprint for native fascism not unlike the Pareto model in Italy. A superb writer too shy to face a microphone, Pegler hated the other two for their ability to swing from column to radio and back again, getting in a fresh lick with each swing at some carefully cultivated prominent enemy. He considered such tactics unfair competition.

Pouncing on Pearson as the more substantial enemy, Pegler termed him "a miscalled newscaster specializing in falsehoods and smearing people with personal and political motivation." Pearson responded with his first libel suit—for a modest $25,000. Journalistic peacemakers persuaded Pegler to apologize on the ground that continued quarreling "might bring unpleasant attention to the newspaper business." Pearson then withdrew a suit which had provided publicity for both of them.

Pegler and Winchell were powerful enough to enforce an extraordinary requirement: their syndicates took sole responsibility for libel. Not so Pearson; he was willing to fight his own legal battles. If United Features censored a crucial "Merry-Go-Round" column, he and Allen would send it out at their own expense to every subscribing newspaper with an explanation of what had happened. They also paid for last-minute corrections to copy.

Bob Allen went along with Drew's almost obsessive conviction that the column belonged to them alone. He had less sympathy for his partner's use of the column and the radio show for personal purposes. Early in the New Deal he and others at the National Press Club heard from Albert L. Warner, Washington Bureau chief of the New York *Herald Tribune,* about an official of the Civilian Conservation Corps who had been phoned by Drew with a request that a presumably qualified friend be appointed to handle a camp in West Virginia. When the appointment was not made, the CCC was hit repeatedly on other grounds.

On another occasion Drew asked Bob Allen to get Speaker Sam Rayburn to speak to his nephew on the Federal Communications Commission about taking a Baltimore radio station (WBAL) away from Hearst and assigning it to a more liberal group of claimants, which included Bob and Drew. He would not go to Sam on such an errand, said Allen, and if Drew went, he would publicly disclose the improper intervention.

One evening in the late 1930s Bob dropped around to Drew's office-home to mention something he had heard during the day which he did not care to entrust to the telephone. Having a key, he came in to find his partner embracing a part-time typist. Bob pretended to be amused, though it was too close to home for his sense of propriety. He did not say anything about the incident to anybody except his wife, Ruth, but he was pleased by a later report that Luvie had squelched that particular diversion.

By this time Bob took for granted Drew's near-insatiability when it came to women or money. These traits placed no great strain on his loyalty. More disturbing was his partner's increasing recklessness in controversy, which affected him directly. On Drew's insistence, the column made lavish use of "anti-Semitic," a highly offensive and difficult-to-prove adjective, in excoriating the isolationists. Edward A. Rumely, head of the conservative but fairly respectable Committee for Constitutional Government, was one of several who sued when this label was pasted on them. During pretrial testimony Rumely bragged about his large mailing list.

This put him under some legal necessity of revealing the names and addresses of those on the list or abandoning the suit. Since the list was his bread and butter, he abandoned the suit.

Hamilton Fish, a Republican Congressman from Newburgh, New York, threatened to horsewhip Pearson for writing that the German Consul General in New York City began paying a higher rent on a building owned by Fish after Hitler came into power. That amounted to a claim that he took bribes from the Nazis, he said. Two other Congressmen offered to help in the horsewhipping, but nothing came of it. Drew provided additional details of Fish's associations with Nazis. The Congressman called him "the most colossal liar in the world," whereupon Drew sued for $250,000. The ante in the libel game was going up.

When Representative Martin L. Sweeney (R–Ohio), Washington spokesman for the Rev. Charles E. Coughlin, brought his chain-libel suit, John J. O'Connor, the New York City Congressman who had been purged with some help from the column, served as his lawyer. O'Connor claimed to be working on a voluntary basis, but Drew suspected somebody with money was putting up the heavy legal fees involved. He instructed his investigator to break into O'Connor's desk in his Washington law office to discover the identity of the hidden enemy. After casing the building, the investigator refused the assignment. He could elude the cleaning women, he said, but a restless night watchman might catch him in the act.

Bob Allen shrank from the excursions outside the law into which their legal troubles seemed to be leading them. He could have settled the Sweeney gripe with one friendly talk, he believed, and others, too. On the other hand, he wanted to take countermeasures against Cissy Patterson, who was beginning to scoff at her "Headache Boys" in articles and editorials defending the very isolationists they were attacking. Drew was reluctant to move against his mother-in-law.

Cissy went so far as to omit segments, then entire columns, of the "Washington Merry-Go-Round." Sometimes she would shift a column she did not like to an obscure position among the want ads. Drew gave his annual party in honor of Cissy's birthday in November, 1941. Though the evening passed pleasantly, with no mention of their increasingly divergent views, he and she never spoke cordially to each other again.

Since U.S. involvement in the war seemed imminent, Allen made plans to get into uniform. Six days before Pearl Harbor the column carried an item, based on a tip from Sumner Welles, that the Japanese fleet had put secretly to sea and might be heading anywhere. The warning did not suffice to lessen the destructiveness of the subsequent sneak attack on Hawaii.

Drew went to Buenos Aires for a meeting of Latin-American foreign ministers on hemispheric defense. While he was away, Bob encountered Eugene Meyer. On impulse he mentioned that if Cissy Patterson failed to declare her intention to renew her contract at least thirty days before it expired, the column would be up for grabs. The publisher of the Washington *Post* wanted the "Merry-Go-Round" badly. He offered to pay not the $35 a week paid by the *Times-Herald*, which was generous—most papers paid only $5 or $10—but $100.

Publishers dropped columns without concern, but the dropping of a publisher by a column was almost unprecedented. George Carlin, head of United Features, came down from New York to discuss the situation. He obtained clearance from Karl Bickel, head of the United Press. The switch, contingent on Cissy's missing her date, had been virtually arranged by the time Pearson returned to Washington. He protested, but Meyer was "persuasive" and Allen, in Drew's word, "adamant."

What influence did accumulated distress over developments in the column and in radio have on Allen's decision to leave? Probably not much. He had been reared in the cavalry, he had been wounded as an underage soldier in World War I, he had an impressive record in the reserves, he had been urging others to fight Hitler and it behooved him, he thought, to do his share. He was pleased over his selection for the Command and General Staff College at Fort Leavenworth, Kansas.

War did not tempt Pearson. He could not understand Allen's desertion in the face of an impending break with Cissy Patterson. In addition to his natural pacifism, Drew had responsibilities to children as well as to a wife, a column more precious than wife and children, a radio show and associated enterprises. His place was at home. Like a wife whose draft-exempt husband has opted for foreign glory and foreign flirtations in preference to the domestic scene, he felt abandoned and betrayed.

Drew came down to Union Station to see Bob off. At the last minute he told his departing partner he did not believe he could afford to pay the flat 10 percent of the gross receipts of the column on which they had agreed. He would have to deduct expenses, he said. Allen left with words of incredulous protest on his lips.

The attitudes of the two men were not subject to compromise. Some months later a personal check from Pearson to Allen came back with a notation that the absentee partner still wanted a syndicate check for his 10 percent share. During the next two and a half years Allen's wife, Ruth, received no payments from the "Merry-Go-Round." For this and other reasons Allen never returned to the column.

2

On February 13, 1942, Cissy Patterson received from Drew Pearson a letter she did not expect, giving formal notice that in six months the "Washington Merry-Go-Round" would shift from the *Times-Herald* to the *Post*. She needed the column in her drive to dominate the Washington newspaper field; it meant prestige and circulation to her. To have it go to Eugene Meyer, who had previously "stolen" her *Daily News* comics, was a stunning blow.

Unable to bear the overwhelming professional and personal implications of rejection, Cissy immediately announced the firing of Pearson as unreliable, irresponsible and reprehensible. She discharged Luvie as dramatic critic and Leon as Latin-American columnist. To emphasize her scorn of the Pearsons, she hired George Abell to conduct a gossip column called "Ready, Willing and Abell." Her sand family was already washing away.

Drew tried to buy a page in the Washington *Post* to assert that he and not the lady had filed for columnar divorce. Meyer refused lest it focus Cissy's rage on him again. The Washington *News* and the Washington *Evening Star* also rejected the advertisement. "Publishers have to stand together," explained the publisher of the *Star*. The *News*, allied to the column through United Features, a Scripps-Howard syndicate, did print the substance of Pearson's plaint in a news story, thereby bringing it to the general attention of the media.

Cissy responded with an editorial putting things in historical perspective:

> When Hitler rose to power in Europe, a collection of un-American crackpot intellectuals, intrigue-lovers, revolutionaries and plain crooks saw an opportunity to get rich over here and at the same time build up their apparent importance.
>
> Pearson is just one example but we use him here because he worked out of Washington and we know him. And how. For years he was both undercover agent and mouthpiece for the Anti-Defamation League, a powerful Jewish organization which, seized by war hysteria, sought to force free Americans to change their way of thinking. He taught many a Jew and non-Jew to fear and hate his fellow-Americans. And he added to that his apology and special pleading for Communist Russia, an old line he had been peddling from the day the United States recognized the Soviet regime in 1933.
>
> This racket made him rich. It put in his pocket money beyond his wildest dreams. More than that it satisfied his natural and over-powering lust for lying, intrigue, character assassination and spying. All of which, next to money, are the aims of his life. We will say for him that he played his part with obnoxious art and success. He and Winchell screeched back and forth to one another on the radio in fine, hair-raising style, and in their various columns peddled to small newspapers all through the country they planted their strychnine cleverly.

Winchell, whose column still appeared occasionally in the *Times-Herald,* sued for libel. Cissy settled the suit to concentrate on Pearson. By this time she and her brother, Captain Joseph M. Patterson of the New York *Daily News,* and her cousin, Colonel Robert R. McCormick of the Chicago *Tribune,* were known as "The Three Furies of Isolationism." They tried to ignore the fact that a virulent anti-Semitism actually existed in the United States, whipped up by the German-American Bund and native lunatics, and the additional fact that the country was at war with Hitler.

Cissy missed no opportunity to harass Drew. She asked the

Department of Justice to indict him for criminal libel. She complained to the publishers of *Who's Who* that he had falsified the sketch of his life. She organized a writing bureau to prepare hostile articles for his enemies on Capitol Hill to use as speeches on the floor and as inserts in the *Congressional Record*. Senator Owen Brewster (R–Me.), the Senatorial champion of Pan American Airways against Pearson, alone distributed 75,000 reprints of one abusive article under his frank.

George Dixon, a *Daily News* satirist who later acquired his own column, came down from New York as a hired gun to write a two-page center spread in the *Times-Herald Sunday Magazine* under the pseudonym of Georgiana X. Preston. "Ladies and gentlemen and fellow Chautauqua lecturers," he began like a sideshow barker.

> This is the story of the Quaker Oat who became a Sour Mash in Washington. We present for your inspection one of the weirdest specimens of humanity since Nemo, the Turtle Boy. People, on seeing him for the first time, often make wagers on which way he is facing . . . because he has two faces.
>
> Don't be alarmed, folks, when you first lay eyes on this oddity but be sure and keep facing him. He has been known to do awful things to people the minute they turn their backs. . . . Don't be frightened when he sniffs at you. This sniff is a nervous habit acquired after reading things he wrote.· . . . In the event we can get our exhibit to open his two faces wide enough you will note the poison sacs. For years now we have had to keep our pet gila monster away from him because in a battle of fangs it would not be a fair fight.

Becoming gradually more serious, Dixon asserted that a visitor to Pearson's office one day overheard the following dialogue:

> "Where in hell has thee been all day, Leon?"
> Leon (testily): "Thee knows very well where I have been, Drew. Thee sent me, didn't thee?"
> Drew: "Thee is right, Leon. Did thee get the dirt? Thank thee, Leon."

That hurt regardless of the degree of authenticity of the conversation. Drew's upright younger brother, not at all pleased over some of the questionable things he had been required to do for the column and the radio show and unable to live on his pay after losing his supplementary salary on the *Times-Herald,* had looked around and found a new job covering Congress for a wire service. He had mastered the reportorial trade and he had made many friends among reporters, including a young fellow named John F. Kennedy, who was breaking in on the *Times-Herald.* Like Allen, Leon never returned to the column.

Dixon listed such well-known Pearson enemies as Secretary of State Hull, General MacArthur and Senator Tydings, along with their expressions of opinion about Pearson. He accorded an accolade to a relatively new enemy, Representative James W. Mott of Oregon, for calling Drew "the polecat of journalism."

Cissy Patterson claimed authorship of some of the juicier paragraphs credited to "Georgiana X. Preston," including one to the effect that Drew had "no friends, only former friends. No man ever had so many doors slammed in his face. He became so corroded with hate that he rolled on the floor in hysterical rages."

Whether he actually rolled on the floor is debatable, but of Drew's torment there can be little doubt. Cissy pounded her ex-son-in-law in print on the average of once a week. When he tried to present a quiet fact or two in self-defense, it only stimulated a flow of fresh insults.

Cissy Patterson set herself up as a one-woman truth squad to correct Drew's mistakes. After one of his attacks against General MacArthur in the Washington *Post,* she placed a signed editorial on the front page of the *Times-Herald* complaining about his efforts "over a period of years by false and sneering innuendo to smear the reputation of a great man."

Her own range of vituperation was extraordinary. In one article she pictured Drew as "a phony Quaker who thee'd and thou'd his way out of World War I." In another she likened him to Danton, the French Revolutionary, who she said sniffed flowers and drank the blood of children. To a reader who asked why she was so vehement, she replied coldly: "When a cockroach gets into your house you have to step on it." She told George Abell it was a pity they weren't in Chicago "because there I could have Drew rubbed out."

Ellen was fifteen when the quarrel between her indulgent father and her fairy grandmother started. She was almost pulled apart by it. Curious questioning from classmates at boarding school drove her home in a disturbed mood. After what may have been an attempt by Cissy to present a gift to her, Ellen retreated to her room and had to be coaxed out. Her grandmother's attacks on Drew gradually aligned Ellen behind her father, though she remained sole heir to Cissy's estate, then estimated at $30 or $40 million. One day Drew took her aside.

"I may have to sue thy grandmother, Ellen," he said gently.

"That's exactly what she wants," replied the teen-ager with wisdom beyond her years. "Don't give it to her."

3

Always more venturesome on the air than in print, Drew became bolder in both media after Allen's departure. He encouraged listeners to send in tips in the column tradition. Since his program was heard widely during the war, many who responded were GIs in remote posts around the world. A characteristic story used by Pearson concerned an admiral who flew a cow to the Aleutian Islands to assure a personal supply of fresh milk but who neglected to bring along a bull to freshen the cow.

Twelve carloads of leather jackets were ripped in small ways so they could be condemned and sold at a profit at the Philadelphia Navy Yard, according to another controversial tip. A third revealed that four hundred U.S. paratroopers were shot down by U.S. and British naval vessels during the invasion of Sicily. When Pearson was called disloyal for these disclosures, General George Marshall, U.S. Chief of Staff, defended him as "my best Inspector-General."

In a particularly strident tone one evening, Pearson accused Representative Andrew J. May of Kentucky of taking bribes from war contractors. His informant was a veteran, he said, who reached him by phone at the studio after an earlier program in which he had mentioned May's opposition to veterans' legislation. He had apparently visited the veteran's home in the Northeast section of Washington, inspected the chinchillas being raised in the cellar there and met the man's wife, Mrs. Eleanor Hall. She described how she had passed an envelope containing $1,000 to May from her employers, the Garsson brothers of the Erie Bason Products Company.

The real source of the newsbreak, according to an inner office account, was an article written by Ronald W. May (no relation to the Congressman), an ex-Navy man from Wisconsin working for the United Press. Wanting to see his article in print and not finding a magazine to print it, May had sold it cheap to Pearson.

The commentator did visit Mrs. Hall, as he said, but solely for the purpose of getting her statement in affidavit form. Attributing the story to an unsolicited phone call was a romanticism to encourage genuine tips. In due time Mrs. Hall supported her affidavit in court against Representative May, who went to jail.

Pearson was willing to use a tip to stab an enemy in the back or pat a friend on the shoulder. On one show he said that Senator Millard Tydings used free government labor to build a yacht basin and a road on his Maryland estate. The story was false. The city of Havre de Grace had built a public yacht basin and it had resurfaced a farm-to-market road near property owned by Tydings. Nothing more than that.

After the network apologized abjectly to the Senator, Pearson explained that a piece of paper had been handed to him just before the show when he had no time to check. "It was a technical mistake," he said, meaning that he knew the Senator and hoped for a tip which would do justice to him sooner or later.

When General Douglas MacArthur, another bone-bitter antagonist, made repeated pleas for naval relief when the Japanese were pressing him in the Philippines—to the annoyance of President Roosevelt, a Navy man, who realized that such pleas were unrealistic—Drew quoted another general to the effect that MacArthur might have to choose between captivity and his medals. (He could hardly swim for it with all that weight on his chest!)

In the middle of the war Pearson declared that his friend Fiorello La Guardia, an energetic Congressman who had become a weary Mayor of New York, would be commissioned brigadier general for important overseas duty. La Guardia wanted nothing better. However, he knew, and Pearson should have known, that the idea had been batted down during a backstage Washington discussion over "political generals." La Guardia countered with a smiling announcement at City Hall that Pearson was due to be appointed a Lithuanian count.

In April, 1941, Pearson predicted that Germany would invade Russia. When that happened two months later, he predicted that Germany would roll over Russia in thirty days, which did not happen. Dealing with delicate and undecided matters of this sort, it was probably inevitable that he would be wrong almost as often as he was right.

Soon after the United States became involved in the hostilities he predicted that all electric power would be rationed and all labor conscripted, drastic steps which were undoubtedly discussed but never taken. He said Secretary of State Hull would become Ambassador to Russia; after the Normandy landing, that FDR would go to the front to direct the fighting; and that Hitler, nearing defeat, would flee to the Alps disguised as a rabbi. Perhaps the Hitler item could be excused as a racist joke.

Pearson claimed he apologized for mistakes, but his apologies could not always be trusted. He remarked on radio that Mrs. Harry Hopkins had received an emerald necklace from Lord Beaverbrook, Churchill's Lend-Lease emissary. As President Roosevelt's confidential adviser, Harry Hopkins felt obliged to deny that his wife accepted emeralds from anybody. A week later Pearson returned to the subject on the air. The Beaverbrook gift to Mrs. Hopkins had been a diamond necklace worth $140,000, he said, not emeralds at all. He regretted the error.

Through carelessness, calculation or some inner excitement which did not appear on the surface, Drew often spilled over the edge of fact into fantasy or fabrication during his radio broadcasts. With great excitement one night, he revealed that President Roosevelt's dog Fala was about to become a father. A female Scottie had been seen frolicking with Fala on the White House lawn. She was attractive enough as dogs go and Fala may even have made advances, but the visitor was well below the age of consent!

Using an unverified tip from Luvie's sister, he declared that FDR, upon leaving for a vacation, forgot to cancel his regular order for Danish twisted buns from the Taylor Bakerette on Wisconsin Avenue, as a result of which the pastry had piled up during his absence. At the first cabinet meeting after his return the President mentioned this item in an apoplectic mood. Secretaries Ickes and Farley warned Drew that Roosevelt was on the warpath. Even Eleanor, usually an ally during rough sailing with the President, chose a joint radio appearance to tell Drew that her Franklin never, no never, ate Danish pastry.

Another time Drew informed listeners that the President's favorite song was "Home on the Range." Actually, the song was the favorite of Marvin McIntyre, the President's secretary. FDR hated it. For months the President was pursued by "Home on the Range" whenever he came within ear's reach of a band.

Writing at a distance about the 1943 Cairo conference, Pearson said President Roosevelt and Prime Minister Churchill had endangered Allied unity by not greeting Chiang Kai-shek when he arrived. It developed that Roosevelt and Churchill were not in Cairo when Chiang arrived. "A technical error," said Pearson. He may have meant that the big powers accorded less than full partnership to the Chinese and that he would prove it sooner or later.

Pro-Russian as well as pro-Chinese, Pearson supported a second front in Europe before the Allied military command was ready to hazard it. He cited various instances where conservative American officials had dragged their heels in extending help to our Russian ally. In expressing this point of view, he believed he had covert support from the White House.

To placate the Southern wing of the Democratic Party, Roosevelt had named Cordell Hull Secretary of State. Hull was a man with only one fresh idea, that on trade agreements. When he resisted pressure for a more flexible foreign policy, the President began to work through Under Secretary Sumner Welles, Pearson's friend.

Hull wanted to squeeze Welles out of the department, but the Under Secretary stood his ground until the summer of 1943. Enemies then planted newspaper references to his homosexual tendencies when drunk. Roosevelt had previously taken the position that Welles, whatever his private habits, was doing a fine job with the Good Neighbor Policy. In the face of evidence apparently obtained by entrapment, he felt obliged to yield.

Furious over Welles's forced resignation, Pearson said on the radio that Hull wanted "to bleed Russia white." The Secretary retorted that this was "a monstrous and diabolical falsehood," and FDR chimed in with his well-known "chronic liar" tag. To Roosevelt's comment that the Russians might be offended by his untrue charge, Pearson retorted that they were well aware of Hull's attitude.

"I am glad if anything I have said now forces the administration to make clear in words what certainly was not clear before in deeds," he asserted. Despite his grandiloquence, he worried sufficiently over the impact of the President's criticism to call an emergency session in New York with Ernest Cuneo, his radio lawyer.

What they needed, said Cuneo, was a new radio sensation to erase the presidential snub from the public mind. He suggested a story about the slapping of a battle-weary soldier by General George S. Patton, the pistol-packing exhibitionist who had commanded the U.S. Seventh Army during the invasion of Sicily. A number of Washington correspondents had already heard about this but had avoided using it. Since he held a counterespionage job, Cuneo had the details at his fingertips.

On November 21, 1943, Pearson broke the story about Patton, explaining that General Eisenhower had reprimanded him and required him to apologize before his own soldiers. Patton, he predicted, would never again receive a responsible war assignment. Winchell, who had reduced an earlier Cuneo tip on the subject to a one-line item in his column, climbed hysterically on the bandwagon with a prediction that Patton would be shot by one of his soldiers. Both he and Pearson were wrong. Fully aware of Patton's great military capacity, Eisenhower picked him to direct the armored push across France which convinced the Germans they were beaten and shortened the war.

With Patton the newest national hero, Washington columnist John O'Donnell wrote in the New York *Daily News* that the soldier slapped in Sicily by the General had been Jewish. He said various high-ranking Jews in the administration "such as

Justice of the Supreme Court Felix Frankfurter of Vienna, White House administrative assistant Dave (devious Dave) Niles alias Neyhus and the Latvian ex-rabbinical student now known as Sidney Hillman had inspired various breast-beaters, world-savers and payroll-patriots, safe in their Washington foxholes, to howl for the dismissal of Old Blood and Guts." The "real suppression," he continued recklessly, had been Patton's "use of the word 'Jew' in reprimanding the reluctant warrior."

The Washington *Times-Herald,* the Chicago *Tribune* and the rest of the battered isolationist organs of opinion joined in the belated display of prejudice. Then Pearson produced a numbing counterrevelation: the slapped soldier, a South Bend, Indiana, carpet-layer, was a German immigrant, a churchgoing Protestant —not a Jew at all! Reviewing the situation repeatedly in print and over the air, Pearson delivered a blow at anti-Semitism in the United States from which it was slow to recover.

Colonel Robert S. Allen lost his right arm during the fighting with General Patton in Europe. Suffering grievously from shock and the mutilation itself, he returned home with no confidence that there would be a niche for him in the postwar world.

Pearson meanwhile was moving from triumph to triumph. In 1944 he made arrangements to work for a much higher financial guarantee through Bell-McClure, a smaller syndicate which was easier to dominate than United Features. He continued to have problems of censorship on the air, but they could be written off to a considerable extent as promotional expense. The Sweeney chain-libel suit, having dragged on like Jarndyce vs. Jarndyce through twenty-five lower-court engagements and been discussed before the Supreme Court itself, was finally dropped in exchange for cancellation of a countersuit by Drew charging malicious defamation of character.

Pearson had yet to lose a libel suit. Enemies were becoming reluctant to tangle with him in or out of court. He had gone beyond restraint by home-town publisher, syndicate or partner. One threat remained, hanging in the sky like a mushroom-shaped cloud: exposure of his former connection with the Irish Hospitals Sweepstake. Senator Tydings had mentioned more than once in public that Drew used to work "for an international gambling syndicate." Cissy Patterson, continuing her pursuit of Pearson with the fury of a mother-in-law scorned, was told by her *Times-Herald* columnist on federal affairs about an investigator who had once worked part-time for Pearson and who had apparently been involved in a lottery. Cissy spoke to Tydings about this. As chairman of an important war committee, it was easy for the Senator to bring the former investigator, by this time a Marine Sergeant, to Washington. Questioned in secret, the investigator told all he knew. When he returned disconsolately to his Washington hotel, Drew Pearson was waiting in a darkened hallway.

"I've been warned not to talk to you," said the investigator. Pearson shook his head and led the way outside. In his car he listened intently to what had happened before the Tydings Committee. The next day he went to Secretary Ickes, who had once employed this same investigator to handle an attempt at blackmail by a discharged female employee. Drew told Ickes that Tydings was striking at President Roosevelt through a secret investigation of the Department of Interior. Ickes burst into a cabinet meeting with this information, as a result of which Roosevelt directed Attorney General Francis Biddle to terminate the investigation, begun under pressure from Cissy Patterson and Millard Tydings.

The struggle took a new twist. James Roosevelt, most anti-Pearson of the President's sons, had friends in strategic positions in the administration. Through them he instigated activity within the Internal Revenue Bureau, which never forgives failure to pay income taxes, and the Post Office Department, which is responsible for enforcing the antilottery statute.

Considerable progress was made in these investigations. Scores of RCA cables from London to the Algonquin Hotel in New York on the drawing of horses in the sweepstake, all signed "O'Sheehy, Public Relations Director," were recovered, along with subsequent Western Union messages from Washington relaying this information to newspapers. To complete the chain of evidence, further testimony by Pearson's investigator was required. He had been dropped by the Marine Corps, rehired by Pearson and sent into hiding as assistant to a Russian friend who operated a flophouse on the Bowery in New York City.

Pearson meanwhile dug strenuously into the circumstances under which various corporation executives facing government tax problems had taken out multimillion-dollar insurance policies with a company for which James Roosevelt worked. After nibbling at this in print and on the air, Pearson agreed to a conference with the President's son. They emerged with feelings of mutual respect. Thereafter neither pointed at the other's Achilles' heel. When other enemies of Drew attempted to pick up the trail, it developed that the files on Pearson in the Treasury Department and the Attorney General's office had disappeared!

CHAPTER XI

Fair Deal

HARRY S. TRUMAN WAS NOT the most inept President in the history of the United States, though he looked like it for a while. He had been a farmer, an artillery battalion commander during World War I, a haberdasher who went bankrupt and an obscure county judge before he came to the U.S. Senate as a front for the disreputable Pendergast machine in Kansas City. Obtaining federal patronage for the boys back home was his chief Senatorial function. He accomplished this by serving as a New Deal wheelhorse. When the prospect of higher office loomed, he cultivated the Washington political reporters, including Drew Pearson.

Early in 1944 the "Washington Merry-Go-Round" reported that Truman, as chairman of a Senate War Investigating Committee and as a border-state politician with many friends and few enemies, might be a compromise choice for second place on a fourth-term Roosevelt ticket. That started a quiet bandwagon.

Truman always said he "never asked to be Vice President," but in fact he intrigued actively for the nomination. When he won it, he used the semipublic forum of a Washington cocktail party to acknowledge the debt to Pearson. Marching up with a grim look on his face, he said: "You got me in a lot of trouble, Drew. I don't know if I can ever forgive you." He may have been half-serious.

After prolonged exposure to FDR's intricate and hypnotic personality, the Washington press would probably have been disappointed in any new President. Truman aggravated this feeling at his first White House news conference after Roosevelt's death.

"Boys, if you ever pray, pray for me now," he said. "I don't know whether you fellows ever had a load of hay fall on you, but when they told me yesterday what had happened, I felt like the moon, the stars and all the planets had fallen on me. I've got the most terribly responsible job a man ever had."

Though he was a stodgy mediocrity, Truman had more brains and bounce, surely, than a Harding or a Coolidge, a capacity to read books and an inner cockiness. He rose to the challenges facing him, including the need for a quick decision on the atom bomb, about which he had not been previously informed. Some months after the end of the war he gave Pearson a taste of his newly acquired authority.

The columnist-commentator visited the White House not as a newsman but as a lobbyist for thirty thousand soldiers in the Philippines who wanted to come home. Disregarding the petition, the President dressed his visitor down. Since the Russians were in no hurry to demobilize, he said in his flat Midwestern twang, an emotional drive to get all GIs out of uniform served merely to weaken the country's hand around the world.

Pearson was in no position to defend himself. After listening to further presidential expressions of irritation over columnar references to Bess and Margaret Truman, he walked out stiff-legged and pale, like an ambassador who has just received a military ultimatum. The two men did not converse privately again for several years.

A major postwar question was what kind of terms we could maintain with the Russians. Pearson wrote that American bankers who had collaborated with Hitler in Europe after the fall of France were already building up Germany and Japan as counterweights to the Soviet Union. On radio he accused HST of lacking FDR's capacity for getting along with Stalin. Truman replied that he "liked good old Uncle Joe."

Unexpectedly, Drew tipped the scale the other way by breaking the story of Igor Gouzenko, a cipher clerk at the Russian Embassy in Ottawa who had defected and "blown" the Soviet spy network in the United States as well as Canada. Since confirmation of this world-wide sensation was lacking for weeks, Pearson received a great deal of hostile mail. This grew when he declared in a second Sunday broadcast on the subject that the theft of American nuclear processes was forcing a showdown with the U.S.S.R.

During the war, he revealed, a Russian spy had been permitted to leave Seattle on a Soviet freighter "with plans of the atom bomb in his suitcase and samples of the metal from which the bomb is made." The State Department did not want to arouse the public against an ally at that time, and it may have figured that the Russians already possessed the basic secrets. Now the Washington attitude was different. Diplomatic officials, Pearson said, were coming to the conclusion that "we cannot go on appeasing Russia."

Gouzenko had removed the cover of no fewer than seventeen hundred spies. At dawn one morning after most of them had fled, the Royal Canadian Mounted Police rounded up those who remained. The FBI moved simultaneously against a few suspects in the United States. Sufficient information was released from Ottawa to take Pearson off the hook and satisfy the public until a comprehensive report by a Royal Canadian Commission of Inquiry could be prepared.

How did Pearson become involved? Naturally, he made a mystery out of it. From subsequent espionage memoirs it seems that the story was spoon-fed to him by Sir William Stephenson, director of British intelligence in the Western Hemisphere. Sir William had been summoned hurriedly to Ottawa from New York after Gouzenko's defection; he had talked to the terrified cipher clerk, accepted his story as credible and arranged a hiding place for him.

Investigation soon verified Soviet penetration of installations at Oak Ridge, Chicago, Hanford and Los Alamos, in addition to the Canadian pilot plant on the Chalk River near Petawawa. In view of Britain's twenty-year nonaggression pact with Russia, to which the United States was not a party, some officials in Canada and England still hoped to avoid publicity.

Sir William did not think the Gouzenko case should or could

be kept under wraps. The United States had been the chief target of atomic espionage directed from Canada. People were still edgy over the bomb. Only a quick, properly accented unofficial presentation of the facts and subsequent public prosecution of some spies, Stephenson believed, could prevent the development of anti-British feeling in the United States.

Through RAF Wing Commander Roald Dahl, Stephenson had become acquainted during the war with Drew Pearson as a responsible publicist with the largest serious following in the United States. In picking Pearson as his outlet, it must have occurred to Sir William that somebody often accused of being pro-Communist would be particularly useful for his purpose.

The Russians possessed the scientific capacity to duplicate the atom bomb, but for the moment it remained in the exclusive possession of the U.S. Army. Pearson felt strongly that such an ultimate weapon should be transferred to civilian hands. When a bill to set up an Atomic Energy Commission ran into a stone wall in the Senate, he invited the chief Republican obstructionists to dinner at his house. For dessert the Senators were treated to the opinions of the country's leading nuclear physicists. The Senate opposition vanished. Chairman Brien McMahon (D–Conn.) of the Senate Atomic Energy Committee always credited Drew's unpublicized dinner with settling the issue.

Though his presentation of the Gouzenko case had formalized the East-West split known historically as the Cold War, Pearson came to suspect President Truman of carrying confrontation with Russia to extremes. He blamed the "hysterical advice" of James V. Forrestal, who had been selected to head up a new Department of Defense which included the Navy, Army and Air Force.

When Forrestal persuaded Truman to take the Arab side against the Jews in Palestine for military reasons, Pearson saw his opportunity. He lathered and shaved Forrestal as a bureaucratic voice for American oil companies with enormous stakes in the Mideast. Walter Winchell and other opinion-makers supported his position.

Ted O. Thackrey, editor of the New York *Post*, was summoned to the White House during this period to discuss his strong support for a Jewish state in Palestine. Since Thackrey was not a Jew and he had known Truman back in Kansas, the President spoke freely. He was getting contradictory advice from Jewish groups, he confided, "the damnedest kind of pressure, no way to please 'em."

"Why should Jews have to think alike?" parried Thackrey.

"All I know," said Truman, banging the desk with his fist, "is that if the goddamned New York Jews would just shut their goddamned mouths, we could find a way to get along with the British and the Arabs!"

Thackrey said he supposed his wife, Dorothy Schiff, publisher of the *Post,* and Bernard Baruch—"whom I always regarded as *your* adviser"—were among the "goddamned New York Jews," and from that point the two men had at each other as violently as they could short of fisticuffs.

Thackrey proceeded to the Washington Bureau of the New York *Post,* on the thirteenth floor of the National Press Building. There he dictated a memo on the talk while it was still hot in his mind. He kept the original, left one copy in Washington and delivered the second to Mrs. Schiff. Later a garbled version of the conversation reached Pearson through Herbert Bayard Swope and was used by Pearson without further checking.

President Truman called a news conference to charge that Pearson had "made up a lie out of whole cloth" in claiming that he had said "Jews in New York are disloyal to their country." In a comment which did not receive much attention, Thackrey declared that the Pearson reference to "disloyalty" was "inaccurate," but that the story in general was not made up out of whole cloth.

For the Washington *Times-Herald,* always eager to gouge the ex-son-in-law of its publisher, the President provided a special statement. "There is one columnist in Washington," he said, "who wouldn't have room on his breast if he got a ribbon for every time he's called a liar. In Missouri we have a four-letter word for those who knowingly make false statements."

Eventually, Truman found it desirable for political reasons to swing back toward a pro-Jewish position. On domestic issues also he vacillated. The liberal cause in the country was falling apart. The President assumed that FDR had been unnecessarily rude to powerful individual Republicans and Southern Democrats in Congress and that they could be conciliated over a little bourbon and branch water. It took him months to realize that an entrenched conservative was about as amenable to persuasion as an embittered rhinoceros.

The Midwestern prejudices which Harry Truman concealed when he was compiling his New Deal voting record in the Senate became glaringly obvious in the White House. During a period when prewar isolationists were regrouping as anti-Communists and vigilantes, he was not even solid on civil rights. A recurrent but false rumor that he had once been a member of the Ku Klux Klan seemed plausible to many people.

The Klan was experiencing a postwar revival. Pearson garnered inside information on it from Isidore Lipschutz, a New Yorker operating as a Committee for the Prevention of World War III, and others specializing in the infiltration of fringe groups. Challenged by the grand kleagle to repeat in public the things he said from his guarded radio studio, Pearson broadcast on July 26, 1946, from the steps of the State Capitol in Atlanta. The liberal Governor, Ellis Arnall, provided troops for protection. There may not have been much risk, but the gesture satisfied Drew's growing inclination to put his body on the line.

In the fall of 1947 he read about a celebration in Marseille over the arrival of a shipload of free wheat from the Soviet Union. Since the United States was sending great quantities of free wheat to France without fanfare, he conceived a humanitarian idea with P. T. Barnum trimmings: a transcontinental "Friendship Train" to collect donations of food for the hungry, war-exhausted populations of France and Italy.

After naming a committee and contributing $10,000 to start the train rolling, Pearson found himself in charge of an immense hands-across-the-sea enterprise. Using newsreels for advance publicity, he supervised the European distribution of seven hundred carloads of food from several trains. Pearson's benevolent internationalism coincided with Harry Truman's espousal of the Marshall Plan.

Pearson had become a free-world hero. Foreign decorations were lavished on him. The Norwegian Storting nominated him along with others for the Nobel Peace Prize. The Army and Navy Union shared its annual award among General Dwight D. Eisenhower, General Omar Bradley and (Honorary Inspector General) Drew Pearson. The Golden Slipper Square Club of Philadelphia, which had previously given its antibigotry bauble to Frank Sinatra, chose Pearson in 1948. The cat lovers of America honored him and his black cat Cinders.

Sponsored by a hat company, on radio the commentator conducted a "Sacred Fire Contest" in which contributed prizes, ranging from suits of clothes to "sedans of a famous make," were awarded for the best essays of less than two hundred words on the meaning of democracy. Radio columnist John Crosby equated the contest with others on the air for "Pepsi cereal and the Whozit candy bar."

Early in 1948, General Eisenhower presented Pearson an award as "Father of the Year" at ceremonies in New York. In front of the newsreel cameras the recipient recalled Indian lore he had absorbed out of respect for a possible redskin on his family tree. "In the words of the Kaw tribe in your state of Kansas," he told the former Supreme Commander of the Allied Forces, "I hope you become 'Little White Father in Big White House.' "

Other Democrats wanted the war hero to seek their party's nomination, but Eisenhower decided not to plump for either party that year. Truman swept the Democratic Convention. His re-election campaign was organized by his counsel, Clark Clifford, a brilliant St. Louis lawyer, around support for farm aid and civil rights; and opposition to inflation, the antilabor Taft-Hartley Law and the misdeeds of a Republican-controlled Congress.

Hoping to catch reflected glory in a cup, the President offered Pearson a civilian Medal of Merit in exchange for a friendly letter about the Friendship Train. Pearson said no. Like everybody else, he expected Truman to lose to Governor Thomas E. Dewey of New York, but he inched farther out on a limb than anybody else. Because of the three-day lag between the production and appearance of a column, he distributed one column for use the day after election—suggesting cabinet appointments to Dewey —and another for use two days after election—on the major issues facing the new Republican President.

As an election-night commentator in New York, Pearson was the first to announce a Dewey victory. That did not solve the problem of his postelection columns. It was already too late to do anything about the first one. He typed a substitute on the major issues (facing Truman, this time) and wired it to all his subscribers at a personal cost of $2,000. Many editors used the wrong column anyway. Some may have done it for the pleasure of sticking a pin in a pundit who at times acted in public like a mountebank.

2

For a while after the war nobody knew whether Bob Allen would return to the column. In a depressed and uncertain state, he spent a full year at Walter Reed Hospital undergoing treatment on the stump of his right arm. Laboriously training himself to type with his left hand, he began to grind out articles for magazines—*Liberty, Collier's, Cosmopolitan*—and, with research assistance, to work on several books. More than anything, he wanted to take over his old job as head of the Washington Bureau of the Philadelphia *Record*, but by the time he was physically ready the newspaper had been closed by a strike.

Millard Tydings visited the hospital one day. He had great respect for Allen, the Senator said, and he would be glad to contribute his legal services without charge if Allen wished to bring suit against Drew Pearson. Allen glowered at Tydings. "I do my own fighting," he said.

Bob and Drew made halfhearted gestures of amity toward each other, but their differences were too deep to permit resumption of the partnership. Eventually, Pearson agreed to pay $45,000 over a six-year period in overdue and disputed allowances to Allen, who in turn relinquished all rights in the column.

During the war years two reporters with Communist Party backgrounds had latched onto the payroll. David Karr, publicly accused of being a former *Daily Worker* reporter, avowed no present taint and remained a while longer in Washington. Andrew Older, who carried a CP card almost provocatively, found it convenient to resign.

Pearson had been hitting the House Un-American Activities Committee ever since it started. He considered it an undemocratic and unfair method of harassing people who held unpopular opinions. Nobody was surprised when he exposed HUAC's post-war chairman, Representative J. Parnell Thomas, for taking kick-backs from his office employees.

Pearson explained in detail that an affair between Thomas and a young secretary had irritated the less youthful spinster who ran the office and induced her to come to the column with evidence. He did not mention that the story had been worked up by Andy Older, his ex-employee, who sold it for a mere $100 in expenses, having found no market for it elsewhere.

Tom McNamara, Allen's former assistant, was still on the "Merry-Go-Round." New staff members included Fred Blumenthal, a brilliant if erratic legman; Jack Anderson, a former Mormon missionary, merchant seaman and free-lance correspondent in China; and Tris Coffin, who had run his own Washington column for a while.

Pay on the column was poor. The assistants remained for various reasons, one being the hope that they might be designated sooner or later as Pearson's chief assistant, junior partner or successor. There was a good deal of jockeying for position in the office. Through a friendly secretary, Jack Anderson read a copy of a Pearson letter which seemed to indicate a preference for Coffin, the most recent arrival in the office. That triggered revolt.

A delegation of dissidents, led by McNamara, paid a formal visit on Bob Allen. They all wanted to leave Pearson, said McNamara. They did not have sufficient prestige to start a column by themselves. If he was willing to stage a comeback in the column field—and they knew he had received offers from syndicates—he could use them as a ready-made staff.

Allen put on his battle face. "I don't want to go back to that treadmill," he said finally.

Some weeks later, Pearson encountered Allen. With a grin, he revealed that he knew all about the attempted secession. Who tipped him off he did not say. Allen shrugged and made no comment.

Pearson fired nobody, not even McNamara. Coffin left of his own volition after the dust-up. Fred Blumenthal moved to New York to work for *Parade* magazine. *Parade* was also interested in Anderson. To the disappointment of Blumenthal, who would have liked the job, Anderson became the magazine's Washington editor under an unexpected agreement with Pearson that he could handle that work on the side—in lieu of a raise. Jack was definitely emerging as the heir apparent of the column.

3

Here is how the master of the "Merry-Go-Round" appeared in mid-career and beyond: a large man with the learned look of a Midwest college professor of Latin; socially aloof but responsive in conversation; physically strong, able to sling a heavy bag of manure across his shoulder at the farm; and mentally tough, not merely hard, from the constant necessity of making painful decisions.

Secure, large-minded public officials with a broad streak of idealism in their makeup were usually attracted to him. During the Truman presidential period they included Chief Justice Fred Vinson, who was trying to mediate between a liberal wing of the Supreme Court headed by William O. Douglas and a conservative wing headed by Felix Frankfurter; Averell Harriman, a wealthy former Ambassador who assumed a troubleshooting role at the White House like that of Harry Hopkins under FDR; and Dean Acheson, a warmhearted, sophisticated lawyer who had not worked well with President Roosevelt but who had been promoted by Truman to Secretary of State.

Pearson had to be circumspect in writing or speaking on the air about friends like these since they were usually informants. As Maury Maverick, liberal ex-Congressman from Texas, warned in a letter bearing documentary proof that Governor Allan Shivers of that state had made almost a half-million dollars in six months on a safe, politically arranged business deal: "Now don't you go calling me 'hard-hitting' or 'able' Maury Maverick in that column of yours for a while or they'll put a finger right on me."

Incompetent presidential appointees had to run the gantlet in the "Washington Merry-Go-Round." Harry Truman did not appreciate warnings from Pearson. He promoted John Snyder, an Arkansas bank teller who had been a disaster as Reconversion Director. On radio the following Sunday, Pearson snapped that there was "no truth to the rumor that many Washingtonians cashed in their war bonds when John Snyder was named Secretary of the Treasury."

President Truman's unofficial adviser on appointments was George E. Allen, a portly insurance lawyer from Okolona, Mississippi. George posed as court jester; his only function at the White House, he declared, was keeping Harry relaxed and happy. When he tied up public-housing funds in what was described as a temporary job as Reconstruction Finance Corporation Chairman, he was fingered by Pearson as "a dangerous influence in government," an inside man for favor-seeking industrialists.

George retaliated with a less-than-hilarious guest column in the Washington *Times-Herald* about "Pere Drewson," a columnist operating by "whitemail," that is, by granting immunity from criticism to federal officials willing to snitch on their colleagues. If he had the power people thought he had, wrote George, he would "abolish" the "Merry-Go-Round," "break the Drewson reign of terror and give officials time and energy for their work."

The column kept tabs on the President's raffish set of assistants, including Jake Vardaman, the head of a bankrupt St. Louis shoe concern who became a land-based admiral as naval aide and later a member of the Federal Reserve Board; and Harry Vaughan, an amiable tea salesman who, as Truman's former buddy in the National Guard, was upped to major general and military aide.

Vaughan, like George Allen, was supposed to be primarily a presidential playmate, but he sounded off in public on important issues until he was abruptly silenced. At the height of the postwar housing shortage, he intervened to procure scarce building materials for a racetrack promoter. He ran tawdry errands for large campaign contributors. Worst of all, he brought into the White House John Maragon, a "lovable" ex-bootblack (and ex-bootlegger) from Kansas City, who promptly established himself as a five-percenter. That is, he did commercially valuable favors for a piece of the action.

When Pearson disclosed that Maragon had been giving presidential intimates bottles of scarce imported perfume—smuggled through customs by Vaughan himself—not to speak of deepfreezes, the President's military aide asked the FBI to look into all sorts of charges against the "Merry-Go-Round" staff. He also did what Cissy Patterson had done earlier: he set up a clearinghouse for the dissemination of hostile information about Pearson.

Cissy's latest move in this direction was to encourage a former Washington *Herald* city editor named Morris A. Bealle to produce a book entitled *Washington Squirrel Cage*. One chapter listed the insults—rogue, blackguard, Judas, Ananias, etc.—lavished on Pearson over the years. The compilation included a statement by Senator Tydings that the columnist used to keep stacks of thousand-dollar bills in a safe-deposit box until the federal government began a drive against income-tax evaders and a half-forgotten remark by Cissy herself that "Pearson's filthy work of plotting, planning, sneaking, lying, stealing, smearing" was designed "in the hope of one day overthrowing our American form of government."

Without doubt, Pearson was becoming the most feared and hated man in Washington. On the other hand, his readers and listeners swore by him, not at him. They sensed that he was rarely fair to anybody, that he unhesitatingly put opponents in a false light and defended friends to the point of imbecility, but they considered him, on balance, incorruptible and good.

Senator John Bankhead (D–Ala.), brother of former Speaker Will Bankhead and uncle of Tallulah Bankhead, the actress, did not qualify as a friend of Pearson, but the Speaker had lived nearby in a Georgetown house rented from Pearson. During a campaign against commodity speculators designed to stiffen President Truman's on-and-off efforts to slow down inflation, Pearson discovered that Senator Bankhead had been gambling on cotton futures in his wife's name while taking governmental actions to boost the price.

Shown a "Merry-Go-Round" column about this during an executive committee session in the Senate, Bankhead suffered a fatal heart attack. Naturally, the family blamed Pearson for his death.

Another concealed cotton speculator was Senator Elmer Thomas (D–Okla.). Under fire from Pearson he demanded a trial by his peers. A Senate committee under Chairman Homer Ferguson (R–Mich.) began an investigation, then stalled. Pearson explained that Ferguson had been frightened off by threats of exposure for accepting favors from the Detroit auto industry. He produced a copy of a very explicit letter from Thomas to Ferguson as proof.

How could anybody acquire such a letter? Apparently, it came from Attorney General Tom Clark, with whom Pearson was on even more intimate terms than he had been with Clark's predecessor, Francis Biddle. Another pipeline, in the person of Theron Lamar Caudle, Assistant U.S. Attorney General in charge of the Criminal Division, dropped around to Drew's house one day for advice. The House Ways and Means Committee planned to investigate a soft settlement of an income-tax-evasion case against a St. Louis manufacturer which Caudle had arranged under instructions from Matt Connelly, Truman's appointments secretary. The least Pearson owed an informant in trouble was lunch. Two hours later, President Truman fired Caudle; the President had heard about the lunch. Connelly and Caudle went to jail for the St. Louis fix.

John Stewart Service, a conscientious Foreign Service officer, had been accused of disloyalty by Patrick J. Hurley, wartime Ambassador to China, for suggesting that in the long run the Mao Tse-tung Communists might be a better bet for U.S. support than the corrupt, disintegrating regime of Chiang Kai-shek. Pearson visited Service's apartment in Washington for a talk about Hurley. Neither knew that the apartment was bugged. As a result, Service was dropped from government employ. It took him years to gain vindication.

Hurley, a vain, unpredictable man, made a confidential proposal to the State Department that the United States publicly demand democracy in Iran and accuse Great Britain of imperialism there in handling Lend-Lease. When the President dismissed the idea as "messianic globaloney," Dean Acheson slipped the phrase to Pearson, who printed it with delight.

In discussing a Pat Hurley or a Millard Tydings, confirmed enemies who could not quite gear themselves up to a libel suit, or a Douglas MacArthur, who had flubbed such a suit, Pearson often adopted a contemptuous tone. During a 1946 broadcast he blamed MacArthur, as postwar chief of occupation forces in Japan, for permitting U.S. soldiers there to become fathers of fourteen thousand Eurasian bastards. Since no substantial number of American troops had been in Japan longer than six months, this would have been remarkable, if true.

Pearson displayed no embarrassment over the mistake. He liked to toss darts at his unfavorite militarist. If one missed the mark, he would keep trying. Perhaps his aim would improve. Somewhat later he charged that a group of Senators led by Tydings had left Japan after a few days instead of staying an intended several weeks because they disapproved of MacArthur's policies. In rage, Tydings tried to rake up the columnist's concealed record as "an agent for an international gambling syndicate."

Senator Tydings mentioned the unnamed lottery assistant in Washington who gave a private statement to the authorities, then hid out in New York to avoid further questioning or public testimony. Pearson dryly embellished his MacArthur charge, avoiding the other matter. So far as he was concerned, that door was closed and locked.

New enemies arose too mettlesome or too stupid to be impressed by Pearson's reputation. To deal with them, he developed a national network of stringers, or part-time reporters, who could be used occasionally, for little more than expenses, as investigators. A particularly promising helper in New York was twenty-two-year-old Sydney S. Baron.

Pearson had listened to Baron testify before a Congressional committee in 1945 about the New York City paving blocks used by Bronx Sanitation Department workers to create a "Belgian courtyard" on the Carmel, New York, estate of Democratic National Chairman Edward J. Flynn, who was also political boss of the Bronx.

Impressed by the young New Yorker's coolness under cross-examination, Pearson hired him to come occasionally to Washington to check tips in instances where a strange face would be advantageous. He asked Baron also to cultivate a Washington operator known as John P. Monroe, whom Pearson had described as "one of the most incredible, irrepressible lobbyists ever seen in a city where lobbyists pop up like fleas," and who had consequently sued the column for a cool million and the Washington *Post* for another $350,000 for defamation of character.

Posing as a Brooklyn butcher willing to pay over-ceiling prices for beef, Baron became a familiar figure at lavish parties thrown by Monroe in his "Big Red House on R Street," which was commodious enough to have been rented at one time by Cissy Patterson. The Big Red House on R Street, not to be confused with the Little Green House on K Street, which had been the gathering place for the Teapot Dome conspirators, drew not only the staple fare of pretty young girls and generals but also extremely important officials, including cabinet members.

Under arrangements made by Pearson, Baron introduced a Manhattan fur dealer—an FBI agent in disguise—to the parties. Monroe offered at once to sell the fur dealer the entire Louisiana muskrat production—which he did not control—in exchange for a quick $25,000 campaign contribution to Representative James Morrison of that state.

It took time, but by 1948 the Baron-FBI-Pearson combination had convincing evidence of eight of Monroe's illegal black-market deals. The libel suit evaporated. Monroe went to jail to the accompaniment of colorful stories in the "Washington Merry-Go-Round" which underscored the columnist's reputation for legal invincibility.

4

Drew's family was his Gethsemane. For every public triumph, he endured a private setback. Most wearing was the malevolence of Cissy Patterson. In every way possible she tried to do him injury.

Back in January, 1945, Cissy began a guerrilla war in court. She first sued Drew for an accounting as trustee for the Potomac farm, which she had given to Ellen. Drew and Luvie had been living at the farm without paying rent. All Ellen got out of it was an upstairs room which she rarely occupied, said her grandmother. Drew replied that he had leased the farm for $100,000 and had made $60,000 in improvements in lieu of rent.

Did Ellen, not yet eighteen, have the right to turn over her property to her trustee? The emotional girl became confused in court. She could not recall signing any lease, but whatever her father did was all right with her, she said.

In an effort to settle the matter, Drew reconveyed the property to Ellen. Whereupon Cissy, who wanted blood rather than clarification, filed a new action to evict her ex-son-in-law for breach of trust. The legal moves and countermoves continued interminably, with Ellen always in the middle.

Drew, whose gross income ranged between $300,000 and $500,000 a year, purchased a second working farm of 160 acres at Travilah, Maryland, just north of Ellen's 285 acres, as if to show Cissy that the value of the original farm was not an overriding consideration with him.

In charge of the combined farms he placed his nephew Paul, one of Leon's sons. For a married man with children and a degree in agronomy from Cornell, Paul received such a meager salary— reportedly $75 or $100 a week—that his mother, Anna, begged Ruth Allen to intercede with Drew for a raise. Bob Allen's wife refused; she wanted nothing more to do with the Pearsons. When Paul finally broached the subject, Drew encouraged him to supplement his pay by outside work on the lawns of their exurb neighbors.

Leon himself was becoming known as a foreign correspondent. In 1945 he accompanied Secretary of State James F. Byrnes to Moscow and was one of three newsmen admitted to the Big Three meeting. Later he took over the Paris Bureau of the International News Service. When he initiated an early-morning newscast out of Paris for NBC radio, his older brother scheduled his shaving period so he could listen without losing time.

To show his lack of concern over the mounting attacks on him, Drew felt obliged to make more social appearances than usual in Washington. Luvie was his invariable companion. Arriving one evening at the home of Baron Silvercruys, the Belgian Ambassador, she noticed the host talking to Justice Felix Frankfurter.

Drew had been consistently critical of Frankfurter, and in return Frankfurter had been telling people he "despised" Pearson. Walking across the room, Luvie inserted herself coolly between the Baron and the enemy. Since she stood a good five feet ten and Frankfurter was a tiny man, her back effectively blocked the Justice out of the conversation. Drew had to go outdoors to indulge his laughter.

Luvie cemented friendly relations with Drew's important friends. Dean Acheson accepted her invitations to stay at the Pearson house during the summer when she and Drew went on working trips. Chief Justice Vinson and Ambassador Harriman vied for the pleasure of being her bridge partner. So did Clayton Fritchey and other correspondents. They claimed she was the best bridge player in town.

Luvie was a superb helpmate under other circumstances. Drew liked to tell of the farewell party he gave during the war when his friend George C. Vournas became a captain in the Army. Each guest was asked to contribute a single line of verse about Vournas in Edmund Vance Cook style. The first six lines and their contributors, which were all Drew could remember, went like this:

As a one-man lynching posse	*(Pat Jackson)*
He'll invade the Wilhelmstrasse	*(Anna Pearson)*
Seize poor Adolf by his asse,	*(Drew Pearson)*
He will do to Schickelgruber	*(Royce Powell)*
What Drew did to Herbert Hoover	*(Peggy Palmer)*
With a can of paint remover.	*(Luvie Pearson)*

Having absorbed Drew's views by osmosis, Luvie joined an organization in 1940 designed to ease anti-Soviet sentiment in the United States in the wake of the Hitler-Stalin pact. After the war she was listed by the House Un-American Activities Committee as a member of a Communist front. Since Mrs. Eleanor Roosevelt and other influential non-Communist American women had also been members, the Pearsons scoffed at the listing.

Noticing that Drew was exhibiting signs of wear and tear one summer, Luvie persuaded him to take his first vacation in years. Husband and wife were sitting on the beach at Santa Barbara when an Associated Press reporter scampered across the sand with news that two Treasury Department experts had been turned loose on their tax returns. Reluctantly, they returned to Washington. In the end, only one small item of business expense was disallowed: a dinner party in honor of Fred Vinson, on the ground that Justices of the Supreme Court were above politics.

Luvie had two deficiencies which were not her fault: she could not give Drew the children he wanted and she could not get along with Ellen, his only child, which added to his concern about the stress under which that hypersensitive girl lived.

Through an intermediary, Cissy Patterson had let Ellen know that she was willing to pay at least $300,000 for the Potomac farm. Ellen refused to consider the offer. She would not talk about it to either her grandmother or her father. The money had no importance compared with the terrible continuing necessity of choosing between them.

At Drew's suggestion, Ellen went to New York in the fall of 1946 to take writing courses at New York University. The following spring she was married in Washington to George L. Arnold, son of Drew's close friend, former federal judge and Assistant U.S. Attorney General Thurman Arnold. Felicia came to her daughter's wedding, but Cissy, though invited, did not attend.

Since George Arnold wanted to live in California, it seemed reasonable to Ellen to sell the Potomac farm to her father for the $100,000 he considered equitable. This small gesture may have turned Cissy Patterson against her granddaughter. Ellen, once sole heir of Mrs. Patterson's estate, was cut off without a cent when Cissy died under somewhat mysterious circumstances on July 23, 1948.

Cissy had made seven different wills over the years. She was mulling over a typed prospective eighth will, revoking a gift of the Washington *Times-Herald* to seven of its executives and increasing her family bequests, the night before her body was found.

Drew Pearson made a dramatic entrance into the case with a reminder to the public that Cissy Patterson had "hinted" she might be murdered. "Somebody might have wanted to prevent execution of that new will," he said. "Before we are done we may find cases of the old circulation skulduggery that was started by the same crowd in Chicago."

He was referring, unmistakably, to the Chicago newspaper wars between Patterson-McCormick and Hearst, in which mobsters were used by both sides. Frank Waldrop, due under the will to become editor-in-chief of the *Times-Herald*, felt that he and his journalistic co-heirs were being incredibly accused of murder despite a coroner's verdict that Cissy Patterson, who toward the end of her life had been subsisting mostly on alcohol and sleeping pills, had died of renal disease.

Several weeks later, Charles B. Porter, Cissy's financial manager, fell to his death from a hotel room in Clarksburg, West Virginia. Again Pearson exploded. He publicly implored the state police to guard Porter's files and diary. Nevertheless, they were turned over at 2 A.M. the next day to a *Times-Herald* reporter who had flown down with a signed request from Sybilla Campbell, Cissy's housekeeper and executor of the Porter estate.

"Efforts have been made to get Porter to return to his native Scotland," Pearson told a Washington correspondent of the *New York Times*. "Some people thought he knew too much. The circumstances surrounding Porter's death are strange indeed, including the fact that he jumped or was pushed through a window screen. This was no ordinary suicide."

Betty Hynes, social reporter and former social secretary to Cissy, also died that week, apparently from an overdose of sleeping pills. Pearson demanded an investigation of this additional death. His own investigators—he now had two instead of one—were already pursuing clues.

With anonymous assistance from Drew Pearson, speculative articles about multiple murder over possession of Washington's largest newspaper appeared in *Time* magazine, the New York *Star* and other publications.

Felicia, who was living alternately in a New York City apartment and an upstate New York farmhouse, decided to challenge her mother's will. Through a Washington lawyer procured by Drew, she asserted that Cissy had been of unsound mind and a victim of fraud, deceit, undue influence, duress and coercion.

After preliminary legal sparring, Felicia came down from New York for a jury trial of her suit. She had been calling herself the Countess Gizycka for literary and social reasons, but she confided to interviewers that she had no real right to the title of her father, Count Joseph Gizycki, and therefore preferred to be called "plain Mrs. Gizycka."

Because what she had to say involved "intimate details" of her mother's life and "scandalous material affecting third parties," Felicia testified in secret. After completing her testimony, she abruptly and unexpectedly accepted a settlement offer of $400,000 in cash, tax-free, instead of the $25,000 a year for life which she would have received under the will. The tax-free $400,000 had a "pocket value" of $2 million or more, her lawyer figured, but even that amount did not seem excessive for the only child of a woman whose estate, though greatly depleted, still exceeded $17 million.

Felicia conceded as part of the settlement that her mother had been of sound mind and that nobody had been influencing her unfairly when she made her seventh will and that she did not make another. Did that dispose of Drew's lurid scenario as paranoiac or simply unprovable? The newspaper executives had a possible libel suit, but they did not pursue the matter.

With part of her money from the estate, Felicia established a $5,000-a-year trust fund for Ellen. Out in California Ellen had begun producing sturdy sons, the first of whom she named Drew after his grandfather. Ellen's husband was doing well as a lawyer, though he lost out in a race for Congress. Under the illusion that his most troublesome family problem was solved, Drew handwrote a new will, leaving virtually everything he owned to Luvie and her son, Tyler, including the farm originally presented by Cissy to Ellen. A two-thirds interest in the other farm was reserved for Ellen and Grandson Drew, the remaining third going to Luvie.

"While the joint ownership of the [Travilah] farm may present some small personal complications," Drew added in the will, "I know my family will be able to work things out harmoniously or live together on the farm harmoniously. After all if there cannot be peace among families how can there be peace among nations?"

CHAPTER XII

A Controversialist in Action

THE POLISHED BRASS and placid decor of Drew Pearson's office-home in Georgetown were so reminiscent of old Washington that a stranger with imagination might expect a gloved gentleman in stovepipe hat to emerge from its portals to enter a coach and four. Nothing could be more misleading. The quiet façade hid an internal buzz of action. Men and women hurried from room to room to consult in tense tones. A UPI ticker clattered and a half-dozen telephones rang all day and well into the night.

From Dumbarton Avenue a visitor came into a ridgelike entrance hall which served as boundary between the residential and working areas. Straight ahead and down a step or two into a relatively modern wing was a living room. Down similarly to the left was a dining room and beyond that a kitchen, with bedrooms and a private sitting room upstairs. With Ellen married and living in California and Tyler away at school, the domestic roster consisted of Drew and Luvie, a cook and a butler, the columnist's cat and a beagle owned by the butler.

Two steps down to the right from the entrance hall was the columnist's study, and debouching from it were various rooms for members of the staff on three floors. In the study, a small room cluttered with books, papers and mementos, Pearson could usually be found at a wide, centrally placed desk, wearing a maroon-colored smoking jacket. Cinders, the cat, might be sleeping quietly in one of the wooden intake boxes ranged across the desk.

Newspaper cartoons about Pearson and photographs of him with political celebrities, including several Presidents, held conspicuous place on the wall above the desk. A rural landscape painted in oil by his mother, Edna, hung near a portrait of his father, Paul. Snapshots of other relatives could be seen on a mantelpiece above a workable fireplace. If verbally nudged, Drew would discuss one or more of these exhibits with a reserve which suggested that his time was precious.

Pearson was particularly proud of a portable Corona typewriter on a stand near the desk. This was given to him by his father in 1922, he said. He took this machine with him on trips. Nobody else was permitted to use it or so much as carry it across the room. When it got out of order, there was only one place in Washington, a small machine shop, where it could be taken for the installation of specially fabricated parts. Some staff members believed that the original typewriter must have been duplicated at least once since 1922 and that the claim to singularity was merely a sentimental gesture. They did not express this opinion to Pearson.

To the immediate right of Pearson's study was a much larger workroom containing quarters for several secretaries, a noisy ticker and thirty or more gray steel filing cabinets lined up like elephants against the walls. These cabinets contained personal as well as columnar secrets. Since the "Merry-Go-Round" had achieved the downfall of prominent enemies by securing their files, Marian Canty, Drew's confidential secretary, had instructions to keep them locked except when in use.

Those working for the columnist must be constantly on call. Miss Canty no longer came in early, but one of the younger girls could usually be induced to arrive at 6 A.M. to type material which Pearson had talked into a machine the previous night and wanted to look at no later than 8 A.M. He thought nothing of phoning a male assistant at 7 A.M. or midnight with a story idea. Woe to that assistant who could not be reached or who, if reached, did not have a pad and pencil handy to record instructions!

Pearson once hired a secretary on a Thursday, with a warning that unless she acquired a telephone in her new apartment by Monday, she need not show up. On another occasion he recalled by telephone an assistant who had hurried out of town without permission to attend his father's funeral.

In dealing with his female employees Pearson was almost invariably courteous, regardless of their degree of youth and pulchritude. He asked about their health and noticed changes in weight, hair style and dress. With the younger ones he employed small endearments in conversation and occasionally turned coquettish— "cutey-pie," one secretary termed it. The women responded according to inclination.

With his male staff members Pearson was often rude and overbearing. He knew all the tricks of a sadistic city editor for keeping an editorial staff on its toes. In the case of one legman who liked an occasional drink he checked around until he ascertained the customary time and place of relaxation, then pounced on the culprit by telephone. Sometimes he gave two or more of his writers an identical assignment. They had no idea of the competition until they encountered each other's spoor in the field. Overlapping titles and duties among the secretarial staff accomplished the same purpose. Trial lawyers were changed from one libel suit to another.

Pearson's paternalism, on the other hand, was easily aroused. He knew the family background of each employee. He made unexpected gestures. He gave Miss Canty a limited leave of absence when he learned that her father, dying of cancer, would eat only if she were there. He ordered a free vacation in Florida for a writer who had been overworking and looked tired.

To preserve their self-respect, several staff members jeered at the boss among themselves, calling him "D.P.," as if he were a tycoon. They noted small discrepancies in his behavior. For example, he permitted no smoking in his study and he barred air-conditioning there on the theory that it would irritate his sinuses. Yet on very warm days he would quietly open his door leading to the larger workroom—where smoking was permitted and air-conditioning had been installed!

Pearson's belief in his lucky number, 13, was often debated in the office. He had cajoled the postal authorities into giving him 1313 Twenty-ninth Street as his office address and 13130 River

Road as the address of his chief farm in Maryland. When he changed syndicates in 1944, he was careful to make the announcement on December 13, his birthday. His associates were both derisive and impressed. John Donovan, whose legal mind precluded superstition, followed Drew's gesture of putting a 13 on his auto license plate.

Pay scales in the office were still inadequate. Pearson quarreled with Heywood Broun over the latter's suggestion that a Newspaper Guild contract might be in order. His kind of independent operation could not continue under such restrictions, Drew insisted. Despite all the grumbling, turnover of "Merry-Go-Round" personnel was low. Those who worked for Pearson throve on daily stress and excitement. They believed in the importance of what they were doing. They were as fascinated as outsiders by the ferocity with which he pursued enemies. They knew from experience that he would back them up and that he gave more to the joint effort than anybody else.

2

Pearson used his combined office-home to squeeze every ounce of value from his time. His schedule was highly irregular. On a given night he might type well past midnight at his desk, climb the stairs to his bedroom, arise at 5 A.M., proceed in bathrobe and slippers to the filing cabinets or the nearby small reference library, make last-minute corrections on copy at his desk, eat an early breakfast (usually orange juice, two eggs and milk, never coffee) and return to bed for a nap before starting the day's work.

His formal morning arrival on the office side invariably created excitement. He was too impatient to tarry in his study. After plowing through the mail and exhausting the contents of his intake boxes, he surged out into the working room to bring the secretariat up to his own pitch with inquiries, reminders and suggestions.

During the morning he might talk to Jack Anderson, known as his "associate," a vague title halfway between employee and partner; a Congressional legman who stuck close to Capitol Hill; John Donovan, who shared with Luvie the right to use a card room

in the more modern central wing; or one of his trial lawyers or
accountants. He might confer with William Neel, the journalistic
jack-of-all-trades who did the weekly radio script and the newsletter; or one of his faceless investigators. The relationship with
each of these men was conspiratorial. If he was talking with one
of them in his study when another arrived, the conversation
stopped abruptly and did not resume until the intruder had left.

Late in the morning he would usually take a jar of wax from
the top of his desk and sharpen the points of his mustache. This
presaged departure. He would study the precise angle of his
hat in the mirror before leaving by way of the garden gate on
Twenty-ninth Street. Climbing into his car, he would drive rapidly—speed soothed his nerves, he believed—on a news-gathering
expedition. No passenger was permitted to smoke in his car. He
would wind up at the Cosmos Club, most prestigious of the
Washington intellectual groups, for lunch with some preferred
informant or friend like Wayne Morse, Averell Harriman or
Walter Lippmann.

Occasionally he accepted the company of lesser club members—insurance executives, real estate developers, lawyers and
the like—who constituted his claque. Lunch could never be
leisurely because he must be back at the office on schedule to
check the column for libel. Marian Canty had instructions to put
the column on the teletype at 2 P.M. sharp. If the column was
late in moving by as much as five minutes, the syndicate in New
York suspected a cataclysm in Washington. Three days later that
column would roar coast to coast.

Having passed the high point of the day, Pearson would take
a nap or cosset himself with a cookie. Despite his dieting he
could not resist cookies. Next he would turn to his enormous
correspondence or to any one of a dozen other chores. During
the afternoon tension built up steadily in the office. If he got
into a shouting row with somebody on the telephone, he might
rush out of the house hatless and with mustache points unwaxed
to work off irritation with an hour or two of physical labor, up-
rooting stumps or digging ditches out at his Potomac farm.

In midafternoon he might leave impulsively for New York
or some other city, despite a confirmed social engagement on

which Luvie had counted for weeks. Sometimes, she believed, he did this on purpose to avoid a particular social occasion. On the other hand, he might dutifully take in a cocktail party—even two cocktail parties—in the late afternoon. As befit the owner of not only a two-hundred-year-old town house but also a great deal of acreage in nearby Maryland, he usually dressed like a country squire for such affairs.

Pearson had presence. Eyes shifted automatically in his direction when he entered a room. With his slight heaviness of head—his former wife Felicia once maliciously called it "plump"—he conveyed dignity, authority, even virility. According to reports from Capitol Hill, where he had many enemies, he was prepared under conditions which promised personal immunity and not too great an expenditure of time to grapple with a well-endowed young woman who appreciated his statesmanlike qualities. He did not attempt to dispel these rumors. They did him no harm socially.

Dinner was ordinarily eaten at home. As a nominal Quaker Drew used "thee" and "thou" at meals with relatives. When he and Luvie went out socially after dinner, he began to look harried if he did not quickly encounter friends, tidbits of information convertible into copy or a few adulatory feminine murmurs. A small facial tic, more catarrhal sniff than anything else, would become noticeable. He would smother an involuntary yawn and disappear.

Back at the office, he typed, read, pored over files, worked the phone or went early to bed. Telephones tempted him. Presumably they were tapped. When he talked to Anderson, who had his own office and secretary downtown, they used a rudimentary code to confuse listeners.

Incoming calls, of course, might be tips, and tips were the hidden resource of the column. During the day his staff tried to discourage him from wasting time on them. Tipsters were asked to leave their names and telephone numbers so they could be reached later from some safe pay phone. Evening calls at the office were handled by Joseph Canty, Marian's brother, a night owl who enjoyed working alone as an indexer and bookkeeper well into the morning hours.

When the phone rang in the more private half of the Pearson house during the evening, Melvin Beal, the black butler, had been instructed to answer: "*Mrs.* Pearson's residence." Since this procedure intercepted some possibly intriguing calls, the columnist had learned to imitate Melvin's voice. After picking up the receiver and answering by rote he could continue in the role of butler or, if the call tantalized him, he could confess deception with a chuckle and talk in his own voice.

One evening Thurman Arnold made an emergency call. Having heard of the custom of the house, he distrusted the dulcet tones of the butler.

"I know you, Drew," he sputtered. "Imitating Melvin again! Cut out the nonsense. This is important. I know your voice. . . ."

But it really was Melvin.

3

Pearson's Potomac farm was an easy half-hour drive out of Washington by the River Road. There on a breathtaking promontory Drew and Luvie had a magnificent mansion with two wings and an upper and lower terrace designed to make the most of striking views in all directions. If he could spit that far, Drew used to tell guests, he could spit 150 feet down into the Potomac River.

In suitable weather the mightiest men in Washington, including cabinet officials, Supreme Court Justices, ambassadors and Presidents, came with their wives to Pearson's Bluff, as the host sometimes dubbed his farm. Those invited were screened for a sympathetic personal attitude as well as for what they knew. Pearson claimed that no use was ever made of anything said on such occasions, which was nonsense. He did not become a dominant columnist by ignoring news under his nose.

Pearson prided himself on being a working farmer, but, owing to a certain haphazard quality in his operations, he lost more than $50,000 a year—a loss deductible on his tax returns. He tried to be up to date, reading the farm journals and attending Montgomery County agricultural meetings. With Wayne Morse, who owned a small farm in the Poolesville area, he went occasionally to the Gaithersburg, Maryland, fair to exhibit some of his prize livestock. John Donovan also owned a small farm near those of Morse and Pearson.

Though Montgomery was the richest suburban county in the country, so far as per capita income went, there were other working farmers nearby, some rich and some not. These farmers respected and liked Pearson. He put on no airs. If they needed emergency help to harvest a crop or rebuild a burned barn, he was quick in Quaker fashion to send over a hand or two without charge.

Pearson enjoyed having groups of city youngsters come out to the farm to goggle at his cows and ponies and buffalo. Early every September, small advertisements were placed in the Washington newspapers that the Pearson bean patch at Potomac, Maryland, would be open as usual the following Saturday and Sunday. Visitors were allowed to pick as much as they wished at $1 a bushel, a fraction of the market price. Hundreds chugged out in rattletrap cars holding family groups of five and six. Pearson himself checked the baskets.

Whenever he could arrange it, Pearson visited the farm on payday. By displaying a personal interest in the hands, he compensated somewhat for a less-than-generous pay scale. He asked each man about his health and that of his family, how things were going and whether he needed special equipment. By allowing farm hands to buy on credit in his name and making unexpected farm outlays himself, he frequently scrambled the office financial accounts.

During the Second World War, when agricultural labor was out of sight and almost unobtainable, Pearson went so far one year as to draft his reporters at haying time. Driving a truck as an example, he assured them that manual work was not only patriotic but also healthy. The experiment had to be abandoned because one writer who was Jewish persisted in making anti-Hitler remarks in German to a group of husky prisoners of war who were working there for 80 cents a day under an arrangement with a nearby POW camp.

The Potomac farm had an outdoor swimming pool, riding stables, a badminton court and other facilities for recreational-minded guests, but Squire Pearson was always pleased when visitors evinced some interest in farming. These he took on tours to see his hay drier, his electric milking sheds and other equipment. He displayed bags stamped "Pearson's Best Manure— Better than the Column—All Cow, No Bull," and bags of mud from an old canal marked to show that they came from the property of "Drew Pearson, the Best Muckraker in the U.S."

He took pride in the fact that his manure and mud were sold at Hechinger's Department Store in Washington. He had gradually pushed his revenue from manure alone up to $150,000 a year. He was also financing experiments in the production of deodorized manure in Ohio, using raw material from the Chicago stockyards.

From mixed motives of prestige and publicity, Pearson was determined to sell his manure at competitive prices. He did not tell visitors about Sergio, the Mexican worker who bagged the stuff, or some other expenses. Sergio was not on the regular payroll because if he had been the production cost would have exceeded the retail price at the store. In international trade, sales of this kind are known as dumping.

For visitors who fell into the spirit of his inspection tours, the squire provided personal introductions to a Hampshire boar who got the pick of the garbage from the Georgetown house and to an unpleasant-looking Holstein bullock whose name changed according to the column's chief enemy at the moment.

He also introduced various cows, claiming to know many of them by name. Whether this was a joke or an expression of vanity, he did seem to be on mooing terms with quite a few of them.

At one time Pearson took the advice of his nephew Paul to give up dairying and grow bluegrass sod, as the only way to make the farm pay. Then Paul, a Cornell-trained agronomist, left because he could not persuade his uncle to raise his salary. One by one Pearson brought back the cows until he had 143 of them again.

George C. Vournas, his long-time friend, who also owned a nearby farm, paused at the Pearson terrace one Sunday morning to deliver the Sunday newspapers and volunteer his opinion on the priorities in Pearson's life.

"First comes your daily column," he informed Drew. "Second

your radio broadcast, third your wife and daughter, fourth the farm and fifth George Vournas. There I am exclusive."

Luvie made a face. "Not at all," she said coolly. "First the column, second the radio, third the *cows* on the farm, fourth the wife and daughter and fifth George."

At mention of the cows, Pearson laughed until he cried. It was a family joke, but quite, quite true, that if a cow fell ill while he was off lecturing in California, they had to call him long-distance to decide whether a veterinarian should be summoned or the cow killed for meat. Only he could pass judgment on this crucial matter, on the hiring or firing of a farm hand, the purchase of new versus secondhand equipment, the sale of packaged manure and mud or any other detail about the farm.

CHAPTER XIII

Communism

THE NATION WAS JUMPY. China had fallen into Communist hands. The Russians had tested an atom bomb sooner than expected. Evidence accumulated that the New Deal, before and during the war, had been infiltrated by Communists and that the late President Roosevelt knew about and ignored the infiltration. From a vantage point on the House Un-American Activities Committee, Richard Nixon made the most of Whittaker Chambers' revelations of bureaucratic spying in Washington for the Soviet Union. Along came Joe McCarthy to put it all together with the instinctive touch of a demagogue.

Against this background, a campaign to destroy Drew Pearson as a supposed Communist took shape during the second Truman and the first Eisenhower administrations. No legal charge being possible, a popular indictment was brought. Though it rested on an unprovable central assumption of conspiracy, the indictment had enough incendiary counts to confuse people.

What hurt Pearson was the overlap of time. In 1947 he testified as a character witness for sixteen leaders of the Joint Anti-Fascist Refugee Committee who were being tried for contempt of Congress after refusing to answer questions before the House Un-American Activities Committee. He cherished the Anti-Fascist

Committee for its help to Spanish Loyalists during the late 1930s. Reporters covering the trial connected the defendants with the more recent undercover activities of Gerhart Eisler, a Comintern representative.

A. A. Berle, Jr., an Assistant Secretary of State, who had been criticized by Pearson during the war for stopping oil shipments to Russia, put a return finger on the columnist after the war. He told the House Un-American Activities Committee that classified information known to Alger Hiss used to pop up with embarrassing regularity in the "Washington Merry-Go-Round."

Hiss had been exposed by Chambers and Elizabeth Bentley, the schoolteacher turned Communist courier, as a Washington source of secret documents. During the period mentioned by Berle, however, Hiss had been highly respected as a State Department official of middle rank. Hiss impaired his own credibility by denying party membership when his conduct came under public scrutiny. He probably deserved to go to jail for pretending he did not know Chambers, but wasn't tipster service for a syndicated newspaper column rather amateurish activity for a spy? Was he, after all, a full-fledged spy?

Despite that haunting question, still unsettled by time, Pearson needed no defense against any implication of complicity with Miss Bentley's spy ring. A full year before she decided to go to the FBI, he disclosed in his column that members of her group had photographed blueprints of the B-29 in a Baltimore espionage laboratory and sent the prints to Russia.

Besides Hiss, Pearson's informant-friends included Owen Lattimore, a State Department specialist on China, and Harry Dexter White, a Treasury Department official. Nobody knew then that Lattimore would be accused of slipping Chiang Kai-shek documents to the Soviet Union—an accusation never proved but which did suggest where Lattimore stood. Nobody had yet drawn sinister conclusions from White's intrigues to turn West Germany into a cow pasture after the war and arrange an enormous U.S. loan for Russian industrial reconstruction.

Following up his Friendship Train success, Pearson sponsored a drive one summer to send toys to European children. Another year he released thousands of balloons from Czechoslovakia to be carried on the prevailing west wind with friendly messages for people behind the Iron Curtain. In 1948 he promoted a letter-writing campaign by Italian-Americans to relatives in Italy which was credited with preventing a Communist electoral takeover in that country.

How could the contradictory evidence be reconciled? Quite simply. Drew Pearson was the leading left-of-center publicist in the United States. He considered himself a patriot, but he had Communists and fellow travelers among his informants and at times on his staff. He was not likely to ignore a substantial story aimed at one of his chief political targets—imperialism, militarism, racial and religious bigotry, crookedness in government and oppression of the poor by the money interests—regardless of its source.

The Forrestal case provided an emotional weapon against Pearson. The Defense Secretary had flirted with Governor Dewey during the 1948 presidential campaign in hope of being retained after a Republican victory. When re-elected, Truman naturally looked around for a more loyal Defense Secretary. His tentative choice was Louis Johnson, a former Assistant Secretary of War who had raised most of the 1948 Democratic campaign funds.

Instead of submitting his resignation, which he probably would have done had he not been ill, Forrestal tried desperately to stay in the cabinet. Early in 1949, Pearson revealed on radio that President Truman wanted to appoint Johnson but hesitated to do so because of Forrestal's campaign. Irritably, the President told friends that the broadcast made it impossible for him to demand Forrestal's resignation without seeming to take advice from a commentator.

The following Sunday, Pearson scoffed at a President who "let important decisions be made or reversed by a radio commentator, whoever he is. Some of us will think twice about criticizing inefficient public officials lest Mr. Truman decide to continue them in office." Furious over the leak, the President added Pearson to a private list of enemies with whom he intended to square accounts after he left the White House.

In March, 1949, Forrestal resigned and was succeeded by Johnson. The "Washington Merry-Go-Round" revealed that Forrestal had run into the street from his home in Hobe Sound,

Florida, shouting: "The Russians are coming, the Russians are coming!" That was the first public intimation of Forrestal's psychotic break. He was rushed to the Bethesda Naval Hospital for psychiatric care. There, two months later, he committed suicide.

Ignoring signs that the Defense Secretary's nervous deterioration dated back at least two years, journalistic stokers of right-wing indignation implied homicide by typewriter. Westbrook Pegler, newly a chum of General Vaughan at the White House, wrote that Forrestal "was hounded to his death by Pearson with vicious lies until his reason broke and he jumped out of a high window." Morris Bealle paid his disrespects in a new book called *The Red Rat Race.* Fulton Lewis, Jr. and George Sokolsky harried Pearson in more subtle ways.

Pearson tried to act as usual. He was in Defense Secretary Johnson's office one day when Secretary of State Acheson made a hurried visit. Later Pearson asked what was up. "We were discussing whether to build a hydrogen bomb or not," replied Johnson. "Are you going to?" asked Pearson. "I'm for it," said Defense Secretary Johnson. "Dean's against it and so is Oppenheimer [Dr. J. Robert, of Los Alamos and the Atomic Energy Commission]. The President will decide."

The "Merry-Go-Round" presented the internal debate in impartial terms. Clearly, the public wanted a hydrogen bomb for reassurance. President Truman gave the signal, and the United States did produce one before the Russians.

Yugoslavia and Russia were at odds over whether many centers of Communism were permissible in the world or only one in Moscow. Pearson persuaded the Yugoslavian Ambassador in Washington to recommend to Marshal Tito the release of Cardinal Aloysius Stepinac from jail as a way of improving relations with the United States. Tito agreed to free the Catholic prelate if his reasons for doing so were printed in full. Pearson obtained the announcement exclusively. When some newspapers trimmed Tito's long statement, the Yugoslavian leader raged over Pearson's "bad faith." He calmed down when Congress, partly as a result of the Stepinac gesture, voted economic assistance to his country.

Drew Pearson baited Joe McCarthy from the moment the

latter arrived in Washington as a U.S. Senator. He exposed the phony war record of the onetime chicken farmer from Wisconsin, his chiseling on income taxes and his ties with the real estate lobby. When Joe began to juggle figures in 1950 on how many card-carrying Communists were concealed in the State Department, Pearson took the names on the list one by one and made McCarthy look ridiculous.

Fixing on Pearson as his chief obstacle in Washington, Joe slugged him at the Sulgrave Club and accused him almost daily on the Senate floor of being the voice and instrument of international Communism. Collecting his most damaging assertions in a booklet, the Senator distributed 300,000 copies to the public. Senator Brewster and other enemies of Pearson also distributed copies.

By stimulating a patriotic boycott, Senator McCarthy forced the hat company sponsoring Pearson on radio to terminate its contract. Drew obtained, then lost, a new sponsor. As he kept a precarious footing in radio on a sustaining basis, friends appealed to Walter Winchell to come to the aid of his old ally.

"Drew can take care of himself," Winchell replied coldly. He had been meeting with Senator McCarthy at the Stork Club in New York. The Broadway columnist never quite understood his own positions on politics, but he recognized that he was vulnerable to a Red-baiting onslaught. To help McCarthy, who was raising his sights to the White House, Winchell revived the chestnut about Truman being a former Klansman.

"I am sorry to have to correct my friend Walter Winchell," replied Pearson on radio. "I have more spies in the Klan than Walter has. That story, which has been kicking around for years, is simply not true." From that moment, WW's hostile yakety-yak rose high above the rest of the anti-Pearson anvil chorus.

McCarthy outmatched the Truman administration in propaganda. He was already howling about homosexuals in the State Department as security risks. When Secretary Acheson, in a misguided expression of old-school-tie loyalty, said he would not turn his back on Alger Hiss, the Senator converted the answer into an unprintable remark which made the rounds of the Washington cocktail parties.

At a news conference, Truman incautiously accepted a suggestion from a reporter that the Congressional spy hysteria was "a red herring" designed to distract attention from serious economic issues. McCarthy retorted that the President was concealing Communists in the federal bureaucracy. When Millard Tydings, as chairman of a Senate investigating committee, found no truth in Joe's charges, McCarthy dismissed him as "Truman's whimpering lapdog" and took revenge by driving him out of Congress.

A public opinion poll indicated that more than half the American public thought Joe McCarthy was "on the right track." His repetitive noisiness led to fears that he intended to challenge the American form of government. Actually, he was having too much fun within the system.

Despite clumsiness in the face of McCarthyism, President Truman was a more assured and competent head of state during his second term. The uphill campaign for re-election had defined his goals. His advocacy of liberal domestic policies gradually enlisted the support of the "Merry-Go-Round." The column did not, however, discern any improvement in the caliber of the White House staff.

Drew Pearson picketed the Argentine Embassy one evening to call attention to the fact that General Harry Vaughan was being presented a decoration from Argentine dictator Juan Perón. By trudging up and down in front of the building during a driving rain, he obtained publicity for a demand that the President fire his military aide for accepting a foreign decoration without the required approval of Congress.

Several weekends later, Drew and Luvie were enjoying a midwinter excursion to the farm when the phone began to ring madly. Various reporters wanted his answer to charges by President Truman. The President had ridiculed Pearson at a banquet honoring Vaughan. He was just as loyal to his military aide as he was to the high brass, the President said, adding that no S.O.B. of a commentator could change his attitude. Before the echoes of the S.O.B. dispute died away, Truman and Pearson ran into each other at a small party given by Peggy Palmer, widow of Woodrow Wilson's Attorney General, A. Mitchell Palmer. The two men shook hands. "We all have our troubles, Drew," said

Truman with a smile before passing on. Behind the scenes the breach between them was being healed.

Pearson's white whale to be pursued in his columnar *Pequod* unto death and beyond was, of course, General MacArthur. In 1950 the General assumed command of the U.S. and UN military forces in South Korea, which were coping with Communist invaders from North Korea. MacArthur was more headstrong than ever. He ignored directives from the Pentagon and even from the White House. These were cited in the "Merry-Go-Round." The column noted that the flamboyant General was already being boomed for President in 1952 by the anti-Communist movement in the United States.

On January 31, 1951, the "Washington Merry-Go-Round" carried an account of a secret conference on Wake Island the previous October between President Truman and General MacArthur. Not realizing that a record was being kept of their conversation, the General pronounced that the Chinese would not intervene, that victory was assured in Korea and that the Eighth Army would be back in Japan by Christmas. Inasmuch as the Chinese had since intervened, the Eighth Army had not returned to Japan and victory remained uncertain, the exposé set the stage for Truman's ouster of the General from his Far Eastern command.

Other reporters picked up and amplified the Pearson exclusive. The *New York Times* won a Pulitzer prize for its version. Competing newspapers reported that a leak from the Pentagon had been permitted by President Truman. In interviews Pearson went so far as to concede that he and Truman had been "on friendly terms for some time and he has done me some favors."

MacArthur returned to the United States with a diminished reputation. In his own phrase, the old General was fading away. During the convention struggle between General Eisenhower and Senator Taft for the 1952 Republican presidential nomination, MacArthur was put forward feebly as an alternative choice, but Eisenhower won the nomination and went on to defeat Adlai Stevenson in the general election.

Soon after Harry Truman retired to private life in Independence, Missouri, Drew Pearson phoned to warn that Senator McCarthy was investigating the theft of $10,000 worth of filing cabinets from the White House. "Joe will wind up with his ass in a sling," chortled the ex-President. "I paid for those cabinets and I have the receipts!" Visiting Washington several weeks later, Truman dropped in to see Pearson. During a friendly chat he agreed to be an early guest on his former enemy's new TV show.

2

No town is more difficult for the production of daily exclusives than Washington. It's blanketed by the media. Drew Pearson kept ahead of and apart from competitors by his own audacity and the strength of his contributors. In his morning mail might come an anonymous (but verifiable) list of free trips taken in government planes by Senator Brewster. At 10 A.M., Chief of Staff Omar Bradley might phone to say he had rebuked four generals for defects in an Army training program revealed in the previous day's column. At lunch former War Crimes Prosecutor Joseph B. Kennan, who had excellent contacts in Japan, might relay a report that Emperor Hirohito wanted a military alliance with the United States. One way or another these and the other intangible gifts of the day were utilized.

Pearson's high-voltage, hypodermic kind of journalism divided readers, listeners and viewers into partisans. He took risks ranging from the use of stock market tips on the air in imitation of Winchell to an injudicious columnar endorsement of krebiozen as a cure for cancer. Some of his political crusades backfired. A case history analyzed by Kenneth G. Crawford, a reputable Washington correspondent, for the *Saturday Evening Post* several years after the event involved Robert Jones, a friend of Senator Taft and a tool of the power lobby who had been nominated to serve on the Federal Communications Commission.

Naming three witnesses vouched for by organized labor in Ohio, Pearson charged Jones with former membership in the Black Legion, a sort of super-Klan favoring black- instead of white-sheeted hoods. The witnesses were presented as former Legionnaires. Under Congressional examination two proved also to be former convicts. The third had been a mental patient. All three contradicted each other and themselves. Jones was unanimously confirmed.

During the McCarthy siege, Pearson received no help from

his colleagues. He was too much of a loner. The Standing Committee of Congressional Gallery Correspondents—annoyed perhaps by his disclosure that they had barred a qualified Negro—charged him with subsidized reporting. He had, it was true, been sponsored on radio by the coffee growers of Brazil and an American retail clerks union, not to speak of Carter's Little Liver Pills and Serutan, a remedy for costiveness. Pleading ignorance of the rules and pulling a few wires, Pearson retained his reportorial privileges in Congress by a one-vote margin.

Pearson's domestic and professional staff, living cheek-by-jowl in the same house like members of some Utopian community, had to absorb extra tension during the Communist-hunting years. Starting with a buxom Yugoslavian lass, who served a brief office apprenticeship during the late 1940s, Drew developed a habit of paying special attention to some sexy, clever young secretary who, in the parlance of veteran employees, became his "fair-haired girl." This girl would be assigned special duties and receive special favors. She would accompany Pearson on trips. She would be invited to family champagne parties on Drew's expressed theory that they needed livening up.

As the latest favorite swished importantly through the office in a new dress before the bar opened in the garden, some other secretary would inevitably wonder out loud just how far that relationship went. Since Pearson was always working, it could not go much beyond a minor affair of convenience, but it had some effect on morale.

Male employees tended to forget minor irritations and close ranks behind the boss during this period. After Drew was attacked physically once or twice in public, they chipped in to buy him a pair of boxing gloves as a hint that he should take better care of himself. Friends again urged him to carry a gun. Drew ignored such suggestions. Looking remote in an ineffably learned way, he drove rapidly around town as usual in his black Buick convertible with red-leather seats and the lucky number on the license plate.

To show public unconcern over the attacks made on him, Drew attended various social functions. Luvie, a thinner, steelier blade for defense or offense, usually accompanied him. Her loyalty to her husband was expressed in a remark to a Washington

Post interviewer that she was "Drew's appendage." If she sensed and was concerned over the harem-like emotionalism in the office part of her own house, she gave no sign of it. At a party she knew at a glance which cabinet member would not stay if she and her husband remained and which Congressman would stay in the same room but would insist on a separate corner. If the conversation turned to politics, she was better equipped than anybody else to interpret the shadings of her husband's thought.

Despite the endless calls on his time and patience, Pearson tried to maintain contact with absent members of the family. Early in his daughter Ellen's marriage, he used to baby-sit for one or another of her sons at his home in Georgetown or even in California if he got out that way. He described such occasions in the column. As the boys grew older and a sister was added to the family, he wrote them open letters of simplistic advice on the rewards for hard work in school, deference to one's parents, the achievements of black and Spanish-speaking citizens in the United States and good-neighborliness among nations.

Finding the patriarchal mode to his liking, Pearson even tried open letters to and about Luvie and Bob Allen, who was at last trying a column of his own out of Washington. Both objected to being publicly praised or preached at. Though Pearson displayed tolerance of human weakness in his public epistles, he bore down heavily in private on any member of his staff or family who fell short of his expectations. When Drew Arnold, his eldest grandson, was threatened with expulsion from preparatory school for a juvenile prank involving drinking, a Washington friend who had established scholarships at the school volunteered to intercede for the boy. Pearson rejected the offer of assistance. His namesake deserved punishment, he said.

The "Washington Merry-Go-Round" advised Ellen how to vote in national elections, but it did not discuss her marriage to George Arnold, which was running into difficulties. During one of George's political campaigns, Ellen was haled into court for sassing and driving away from a traffic cop who accused her of tipsiness at the wheel, and even though she was later acquitted, the incident revived all of Drew's half-buried concern for the future of his daughter.

To stepson Tyler, an undergraduate at Amherst College, and other members of the family on significant occasions such as birthdays, Pearson squeezed out time for affectionate private letters. He spent Thanksgiving every year with his sisters in Swarthmore, but he seemed to have lost touch with his brother, Leon, who had returned from Paris to work in New York for NBC Radio, first as a correspondent at the United Nations, then as a dramatic critic.

A pattern of niggardliness and human concern marked Drew's relations with those close to him. He had lost the services of Rudolph Gaull, his butler, because he allowed Gaull, in lieu of a salary increase, to pick up spare-time cash by catering to the neighbors. Gaull made so much money at this secondary job that when Drew, jokingly or not, suggested sharing the profits, Gaull quit and set himself up as a local contractor, and was succeeded by Melvin Beal.

While Leon's son, Paul, was manager of the Potomac farm, he had been allowed to do custom farming for the neighbors to supplement his income. When he resigned to go into business for himself as a bluegrass sod specialist, he was succeeded temporarily by William Neel, Pearson's New York radio production man, who had been talking for years about the healthiness of outdoor work. Despite his lack of experience, Neel proved competent in the new role and did some writing for Pearson on the side.

Though Pearson's gross income from his various ventures never dipped below $250,000 a year, the salary of John Donovan, his closest associate, was frequently in arrears. Having his own office and practice downtown, the lawyer good-naturedly let the amount accumulate until it got too high for comfort. Then he protested. Instead of paying promptly, Drew promised to design and build a house on Donovan's Montgomery County farm resembling the stone mansion on Drew's place. He did draw up plans, but he never built the house.

Pearson sympathized with anybody who reached out for independence. This impulse had been the touchstone of his career. One reason he turned to free-lancing in youth was the relative freedom it offered. He wrote his first books under a conviction that he could say more between bound covers than he could in newspapers—even the best newspapers—which in his opinion were increasingly dominated "by a cash-register philosophy." He approved syndication to get out from under the thumb of a single paper, he plunged into radio to offset syndicate censorship and he tried TV finally to escape the restrictions of radio.

The TV critics were lukewarm over his debut. One described him as a "misunderstood knight in shining armor." Another dismissed him as a "hair-tonic salesman." When he talked straight at the camera for fifteen minutes, a third said, he proved "irritating to a hypnotic degree." He did better with guests. Meanwhile, he was making a partial comeback on radio through his own syndicate, which sold transcriptions of weekly broadcasts to networks, independent stations and sponsors. It was ironic that he and other controversial talkers on the air found themselves in less demand at the very time that Senator Joe McCarthy was diminishing as a menace.

Pearson shored up his journalistic position. In Boston, Kansas City, Cleveland and other cities he had lost important subscribers, partly through right-wing pressure, partly through his own unwillingness to recognize sacred cows among publishers.

To compensate for the cancellation of a large-circulation newspaper, he would try, personally or through John Osenenko, his syndicate manager, to round up a group of local weeklies. For the weeklies he provided a condensed miscellany of stories from the preceding seven days, spiced with radio-type predictions. He soon had scores of these weekly outlets.

He did more and more lecturing. One purpose, he told friends, was to raise money to meet the increasing expenses of the column. To outsiders who did not know the sexy meaning of the phrase in the trade, he said he went on lecture tours "to sample grass-roots opinion." Among veteran lecturers it is a truism that every small-town audience contains at least one attractive matron willing, even determined, to romance the visiting celebrity. It is these receptive women who constitute "grass-roots opinion." Some lecturers insist on a higher fee if they are asked to stay overnight in a private house; others grin and take the risk. Pearson fell in the second category.

During an interminable wait at an airport on one lecture tour in 1963, Drew Pearson told a writer accompanying him the story of a well-to-do Midwestern farmer who patrolled an upstairs hall-way in the middle of the night—with a pitchfork in his hand—because his wife had glanced indiscreetly at the visiting lecturer at the dinner table. Whether Pearson himself was the hero of this horrendous incident was unclear. Perhaps not. He had too many enemies to take unpredictable risks.

The Pearson lecturing fee was flexible, ranging from $50 for a civil liberties group which he hiked to $1,000 for a business association which he felt obliged to address as a way of mending his political fences. Before both kinds of audiences he told stand-ard jokes and intimate small stories about Presidents he had known. A favorite joke involved brassieres: the Salvation Army bra (uplifts the fallen), the Communist bra (supports the masses) and the Drew Pearson bra (makes mountains out of molehills).

"The greatest single factor in preventing juvenile delinquency and crime," he would tell a Junior Chamber of Commerce in his peroration, "is the family. The Jaycees, the Big Brothers and similar groups reflect the best in the Free Enterprise–Capitalist system. The remedy for lawlessness is not more laws—the remedy is love!"

3

News that President Eisenhower had received a vicuna coat as a gift from Bernard Goldfine, a conniving New England industrial-ist, broke in the "Washington Merry-Go-Round" in mid-June, 1958. After denying the story angrily at first, White House Press Secretary James Hagerty admitted that vicuna cloth from Gold-fine had been accepted by the President. Since Eisenhower already owned two vicuna coats, so Hagerty said, he had turned the cloth over to a friend—a friend whom nobody was able to produce or name.

Goldfine's memory was also poor, but he recalled giving vicuna cloth or vicuna coats to twenty-three governors as well as to the President. Instead of proving Ike's innocence, this disingenuous-ness lowered the threshold of possible White House corruption. Nightclub comedians began to joke about vicuna coats for men as the equivalent of mink coats for girls.

Vicuna sales boomed. The London *Daily Mail* awarded first prize in a vicuna-coat contest to a woman who explained to her mother that a diamond bracelet from her wealthy admirer was "nothing more than what President Eisenhower calls a tangible expression of friendship." Within a few weeks a peerless war hero and President-above-the-battle shrank in the minds of many to an equivocal figure of folly and fun.

Late in June, the columnist was asked by Mike Wallace during a radio interview where he got his information. With customary opacity, Pearson replied: "We worked on it four days in Massachusetts, New Hampshire, here in Washington and one source right in the White House." The hidden story was more diverting.

Dr. Bernard Schwartz, thirty-four, an idealistic and capable professor from New York University, had been hired by the House Commerce Committee in 1957 to study the operation of the six large federal regulatory agencies. To his dismay, Schwartz discovered what insiders already knew: these agencies—a relatively uncharted middle ground of government between Congress and the White House—were manipulated by big business.

Early in 1958, Dr. Schwartz submitted a memo on some of the more flagrant cases of improper influence uncovered by him. Some trails led into the White House. The Commerce Committee found the spoor too dangerous to follow. No investigation was needed, it decided. Three days later parts of the Schwartz memo appeared in the "Washington Merry-Go-Round."

Accused of leakage, Schwartz denied the charge and demanded that committee members be polled on their dealings with Drew Pearson. Having bluffed his way to safe ground, the investigator began to hanker to see his full recommendations in print. Like Tito, he wanted complete discovery of his thoughts on an historic matter. Pearson advised him to cache a copy of the memo in a certain bush on the right-hand side of the Capitol going toward Pennsylvania Avenue. A little later, a *New York Times* reporter came by, reached in for the document and bore it away. After the text appeared in the *Times*, Schwartz was fired, despite his anguished pleas of innocence. He thereupon stole his own file from the committee office.

Clark Mollenhoff of the Des Moines, Iowa, *Register,* an excellent investigative reporter who turned up a decade later as a personal undercover man for President Nixon, heard rumors about a missing file. The professor had been brooding over his impulsive act. Approached by Mollenhoff, Schwartz said he would yield his precious material to a U.S. Senator if he would promise to press for an impartial investigation.

Mollenhoff steered Schwartz to the hotel apartment of a Republican friend, Senator John J. Williams of Delaware. There the discussion continued. Drew Pearson was also hunting for the file. When he reached Schwartz's home by phone, Mrs. Schwartz revealed her husband's whereabouts. Pearson clucked disapproval. This was a file of great potential damage to a Republican administration, he pointed out. Entrusting it to a GOP Senator was tantamount to suppression.

"Call Bernie at once and tell him to come to my office," ordered Pearson. "Tell him to come at once. No discussion, none at all! This is too important to handle over the phone."

Mrs. Schwartz phoned her husband, and the good doctor came by cab to Pearson's combined home and office in Georgetown. Clark Mollenhoff tailed along, arguing all the way. At Pearson's office, Dr. Schwartz was persuaded to deliver the file to Senator Wayne Morse of Oregon, a crusading liberal, once Republican but by then a Democrat.

Senator Morse was an old friend and frequent luncheon companion of Drew Pearson. As a conscientious public official, he felt obliged to turn the Schwartz file back to its owner, the House Commerce Committee, just as soon as Pearson's staff finished photostating the essential documents.

While loose ends were tidied up here and there, Pearson planned his exposé like a military campaign. He started mildly in May with an announcement that a Congressional investigation of "the second most powerful man in government—President Eisenhower's crisp, curt little overseer, Sherman Adams"—had been abandoned despite Adams' known role as intermediary for a colorful business tycoon who managed to bend to his will such powerful agencies as the Securities and Exchange Commission, the Federal Trade Commission and the Federal Communications Commission.

Within a week, the St. Louis *Post-Dispatch* and the New York *Herald Tribune* were following up tantalizing "Merry-Go-Round" references to Bernard Goldfine's quixotic generosity—cases of liquor, suits, Oriental rugs, hotel accommodations and cash—and his magic coups before the regulatory agencies. Pearson spaced out his revelations. By the time he introduced the President's preference for the wool of a wild ruminant of the Andes, the whole Washington news pack was baying along the trail.

Eisenhower's pitch of outrage was so strong at first that editors balked at Pearson's columns. A confidential memo to these editors specified that Adams, Goldfine's close friend, got the first vicuna. When the gift became known at the White House, Pearson declared, Adams babbled to colleagues: "The Old Man got one, too, a three-quarter-length coat."

Gradually Pearson went beyond Goldfine in his attacks on the integrity of Adams. The presidential assistant had personally overruled a Commerce Department allocation of a great-circle airplane route over the Arctic to Japan and given the route to a competing company. He had asked the Securities and Exchange Commission Chairman to postpone hearings on the Dixon-Yates deal to undermine the federal public-power policy embodied in the Tennessee Valley Authority, lest embarrassing details about the deal become public and prevent Congress from making an expected appropriation.

In the wake of these and other revelations, President Eisenhower said: "What Sherman Adams has done was imprudent, but I need him." Some days later Jack Anderson was caught in a Sheraton-Carlton Hotel room in company with Baron Schacklette, an investigator for the House Commerce Committee, with a device for bugging the Goldfine suite next door. "Anderson might have been imprudent," said Pearson, "but I need him." With incredible impudence, he added: "What would happen if Sherman Adams died and Eisenhower became President?"

By July, Republican leaders in Congress were demanding the ouster of Adams as a handicap to the party in the fall election. In August, Vice President Nixon told the President flatly that Adams had become a political liability. On September 22, Adams resigned, with a statement that he could no longer endure "a campaign of vilification calculated to destroy me and embarrass President Eisenhower." The President said he would be "sorely missed."

Pearson's next step was to overtake the Dixon-Yates deal. A utilities expert named Adolphe Wenzell had been planted in the Budget Bureau to work out the details, he revealed. When Democratic Congressmen suggested in speeches that a scandal "worse than Teapot Dome" was in the making, the President canceled the deal.

Drew Pearson first met Ike in Washington in the spring of 1932, when Eisenhower was a major on General MacArthur's staff acting as liaison between the Army and the metropolitan police force which was trying to restrain twenty thousand hungry and homeless veterans encamped on the Anacostia Flats. The young reporter sympathized sufficiently with the bonus-seeking veterans to spend his own money on food for some of them. Eisenhower, he noticed, spent his time reading westerns, when he wasn't picking up the latest news from the reporters who trudged in and out of the District of Columbia press room. The Major's goal in life, Pearson decided scornfully, was "to stay out of trouble." It did not occur to him then that Eisenhower was carrying out a difficult assignment with unobtrusive efficiency.

Over the years Pearson learned to appreciate Eisenhower as a flexible and diplomatic man with high ideals. The General made up his mind to run for President as a Republican in the spring of 1952. Pearson thought enough of him at that time to travel all the way to SHAPE headquarters near Paris, where Ike was organizing the first NATO army, to warn that supporters of Senator Taft were buying up Southern delegates to the Republican National Convention.

"Can things like that happen in the United States?" said the General incredulously. Instead of asking friendly Republican Senators like Henry Cabot Lodge and James Duff to investigate and expose the Taft maneuvers through the Rules Committee, as recommended by Pearson, he left the unseating of illegal delegates up to the convention, where it became a crucial problem.

During the early skirmishing for President, Eisenhower met a group of Republican fat cats at the F Street Club in Washington. In discussing taxes, the candidate said American lives must be put above property in wartime. The businessmen threatened to swing to Taft if the General persisted in this heresy, so Eisenhower recanted.

To Pearson the incident illustrated the recurrent struggle between Eisenhower's decent instincts and his awe of wealth. Never having put much money aside during his military career, the General deferred to the plutocrats. Despite a "respect for worldly goods verging on cupidity," Pearson concluded, Eisenhower was not crooked. The public sensed this and trusted him.

Dwight D. Eisenhower was past sixty when he entered the White House. Having been tucked away in uniform most of his life, he did not know as much as he thought about law, civilian politics or the day-to-day manipulations of government. Otherwise he would not have delegated so much authority to Sherman Adams as his chief lieutenant.

Every President must have somebody responsible for the care and feeding of campaign contributors. Harry Vaughan performed the chore for Truman. Adams went far beyond that task for Eisenhower and, unlike Vaughan, he felt obliged to conceal his sleight-of-hand from the boss.

There were more conflicts of interest during the Eisenhower regime than in any administration since the days of Hoover. Of the many officials exposed, ranging from Sherman Adams to Air Force Secretary Harold Talbott, who channeled government contracts into his own company, none was prosecuted, in Pearson's opinion, because the President himself had been compromised.

Corporate control of Eisenhower was disguised as an effort to make him feel comfortable. One wealthy clique known as the Augusta Golfing Cabinet provided an eighteen-room, seven-bathroom cottage called Mamie's Cabin—who could object to a little luxury for a President's wife?—in the foothills of Georgia. This clique picked members of the real cabinet and dictated the country's fiscal policy. Three oil millionaires contributed $500,-000 for operating expenses and improvements at the Eisenhower farm at Gettysburg, Pennsylvania, during a period when Ike did more favors for the oil industry, according to Pearson, than any preceding President.

George E. Allen, Truman's court jester, appeared in both groups. He golfed at Augusta and helped buy the Gettysburg farm, which pleased the General partly because of his historical interest in the Civil War battle.

Pearson did not assemble his full Gettysburg exposé until after Eisenhower left the White House. "Pearson's yen for lying about somebody," Eisenhower told reporters excitedly, "brings stupidity to the fore in concocting his lies!" Pearson responded by citing claims of the sponsoring millionaires for tax deductions on their contributions as a business expense, though they had no intention of running the farm at a profit. Later he printed a copy of a letter from the Gettysburg farm manager begging Ike's bene-factors for more money to keep the farm functioning properly.

Asked again and again about Pearson's references to the farm, Eisenhower pleaded ignorance. "I don't read any newspaper I consider irresponsible," he said, with measured distaste for his archcritic, "and I consider any newspaper that carries Pearson's column to be irresponsible." The former President donated the farm to the nation but continued living there under a special arrangement until he died. He left an estate of nearly $3 million.

Eisenhower infuriated many correspondents by his drift on domestic issues, his swift retreat from principle to platitude when questioned, and his everlasting pose of the good man whose good-ness need not be proved. Yet he had—as Pearson conceded—two great achievements on his record: liquidation of the Korean War and Senator McCarthy.

The terms on which the war ended had been offered previously to President Truman, but Truman could not accept them—nor could Adlai Stevenson have accepted them had he become Presi-dent—because of the McCarthy charge that the Democrats were soft on Communism. By this time the North Koreans and the Chinese Communists were being effectively contained north of the 38th parallel. Though compromise fitted the military situation, Ike needed his full prestige to swing domestic opinion.

McCarthy was finished politically by late 1954, less than two years after Eisenhower entered the White House. Pearson and liberals generally kept up their pressure and McCarthy contrib-uted to his own downfall, but the Senator could be discredited only by his own party. The President achieved this by aligning the country's military establishment against McCarthy in a Congres-sional showdown.

In foreign affairs Eisenhower displayed a great deal more initiative than in domestic affairs. In 1953 he advocated a Food-for-East-Germany program originated by Drew Pearson. He tried for a while to open the Marshall Plan to the East European nations. He took up Pearson's reiterated plea for "people-to-people negotiation" with the Soviet Union. After the death of Secretary of State John Foster Dulles, who was almost as paranoid as Forrestal in dealing with the Russians, he invited Nikita Khrushchev to Washington, thereby initiating a series of contacts continued by John F. Kennedy, Lyndon Johnson and Richard Nixon.

President Eisenhower put one thousand troops in South Vietnam, but he backed away from the far more extensive military commitment there urged by Vice President Nixon. Ike sidestepped a Bay of Pigs invasion of Cuba recommended by the CIA. In a farewell message to the nation, he warned sharply against the menace to democratic institutions posed by the ever-growing military-industrial complex.

Having been a general so many years, Eisenhower knew very well what the generals and admirals were up to. He resented unnecessary war contracts to repay campaign contributions. He brushed aside the supposedly secret but much discussed Gaither Report, which projected a first-strike nuclear attack on the Russians. He did not believe that the Soviet Union would try a comparable long-distance attack. None of this was fully appreciated by Pearson because of his personal and political entanglement with a Texas chauvinist named Lyndon Baines Johnson.

As Senate Majority Leader, Johnson had been cuddling up to the military men who were cold-shouldered at the White House. Under his influence, Pearson collaborated in 1958 with Jack Anderson on the least creditable book of his career, entitled *U.S.A.: Second-Class Power?* This alarmist opus argued that the country was in crisis because it put a balanced budget ahead of missile superiority. Its inflammable language—presumably contributed by a ghost writer—must have delighted the saber-rattlers with whom Pearson was normally at odds. Cabell Phillips, a Washington correspondent for the *New York Times*, said in his review of the book for the *Times* that its effect was that of "a man crying havoc in the street on slender provocation."

CHAPTER XIV

Presidential Agent

To LYNDON JOHNSON, who gulped his food, smoked three packs of cigarettes a day and never got enough rest, politics was vocation, avocation and relaxation. Drew Pearson felt the same about his column. Johnson had made the necessary deals down in the ditches with the rednecks in his native state in order to get ahead, just as Pearson had used gambling as a crutch during his desperate days. Yet nobody owned either of them. Johnson and Pearson were durable, direct, effective, kind, cruel, devious and suspicious to the verge of paranoia. They recognized kinship at first sight when they met during the early 1930s at the Washington home of Charles Marsh, a pro-New Deal publisher of Texas newspapers. Similarities contributed more than differences to their stormy relationship over the years.

Pearson and Johnson were sentimental about their country, their families and their careers. Pearson claimed credit for putting Johnson on the road to the White House in 1948. That year Johnson was running for U.S. Senator against Governor Coke Stevenson of Texas. Stevenson had been straddling one crucial issue so skillfully that he enjoyed the support of both the American Federation of Labor and the labor-baiters in the state. At a Stevenson news conference in Washington, Pearson's sharp questioning elicited answers which turned both camps against Stevenson and gave Lyndon a wafer-thin triumph. Johnson accepted Pearson's romantic version of his victory—even if nobody else did—because his henchmen stole that election at the polls.

Johnson on his part developed an avuncular fondness for Drew's stepson. Tyler was a likable youngster, with a large bump of hero worship. He let it be known that the overpowering Texan, with whom he came naturally in contact, occupied a pinnacle in his esteem comparable to the one reserved for Drew.

Tyler had been graduated *rite* from Amherst College in 1954— that is, "with a pass"—*"rite,"* according to Webster's Third International Dictionary, being "a mark of undistinguished achievement in the academic requirements for graduation." Ellen Pearson Arnold, always envious of her stepbrother's claims on her father's attention, used to say that except for special arrangements Tyler would never have graduated with his class. Registrar Robert F. Grose of Amherst College treated the remark as a joke. Tyler said he graduated, period; whether *rite* or *summa cum laude* was nobody's business.

When Tyler was married on January 12, 1955, to Bess Clements, daughter of Earle C. Clements, Washington lobbyist for the tobacco industry and former Governor of Kentucky, Senate Majority Leader Lyndon and Lady Bird Johnson gave the couple a reception at the Sheraton-Carlton befitting the political aristocracy of their families. Guests included Speaker Rayburn, former Speaker Martin and such Senators as Morse, Kefauver, Neuberger, O'Mahoney, George and Thurmond.

Tyler was in uniform at the time. After the wedding trip, by special dispensation, to Florida and Nassau, he served out his tour of duty in the Signal Corps. He became the target of open letters in the column on such august matters as Soviet-American friendship. One column cited a "Pentagon rumor" that Tyler was leaking military secrets to the column.

Pearson must have been writing humorously. Tyler had no talent for newspaper work, no nose for the conspiratorial in acquiring news. After graduation from college he did try out for several months as a legman for the "Merry-Go-Round," but his performance was not such as to encourage Drew in any hope of

training the young man as his successor. When Tyler was discharged from the Army, he sidestepped journalism for good by
taking a law course at Georgetown University.

Despite the new intimacy between the Pearson and Johnson
families, there were times during the Eisenhower regime when
Drew reminded the public that Johnson had flirted with Senator
Joe McCarthy and the Dixiecrats and had sponsored a bill to
exempt natural gas from federal regulation "for the benefit of his
friends, the Texas gas and oil men who contribute so heavily to
his campaigns." Then the two men had to be kept apart at parties
for fear of furious dialogue if nothing worse. Other times they
saw eye to eye on a dominant issue or had something going between them, like the deal to deny confirmation to Lewis Strauss as
Secretary of Commerce.

Overwork took its toll on Johnson during the summer of 1955.
He suffered a nearly fatal heart attack at the Middleburg, Virginia,
estate of the Texas contractor whose income-tax difficulties he had
squared with the late President Roosevelt. Most politicians would
have given up. Not Johnson; he dieted from 200 to 170 pounds,
took siestas, read Plato instead of the *Congressional Record* and by
the following January was able to resume his Democratic leadership in the Senate.

The "Merry-Go-Round" welcomed him back. "When I'm
down," commented Johnson ruefully, "Drew praises me, but when
I'm up, he takes a cut at me."

Tyler Abell named his second son Lyndon. He gave up
clerking for a local judge to join the Johnson vice presidential
campaign staff in 1960. With considerable help from the "Washington Merry-Go-Round," the Kennedy-Johnson ticket edged out
the Nixon-Lodge slate that year. Tyler Abell was rewarded with a
patronage appointment as special assistant to the Postmaster General and his wife, Bess, went to work for Lady Bird Johnson.

Half of Drew's patriarchal burden was eased. The other half
involved Ellen and her children. After years of domestic tension,
Ellen had finally obtained a divorce from George Arnold. While
in Mexico getting her decree she met and married Dwight Whitney, a Hollywood reporter. Though their marriage was soon an-
nulled, they had a daughter, named Felicia after her grandmother.

George Arnold provided for his three sons by Ellen. However, she was emotionally at loose ends. When she turned to her father for advice, as she always did, he promptly invited her to bring Felicia to the Potomac farm, which had a luxurious guest cottage. Though she got along with Luvie no better than with Tyler, Ellen accepted the guest-cottage invitation.

Drew Pearson, dressed as an Irishman, and Luvie, dressed as the gold drain, attended the most exclusive of the five Kennedy inaugural balls, a costume party at a private home. Socially, they were in with the New Frontiersmen. Professionally, Drew was out. He never believed that the golden boy of the Kennedy clan of freebooters from Boston could be as good as he looked. The President and his brother Bobby, the new Attorney General, recognized this; they acted accordingly.

Lyndon Johnson stood no higher than Pearson at the White House. The President treated him with scant consideration, and Bobby, who never wanted him on the 1960 ticket, spread rumors that he would be dropped in 1964. Meanwhile, Johnson was reacting to his new national constituency. His expression of liberal views on civil rights and other issues won published praise from Pearson.

In 1963 Lyndon contributed to Drew's dream of independence. The Bell-McClure syndicate, which had been peddling the "Merry-Go-Round" for almost twenty years, came up for sale. Leonard H. Marks, Johnson's radio-TV adviser, joined Pearson in buying it for $400,000. The third partner in this virtually unpublicized, highly intriguing purchase was Fortune R. Pope. For good luck the sale was consummated on Drew's birthday.

Fortune Pope's father was the late Generoso Pope, a fabulous character who exercised national influence as a Democratic politician and associated openly with Frank Costello, the Mafia leader. Pearson had a long, puzzling alliance with Generoso, who supported Mussolini in the days when the column was strongly anti-Fascist. For years Pearson wrote, or had written in his name, a special Sunday column for *Il Progresso*, Pope's widely read Italian-American newspaper in New York.

Fortune Pope acted as grand marshal in the annual Columbus Day parade which marched down New York's Fifth Avenue. He was prominent in other Italian-American activities. Unexpectedly, in 1960, he pleaded guilty to diverting $375,000 in assets from the Colonial Sand & Stone Company which he had inherited from his father. He made restitution and received a suspended one-year prison sentence. Later his conviction was erased by a pardon from President Johnson.

When in 1965 Leonard Marks was appointed by President Johnson to direct the U.S. Information Agency, he placed his newspaper syndicate stock in his wife's name, thereby becoming invisible in the setup. Since Fortune Pope was concerned solely with the fiscal aspects of the operation, that gave Drew Pearson what none of his competitors ever achieved, full control over his journalistic destiny.

2

At a Communist conference in Moscow during the fall of 1960 Soviet Premier Nikita Khrushchev came under attack for appeasing the West. The Chinese and their allies among the Russian conservatives and militarists gave the Premier six months to show that his international policies would work. Khrushchev kept his domestic enemies at bay with a vigorous anti-Stalinism while he tried to straighten out his foreign difficulties.

When John F. Kennedy was elected President that fall, Khrushchev released the RB-47 naval fliers who had landed in the Soviet Arctic and U-2 pilot Francis Gary Powers, who had been downed over Russia. Khrushchev let Averell Harriman know he had delayed the release—to avoid helping presidential candidate Nixon—until the American political campaign ended. Anatoly Dobrynin, the Soviet Ambassador to Washington, conveyed Khrushchev's wish to be represented at the inauguration by an extraordinary ambassador of cabinet rank. Kennedy rejected the idea. On inauguration day, Khrushchev sent the President a long, enthusiastic telegram of congratulation. Kennedy replied curtly.

Adlai Stevenson, the new Ambassador to the United Nations, said during a news conference in New York that President Kennedy would meet Khrushchev if the latter attended a special UN meeting in March. From Washington Kennedy denied any such intention. Llewellyn Thompson, the American Ambassador in Moscow, was assigned to explain the rejection personally. He tracked his man down in Siberia. President Kennedy wanted to defer any discussion of the Cold War for six months until he got his bearings, said Llewellyn. Khrushchev roared with laughter at such naïveté.

In mid-April the CIA staged its inept invasion of Cuba by Cuban exiles. The invasion probably would have gotten nowhere even without the last-minute withdrawal of U.S. air cover by President Kennedy. Stevenson had to defend the blunder before the UN on the basis of a version of events from the State Department which he later found to be false. Kennedy won some domestic sympathy by claiming full responsibility for the Bay of Pigs fiasco, but he did not thereby lessen Soviet suspicions.

Disgruntled by American adventurism and the preceding personal rebuffs, Khrushchev retaliated in the Congo, at the Geneva nuclear-testing conference and in Laos. Kennedy threatened intervention in Laos and secured Congressional appropriations for more missiles and long-range B-52 bombers. Khrushchev warned that Berlin was an open wound in Russia's side, which must be healed.

Drew Pearson followed every detail in the heightening international quarrel. His journalistic contacts at this time were unsurpassed. In addition to Harriman and Stevenson, he talked without constraint with former Under Secretary of State Chester Bowles and with Senators Fulbright and Cooper of the Senate Foreign Relations Committee. When Kennedy agreed to go to Vienna in May for the meeting with Khrushchev which he had previously scorned, Pearson tried desperately but without success to see the President before he left.

Though he had geared himself up with medically prescribed amphetamines for the confrontation, Kennedy did not expect Khrushchev's brusqueness in Vienna. He was stunned by it. On the plane coming home, he groaned he had never been so depressed in his life. He did not see how the country could get through the summer without war, he told Pearson at dinner three days later. Khrushchev was under obligation to the East Germans, he said, to sign a separate peace treaty. That could set off an explosion over access routes to Berlin. The President mentioned an estimate especially prepared for him of the number of Americans who would die in the first atomic attack.

The following day Kennedy took to his bed. He stayed there

several weeks, suffering, it was announced, from an old back injury. The suffering may have been partly psychosomatic. It was to compensate for Vienna, Pearson always believed, that Kennedy increased American military strength in Vietnam from one thousand civilian advisers to fifty thousand troops. Knowing Vietnam's long struggle against outsiders, Pearson felt that each additional large white man in uniform made the United States more unpopular in that country of smaller, darker-skinned people.

Several days after dinner with the President, Pearson was among the guests of Vice President Johnson on a yacht sailing down the Potomac. Walt Rostow, Kennedy's national security adviser, bragged that Kennedy "looked straight down the gun barrel of atomic war in Vienna but did not flinch!" Pearson remarked that the President might not have had to look down the gun barrel if he had taken advantage of the earlier Russian thaw.

In July, having signed no separate peace treaty, the Communists began building a wall to cut Berlin in half. President Kennedy urged citizens to improve their air-raid shelters. "We do not want to fight," he said, "but we have fought before. It would be a mistake for others to look upon Berlin as a tempting target."

At this time Drew and Luvie Pearson were cruising through the Norwegian fjords as guests on a yacht chartered by Mrs. Eugene Meyer, publisher of the Washington *Post* since her husband's death. Acting on an idea in his mind since he had met Khrushchev in New York in 1959, Drew took Luvie to Moscow. There a lunch with Aleksei Adzhubei, Khrushchev's son-in-law and editor of *Izvestia*, led to an invitation to visit Khrushchev immediately at his summer home near Gagra on the Black Sea.

With Luvie at his side, in the presence of an interpreter and a stenographer, Drew talked four hours with Khrushchev that first afternoon, and at breakfast, lunch and dinner the next day. They swam together in the Black Sea, that is, Khrushchev dunked himself within a rubber tire as a life preserver while Pearson practiced his Swarthmore College crawl.

After displaying irritation at first, Khrushchev spoke frankly. He had told Kennedy, he revealed, that sending fifteen hundred more American soldiers to Berlin was "a clear threat" and "an unwise step." Being nearer, Russia could pour in fifty thousand soldiers overnight. "I told your young Mr. Kennedy that if he wants war he can have war," said Khrushchev. Kennedy had replied that that meant mutual destruction. Perhaps, said Khrushchev, "though in my heart I feel we are stronger."

Under Pearson's tactful questioning, Khrushchev outlined a step-by-step program for relaxing tension, including stabilization in Berlin, withdrawal of U.S. and Russian troops within their borders, the freezing of armament budgets and eventual disarmament. At one point Pearson explained how American newspapers operated and suggested that belligerent statements by Khrushchev irritated American public opinion and made compromise by Kennedy more difficult.

"Please tell Mr. Kennedy," Khrushchev said as the Pearsons were leaving, "that if the U.S. and the U.S.S.R. stand together no country in the world can start a war."

When Pearson came to the White House to report, President Kennedy had just been informed that the Russians were resuming nuclear testing. He listened with only half an ear to the correspondent. To illustrate his difficulties with the Soviet leader, he recalled that in Vienna he had tried to lighten the atmosphere by suggesting that "we go to the moon together." Khrushchev had brushed off the idea with an indignant "*Nyet.*"

The Khrushchev columns framed by Pearson stressed the Soviet desire for "a friendly wrestling match between countries," competition through trade, not war. Khrushchev wanted to get along with the United States, Pearson insisted. His was a diplomatic presentation in the journalistic tradition of an exclusive interview with somebody special—an Albert Einstein or an Al Capone—whose viewpoint had not previously been given in detail. An unexpurgated account went to Pearson's State Department friends, his Senatorial informants on foreign affairs and the CIA.

With a docile editor, Elmer Roessner, in charge at Bell-McClure, Pearson had no worry about censorship by his syndicate. Jack Anderson objected to the sequence of columns, predicting accurately that they would cause boycotts by Birch Society members and cancellations by newspaper editors. Pearson went ahead anyway. He placated subscribers to some extent by providing background memoranda.

The wife of an embattled public figure is always a civilian casualty. This time Luvie moved into the front line by producing an article on her thirty-six hours with Khrushchev for the *Saturday Evening Post*. "Khrushchev wants peace," she wrote flatly. "Peace is essential for the development of his country and he knows it." Editorially, the *Post* said it did "not share Mrs. Pearson's estimate of Mr. Khrushchev's peaceful intent." Luvie walked out of a Washington party after another female guest shrieked that she had "praised that S.O.B. who started the Korean War." Though accustomed to abuse as the office fan-mail sampler, Luvie had to stop reading the Khrushchev letters; they were too vitriolic.

Khrushchev's grip on the Presidium remained precarious, though he had won an implicit extension of his six months' period of grace. He had enraged his country's military leadership by proposing a cut of 200,000 officers and 1,000,000 men from the Army. He found it necessary to back away from that idea for the time being.

Khrushchev was under particular fire for not forcing President Kennedy to remove American missiles from Turkey, a hundred yards from Russian soil. The President had agreed privately to do this. He had twice asked Secretary of State Dean Rusk to get those missiles out of there, but Rusk, according to Pearson, took no action.

During the summer of 1962 the Pearsons and Adlai Stevenson were guests of Agnes Meyer on another cruise, this time through the Adriatic. Pearson and Stevenson made a side trip through Yugoslavia. At Gagra, Khrushchev was serving as a propitiatory host to Robert Frost, President Kennedy's favorite poet. Having issued secret orders for planting Soviet missiles in Cuba, Khrushchev pumped Frost full of his pacific intentions, presented the poet with a farewell gift of Georgian wines for the President and an invitation to the whole Kennedy family to come to the Black Sea for a visit.

Robert Frost wanted to trust Khrushchev, but his sensitive ear caught an undertone of nervousness in the Soviet leader's conversation. Talking to reporters when he arrived back in New York, the physically shaky, emotional eighty-eight-year-old poet blurted that Khrushchev had said Americans "are too liberal to fight—

he thinks we will sit on one hand and then the other." Khrushchev never said anything of the sort. The phrase formulated Frost's buried concern over the likely behavior of his fellow countrymen. Both Khrushchev and Kennedy were furious over the poet's stumble into their deadly dance on the brink of disaster.

Chagrin over his fluff weakened Frost. Two months after the incident he was admitted to a Boston hospital in critical condition. Before he died, messages of encouragement and admiration poured in from celebrities all over the world, including the Russian poet Yevtushenko and Soviet Ambassador Dobrynin, but none from the White House.

As nobody forgets, Kennedy drew a war line around Cuba to force removal of the Soviet missiles. Khrushchev backed down. Khrushchev even agreed to American inspection of the missile sites. Fidel Castro balked at this. So did Marshal Rodion Malinovsky, the Soviet Defense Minister. Khrushchev reneged on the inspection-site promise, but he permitted inspection of Soviet vessels on the high seas. Under his orders, Soviet soldiers manning antiaircraft guns in Cuba ceased shooting at overflying U-2 planes which wanted to photograph the missile sites.

Five years earlier, Khrushchev had defeated an effort by the Kaganovich-Molotov "antiparty group" to oust him. Now he worried over a possible new attempt at a coup. While Malinovsky was visiting India, Khrushchev fired the Marshal's allies, Chief of Staff Matvei Zakharov and Intelligence Chief I. A. Serov. To placate lesser military critics, he warned the United States that giving atomic weapons to Bonn would be considered ground for an invasion of West Germany. The State Department took notice. U.S. missiles were removed from Turkey. The world breathed easier.

In the summer of 1963, Drew and Luvie Pearson were accompanied by Agnes Meyer and Earl Warren on a second visit to Khrushchev. They were warmly welcomed, if only because a Pearson scrapbook of his columns had thoroughly dispelled the Soviet leader's suspicion that his remarks might not be fairly rendered.

Mrs. Meyer joined in the interviewing, but the Chief Justice felt obliged by his high judicial position to stay away from the conference table. Khrushchev again spoke freely, covering everything from his excellent health at sixty-nine, which he attributed to "the good Socialist life I lead," to the drought which was plaguing new wheat-growing areas in Kazakhstan and southern Siberia. He hedged when Pearson asked whether the Chinese Communists, out from under the Soviet wing, "might cause world trouble."

"I am not instructed to speak for the Chinese," said Khrushchev, "but if I am to express my own personal view, I don't expect they will start anything."

Pearson persisted: wasn't Chinese reluctance to concede coexistence one cause of the rift between China and Russia? "Let us agree on one thing," shot back Khrushchev. "Put the responsibility for negotiating with China on our shoulders, not on yours."

After Khrushchev left on a trip to Yugoslavia, the Pearson party toured southern Russia. On the way home they visited two East European satellites of the Soviet Union. Drew interviewed Premier Todor Zhivkov of Bulgaria, Chairman Gheorghiu-Dej of Rumania and other Communist leaders. He described the liberal attitude toward abortion in those countries, the assignment of women to heavy manual labor and other socioeconomic points of interest. Bulgaria was assuming a leading anti-Chinese position among countries in the Soviet bloc, and Rumania was struggling against the subordinate economic role assigned to it by Russia, he reported. Both countries, Pearson wrote, were anxious for closer American ties.

From one of his intelligence sources Pearson heard that Premier Chou En-lai of China had predicted it was "just a matter of time before Khrushchev is swept out of power." The new piece of information helped to fill in the jigsaw puzzle. Pearson's new Russian series focused on the Sino-Soviet break, which presaged the end of any single world Communist conspiracy and which called for new diplomatic initiatives by the United States.

Jack Anderson was as displeased by the new series as he had been by the old. He felt that the ideological ties between Russia and China were stronger than their nationalist interests. President Kennedy, however, reacted differently when the subject was broached by Pearson. Having by this time developed a cooler, more sophisticated hand in foreign affairs, the President listened in detail to Pearson's report. He questioned Drew closely on the

Chinese angle. After further consultation with his official experts, Kennedy planned an approach to Peking. Before he could complete arrangements, however, he was assassinated.

3

With his eerie quality of seeming to be on the spot when news broke, Drew Pearson was in Dallas the day a disturbed young man who had made pilgrimages to Russia and Cuba shot President Kennedy. In the months which followed, Pearson produced some carefully angled exclusives. The CIA, he revealed, had twice assigned Cuban agents to kill Castro. He raised the point that the bungled attempts might have come to the attention of Lee Harvey Oswald and focused his diffuse hostility toward a world where he could find no comfortable place.

The Soviet Union turned Oswald's file over to U.S. investigators, Pearson noted in the "Merry-Go-Round," adding that the United States had never done as much for the Russians. The purpose of the columnist-turned-diplomat was to reduce hysteria, which might upset the delicate balance between the two countries.

Early in the thirty-day period of mourning for President Kennedy, Pearson convinced Lyndon Johnson that an interfaith memorial service in Washington would help to avert any panicky search for a scapegoat among the country's minority groups. The new President approved the idea, then tried to back out on the plea that he was tired and wanted to go to his Texas ranch for a rest.

Pearson persisted. Final arrangements were made during an informal outdoor meeting on the steps of the Lincoln Memorial. It was a cold windy afternoon. Individually and in groups of two and three, the heavily dressed guests climbed up to the tall man standing stolidly on the top step dressed in a long black coat and a Russian black fur hat.

No introductions were required. Among these community leaders everybody knew everybody else. To each of them Pearson explained that President Johnson would deliver the chief address. Federal and local agencies were already cooperating. Only small details of sponsorship and program remained to be settled.

Two passers-by watched from the sidewalk as Pearson conducted his consecutive quiet interviews. "That fellow on top of the steps looks like an advertising director assigning routes to door-to-door salesmen," said one. "No," declared the other. "He looks more like the mayor of a town that has no mayor."

On the same site the following Sunday evening, before an enormous hushed audience holding flickering candles, President Johnson delivered an impressive appeal for national unity written by Drew Pearson. A New York committee assembled by Sydney S. Baron sponsored and paid for another interfaith celebration at the 34th Street Armory. Similar gatherings arranged by stringers and friends of Pearson were held in San Francisco and other cities across the country, with Pearson paying any necessary expenses. After the Washington affair, President Johnson took Drew and Luvie to the White House in his car, arranged a midweek session with Pearson, then sent the couple home in the car.

In the form of an open letter to Lyndon Abell, the "Washington Merry-Go-Round" hailed President Johnson as the best-qualified man to reach the White House since Woodrow Wilson. This may have gone over the head of Drew's three-year-old step-grandson, but to official Washington it was evidence of a budding alliance between a freewheeling columnist and a wheeler-dealer from Texas.

On December 4, 1963, Premier Khrushchev cut the Soviet military budget by 4.7 percent. On Pearson's advice, President Johnson announced a matching reduction in U.S. military spending. The *Red Star*, official organ of the Russian Army, openly criticized Khrushchev. Barry Goldwater and Strom Thurmond denounced the new President from the floor of the U.S. Senate. To Pearson, the dual wave of reaction doubly justified the gesture.

In Pearson's eyes, Khrushchev was a reformer comparable, under his system of government, to the Wilson-Roosevelt-Truman-Johnson line of ameliorists in the United States. He pressed his opinion on Johnson at their regular meetings. More than once the President commented that Pearson would make an ideal Ambassador to Moscow since he knew more about Khrushchev than anybody else. Pearson took the recommendation seriously, but Johnson never made the appointment. It was politically impractical.

In June, 1964, Pearson went to Egypt for what proved to be his final conference with Khrushchev. The Soviet leader had just dedicated the huge Aswan Dam, whose financing he had taken over as a way of penetrating the Arab world after the United States repudiated its pledge to put up the money. Khrushchev told Pearson frankly about his domestic troubles. Opponents in the Politburo were blaming him for the loss of China, crop failures and other supposed faults of leadership. He could use a strong favorable diplomatic gesture from the United States, he indicated.

Upon his return, Pearson spoke to President Johnson about the unusual Khrushchev appeal. However, the presidential campaign season was too well advanced. The Republicans were already charging Johnson with being too friendly with the Russians. In October, before the end of the one-sided Johnson-Goldwater campaign, Khrushchev was quietly shelved by the Brezhnev-Kosygin clique, which took a half-turn back toward Stalinism and pursued cooler relations with the United States.

Professionally, Pearson was doing well. His emergence as a respected precursor of cautiously improved relations with Russia had brought a new wave of subscriptions to the "Merry-Go-Round," fresh radio-TV prominence and requests for articles and interviews. Because of his intimacy with President Johnson, oddly enough, he lost some liberal Southern newspapers, which had become accustomed to seeing the misbehavior of Southern Democratic politicians pin-pointed in the column.

Washington society rediscovered Pearson. Years before, he had been dropped from the "Social List" on the curious ground that he "engaged in too many controversies." Abruptly, it became fashionable to remark that the Hollywood prototype of watchdog journalist was patterned on this peaceful-looking but dangerous man. Here was an enlarged lion—"the" Lion of Felicia Gizycka's novel—a celebrity of the caliber of Eric Hoffer, the longshoreman-turned-pundit; Jack Dempsey, the ex-prizefighter; or Jeane Dixon, the astrologist. Hostesses who disliked Pearson felt obliged to invite him to their parties. His rare appearances, brooding and often alone, amounted to pseudo events.

Pearson owed an autumnal romance to his reputation as a defender of Khrushchev. Margaret Herring Laughrun, a twenty-seven-year-old Southern girl, became his personal secretary early in 1963 when he was sixty-five. Married and the mother of two very young sons of whom she had custody, Margaret lived apart from a husband who was attending medical school under the GI Bill of Rights. Having become a leftist while her husband was serving abroad in the Army, she had intrigued for the job with Pearson through a friend of Bess Abell.

Margaret Laughrun was a plumpish girl of medium height who seemed younger than her years. Her style of dress tended toward the comfortable rather than the seductive. She had naturally rosy cheeks, large brown eyes, long black hair, a soft voice and a breathless, vulnerable manner.

Marian Canty, Pearson's confidential secretary and office manager, disliked personal secretaries on sight: their title and duties conflicted with her own. She conceded Margaret's qualifications for the job on the basis of previous experience in the office of Senator Young of Ohio, but she objected to the new girl's diffidence.

"I wish Margaret would speak up," she said to the other girls. "She's a regular female Uriah Heep."

Pearson was vastly pleased with Margaret. From small endearments he proceeded to what the office called his "cutey-pie" phase. Soon Margaret was invited to Pearson family cocktail parties, a sure indication that she was his current "fair-haired girl." In addition to her secretarial duties, Margaret was assigned to report on the activities of the country's new radical youth groups, of which she frequently spoke to him. In September she accompanied Drew to New York on a business trip, during which they became intimate.

Though Drew did not permit romance to interfere with work, he was a vigorous lover. Demonstrativeness in the office displeased Margaret because of the proximity of the domestic half of the house. Luvie had nothing to do with them, Drew insisted. He and his wife were extremely close, he pointed out; they shared most things. When they did the supper dishes together in the absence of a servant, he added as an example, one always washed and the other dried.

In August of the following year Margaret attended the Democratic National Convention in Atlantic City as Drew's secretary and assistant. Drew drove up with Luvie in one car, and Margaret rode with Jack and Olivia Anderson in another. Margaret distrusted Jack politically and felt confirmed in her distrust when he concentrated his coverage on police precautions against ultraleftist violence in Atlantic City.

The Democratic Convention of 1964 was a pretty cut-and-dried affair except for two major elements of suspense: who would be picked by Lyndon Johnson to run with him for Vice President; and how the biracial Mississippi Freedom Party would fare in its determined bid to crack the lily-white delegation from that state.

Drew concentrated on Humphrey's chances of landing on the Johnson ticket. He assigned Margaret to keep in touch with the Mississippi Freedom Party, but he did not use much of her information. At one point he offered her a rare press ticket. Margaret looked at him without expression; she and other Freedom Party workers were already romping uninvited through the convention hall while the reporters looked remotely down from their high gallery.

Despite the presence of the others, Drew kept tabs on Margaret when she was not working directly for him. He was waiting outside her Haddon Hall Hotel room when she walked down the corridor at 8 o'clock one morning.

"Where have you been all night?" he said.

"Out," she replied.

"With your Mississippi Party friends?" he demanded. She nodded.

"Take your typewriter and return to Washington at once," he ordered. Margaret said she did not have enough money with her for the trip by bus and train. At this, Drew relented and said she could wait and go back with the Andersons.

In Washington, Margaret announced she had volunteered to help in the Alabama and Georgia voter-registration drive of the Student Non-Violent Coordinating Committee (SNCC), with whose members she had become friendly during the partially successful drive for representation at the convention. Pearson gave a farewell champagne party at the office for his retiring personal secretary. He made a speech about "this brave little girl who is leaving her children and risking her life for her principles." Margaret wept. One secretary said sardonically in an aside that

Margaret would do better to provide a home for her boys instead of entrusting them to a Unitarian Church friend in Arlington. The others seemed impressed by Margaret's idealism and daring.

To office secretaries, Drew openly dictated occasional encouraging letters to Margaret. Sometimes he enclosed gifts of money. When he was away from the office on trips, he wrote notes expressing his feelings in more intimate fashion.

Margaret Laughrun returned to Arlington briefly in December. Her husband, she had been informed, was bringing a suit for divorce and custody of the two boys, which she did not feel able to fight. Though she lacked proof, Margaret always believed that her husband had taken action on the basis of rumors of her affair with Pearson. The official purpose of her trip was to lobby in connection with the poorly enforced new voting-rights law. When she telephoned Drew, he invited her to the office, giving her one of his precise appointments, for twenty-one minutes after the hour. In anxiety not to be late, she arrived early.

SNCC had been under FBI investigation, Drew warned. Margaret and other activists were due to be Red-baited. From the evidence of her own letters, the work down South was grim, dangerous and almost beyond the endurance of a gentle girl like her, Drew argued, suggesting that she return to her old job. He missed her, he added.

Margaret shook her head. She did not want to hurt Pearson's feelings, but from her point of view he was "no longer with it." He had "sold out" at the Atlantic City convention, she explained later to her Arlington host. "He stuck with Hubert Humphrey and his peers of the fifties against the black people," she said. "I could never go back there."

As Margaret hurried from Pearson's office on the verge of tears, she passed a man coming in who looked familiar. It was Dr. Martin Luther King! She always wondered whether King's visit had been timed to match hers in order to influence her decision.

4

Senator Barry Goldwater, the right-wing Republican candidate for President, proposed the bombing of North Vietnam. President Johnson, whose confidence in the advice of the military equaled that of Goldwater, allowed Democratic strategists during the 1964 campaign to deplore as irresponsible a step he himself was already preparing to take and did take after his election. Political observers in Washington, aware of Pearson's consistent opposition to escalation of the struggle in Indochina, could not understand how he kept on friendly terms with Johnson.

Frank Kluckhohn, a spokesman for Washington conservatives since his retirement as a correspondent for the *New York Times*, theorized in print that Pearson was "eating crow" for fear of being jailed on the basis of FBI reports in President Johnson's possession. Robert Sherrill, Washington correspondent for *The Nation*, deplored kindness on Pearson's part toward a "treacherous, dishonest, manic-aggressive, spoiled and above-all, accidental President." Neither Sherrill nor Kluckhohn fully appreciated the Pearson-Johnson cycle of amity, opposition and reconciliation.

At the present phase of that cycle, Pearson had unprecedented leverage at the White House. His columns almost invariably showed Johnson in a favorable light, being opposed or thwarted by stupid advisers or adverse events. The public flattery employed to influence the President was often glaring. Johnson, in turn, could not resist trying to manage the news in the "Merry-Go-Round." Watching their daily tug-of-war became an indoor sport in Washington.

Pearson did not let anybody feel entirely sure of him. He was faithful to the President in his fashion. If he explained that Johnson's State of the Union message was not too long, as critics claimed —only six thousand words compared to the Kennedy average of seven thousand—he was likely to add: "It only seemed too long."

The columnist rode to the President's rescue in the Bobby Baker case, the worst scandal during Johnson's tenure at the White House. Baker was Lyndon's protégé. He had become a millionaire while serving as a Senate aide at $19,600 a year. As a result of activities of which Lyndon Johnson must have been aware, Baker eventually went to prison for larceny, fraud and income-tax evasion. A key witness against Baker, an insurance man named Don Reynolds, particularly embarrassed the President by revealing that he had been required to purchase $1,200 in advertising on the Johnson family radio-TV station in Austin after he wrote a million-dollar policy on Johnson's life.

Crusading against Don Reynolds, the "Washington Merry-Go-Round" disclosed that the insurance man had been "an informer" for the late Senator Joe McCarthy and "an irresponsible witness" before the McCarran Immigration Committee. It cited derogatory information about Reynolds which could only have come from his confidential Selective Service record.

Noting that the use of such material must have been authorized at the highest levels in the administration, the *Wall Street Journal*, the Chicago *Daily News* and the *New Republic* charged Pearson with being Johnson's "axeman" and "White House mouthpiece." Pearson distributed a defensive memo to his editors reminding them that he had specialized over the years in obtaining "closed-door transcripts and conference documents." Somehow the reminder undercut his own denial.

Pearson was notorious for using legislative puppets. If he effusively praised a foreign affairs expert like Senator Wayne Morse or a consumer advocate like Senator Warren Magnuson for introducing a bill, Capitol Hill figured he was patting his own back. Similar calculations began to be made in connection with Vice President Humphrey and President Johnson. When Hubert proposed a "Marshall Plan to rebuild the cities of the United States" and Lyndon espoused "a common market for the Americas" —ideas previously broached in the column—it was safe to bet that the initiative, as well as much of the applause, came from 1313 Twenty-ninth Street.

In compensation for unacknowledged brain-trusting, Drew felt entitled from time to time to bring worthy individuals to the President's attention. One was George Arnold, Ellen's former husband. A high position in the Attorney General's office similar to one previously held by Thurman Arnold, George's father, had fallen vacant. Pearson's advocacy of George may have been designed partly to please Thurman Arnold and partly as a ploy to aid Ellen.

The family experiment at the Potomac farm had failed. Ellen and her daughter tried living in a guest cottage there, but Luvie and Ellen could not get along. Eventually, Ellen felt so much like a pariah on property once owned by her that she left and went to live in Washington. Drew may have trifled with the romantic notion that bringing George to Washington would patch up the former relationship with Ellen. However, the Justice Department appointment went to a son of former Attorney General Tom Clark of Texas. George Arnold remained on the West Coast.

A drug-industry tycoon who had once sponsored Drew's radio program came to the columnist's office one day with a problem. His corporation wanted to absorb a small competitor. The problem consisted in getting advance approval for the merger from the Anti-Trust Division of the Justice Department. Drew suggested that the former sponsor hire one of his friends, a member of a small group he met frequently for lunch at the Cosmos Club, because this lawyer had once worked in that division.

The tycoon took the advice. The acquisition was approved. The arrangement became slightly notorious in Washington because the businessman who benefited complained loudly and long to local friends that the lawyer's bill was "exorbitant." The only thing done for him, he said, was "one phone call by Drew Pearson to the White House." Did he know this or was he guessing? Certainly Pearson received no money as intermediary.

Late in 1965, Pearson made an ill-considered effort to place Tyler as U.S. Attorney for the District of Columbia. Johnson's original nominee, David G. Bress, a former president of the local bar association, was under attack in the Senate Judiciary Committee, which had to confirm or reject the President's choice.

Despite his personal relationship with Tyler Abell, the President declined to withdraw Bress. Pearson was furious. Thrusting aside his official portrait of the liberal and humane man in the White House, he clobbered the President in a series of columns. He made reference to a current romance, strongly disapproved by Johnson, between the President's daughter Lynda Bird and Hollywood actor George Hamilton. One column cited "three personal things" about Johnson which, Pearson wrote, "most irritate the public":

> George Hamilton's draft deferment while he hobnobs around the world with Lynda Bird Johnson; Lynda Bird's trip abroad while other Americans were asked to stay at home; and Luci's gala wedding to Pat Nugent while a lot of boys were fighting in Vietnam.

The President usually got his way with Congress, Pearson noted derisively, "but he can't seem to get his way with his own family."

An almost apoplectic Lyndon Johnson forgot all about Pearson as a great constructive force in American journalism and began to study those old FBI reports which supposedly justified an indictment of the columnist for stealing government secrets.

Meanwhile, Pearson emissaries were tackling individual Senators on Tyler Abell's behalf. During Johnson's second term Tyler's status had improved. He was now associate counsel to the Post Office Department at a higher salary. His wife, Bess, was Lady Bird's social secretary at the White House. Nevertheless these were personal appointments.

Young Abell was an ornament in local society, a yachtsman who competed in sailing races and a part owner of a fashionable waterfront restaurant called the Gangplank. He possessed a law degree, but he was not known as a practicing lawyer in the local courts. In the opinion of even friendly Senators, Tyler Abell did not shape up as a plausible choice for chief legal officer in the nation's capital.

Acknowledging the inevitable, Drew Pearson broke off his campaign and resumed hand-holding with the man in the White House. Lyndon Johnson relished his victory. "Drew was sore at me for a while because I wouldn't make his stepson U.S. Attorney," he told a news magazine reporter with a guffaw, "but he's all right now!"

The President was on closer social terms than ever with Tyler and Bess. In the spring of 1966 he and Lady Bird attended a housewarming in an eleven-room Federal-style building at 1830 Twenty-fourth Street which the Abells had purchased. This was an "Express Yourself Party," at which guests were invited to use cans of paint on the bare walls. Society reporters paid less attention to the White House visitors than to the behavior of architect John Warnecke. "Inspired by the bare back of beautiful Mrs. Tazewell Shepard," the town was informed, "Warnecke painted a large red valentine, with cupid's arrow, in tattoo on her flesh."

CHAPTER XV

Double Exposure

Drew Pearson's quarrel with Senator Thomas J. Dodd lasted a decade, which was not long in comparison with his thirty-year pursuit of General MacArthur. It did not have the historical impact of his part in the rout of Senator Joe McCarthy. Nevertheless, his final exposure of the Senator was as impressive as anything else in his career since it enabled him singlehandedly to down a conservative faction in Congress which he had been harassing for a long time.

Dodd fought back at first through friends, the FBI and various lawsuits. He did not reply in personal terms until 123 complete columns had stripped him of every vestige of decency and dignity. Then he retaliated with the meanest libel ever applied to Pearson, an unprovable charge that the columnist was "a molester of children who had the records of his arrest destroyed."

The Dodd case did not represent any peak in savagery for Pearson. He had become more contentious with age—readier to snap at colleagues, friends, even relatives, more willing to try desperate expedients against enemies—but he had always known that in the closed-society squabbles of Washington one man had to win, the other to yield, be crippled politically or die. Several of his pre-Dodd encounters—notably the one with Norman M.

Littell, the only person ever to collect damages from the "Washington Merry-Go-Round" after a court trial—showed to what lengths he had learned to go in controversy.

Norman Littell was the son of a Presbyterian minister. He had been a sailor, logger and newspaper correspondent before he turned to law and reform politics. Soon after his arrival in Washington in 1939 as an Assistant U.S. Attorney General in charge of the Land Division, he won praise from the column for his defiance of unscrupulous lobbies and individual New Dealers who tried to exploit their positions for financial gain.

Norman and his wife, Katherine, were occasional guests of Drew and Luvie in Georgetown and on the Potomac farm. They were visited in turn by the Pearsons. The families saw less of each other after Littell left the Department of Justice in 1944 in the wake of a public quarrel with his boss, Attorney General Francis Biddle.

On April 10, 1949, without a preliminary phone call or other warning, Pearson attacked his onetime friend. "The Justice Department is casting a quizzical eye on ex-Assistant Attorney General Norman Littell," the column item read. "They have reports that Littell is acting as a propagandist for the Dutch government though he failed to register as a foreign agent." Since unregistered lobbying for a foreign country was a crime punishable by $5,000 fine or imprisonment up to ten years, Littell sued for $300,000 in damages.

Pearson should have apologized to Littell, but instead he compounded the injury. Almost a year later, during radio comment on Senator Joe McCarthy's charges about Communists in the State Department, he declared:

> I would like to urge a full investigation of all subversives, all attorneys for Communists and of our national security, perhaps by a committee of prominent citizens. As a sample I suggest that such a committee look into the attorney for a Communist embassy and ascertain how, after Gerhart Eisler was spirited out of New York on the Polish steamer *Batory*, this attorney arranged for Polish Communists to board the returning steamship and interview the crew ahead of the U.S. officials who wanted to find out how Eisler escaped. This attorney was a former high official of the Justice De-

partment and because, unlike McCarthy, I believe in naming names without Congressional immunity, [I reveal] that gentleman is Norman Littell.

Pearson was covering up an old mistake with a new (McCarthyite?) charge. Littell did work quite openly for the Polish Embassy in 1949 and 1950. In the *Batory* case he went so far as to make a personal appeal to Tom Clark, the current Attorney General, but he contended that any American lawyer was entitled to advise a foreign country for a fee without being tagged as subversive. He sued Pearson for an additional $300,000.

As always, Pearson had political reasons for what he did, ranging from the attitudes of his friends and enemies to the military situation in Indonesia. He knew that Littell, turning to the right after an explosive exit from the New Deal, had gotten on cozy off-the-record terms with several conservative commentators, including Westbrook Pegler, Pearson's most bitter newspaper rival. Pegler praised Littell publicly as "the only New Dealer who left with empty pockets."

During the Second World War, the Japanese ruled Indonesia through a native orator named Sukarno. When Sukarno proclaimed an Indonesian republic after the war, the Netherlands made an attempt to regain its prewar control over the islands. Fleeing to New York, Sukarno lived in a cheap boardinghouse with men who later became his cabinet ministers.

As an anticolonialist from way back, Pearson sympathized with Sukarno. He favored cutting the flow of American money to the Netherlands for economic recovery on the ground that much of it was being used to put down the Indonesian insurgency. One of his close friends, Joseph Borkin, was the registered lobbyist for the Indonesians. Pearson was annoyed when Littell was quoted by a local columnist as saying that Borkin should be ashamed to work for "those Japanese puppets" in Indonesia.

Littell went further. He testified before Congressional committees that a proposal to set up an American Indonesian Development Corporation to help Sukarno would permit "fly-by-night American businessmen," who made a relatively small investment, to collect 7 percent indefinitely on all Indonesian exports and imports. That, he charged, amounted to exploitation beyond ordinary economic imperialism. He introduced Dutch officials to columnist Dorothy Thompson, who wrote harsh columns about the American Indonesian Development Corporation, and to Senator Owen Brewster, a key figure in Congressional debate over paring American economic assistance to the Netherlands.

Pearson concluded that Littell was working secretly for the Dutch Embassy or bucking for a job there. The distinction did not seem important to him. What he did, however, was indefensible: through somebody else he planted reports with the Foreign Agents Registration Section of the Department of Justice that Littell was writing speeches for the Dutch Ambassador, lobbying for the Dutch in Congress and socially pushing the Dutch cause without registering as an agent. Several weeks later he made formal inquiry at the Criminal Division as to whether such reports had been received. The inquiry stimulated a Department of Justice request to the FBI to investigate Littell. When an FBI agent reached Joe Borkin in the course of the investigation, Pearson felt justified in launching his item.

Littell possessed one unsuspected advantage in the lawsuit: he had access to what might be described as the internal Mafia of executive power. Through General Harry Vaughan, President Truman's military aide, he was permitted to inspect the FBI file on Pearson. (He was not allowed to take the file from the Department of Justice building, so he phoned the contents to his office.) The file disclosed that Littell was not being paid by the Dutch. More important, it led Edward Bennett Williams, Littell's resourceful lawyer, to a Pearson investigator who had been dropped by the column as an economy measure in the face of the radio boycott inspired by Senator Joe McCarthy.

The investigator was unemployed and angry at Pearson. Williams persuaded him to sign an affidavit giving the inside story of the "frame-up" and to agree to testify at the trial in the spring of 1953. Pearson turned mental somersaults when he saw the name of his investigator on Littell's list of prospective witnesses. Making quick contact with the investigator, he hired him at a higher salary to go to Las Vegas to help in a secret national campaign against Senator Joe McCarthy.

Out of a new concern over possible office betrayal Pearson

ordered changing of all the locks, interior and exterior, in his Georgetown home. He became more secretive in dealing with his other employees and devised subtle checks on their loyalty as the Littell case progressed to its conclusion.

Littell had promised not to publicize the FBI file on Pearson, but Edward Bennett Williams considered it too precious to waste. When a key official of the Department of Justice, a particular friend of Pearson, took the stand at the trial, Williams showed him a copy of the FBI report. One glance was enough to jog the memory of the witness and discourage any attempt to conceal Pearson's trickery. The file was not put into evidence.

Carrying psychological warfare a step further, Williams thrust the investigator's affidavit at Pearson when the latter was on the stand. Pearson showed no sign of distress. Williams offered the affidavit in evidence, but H. Graham Morison, Pearson's trial lawyer, blocked it by pointing out that the investigator had defied the court by vanishing after accepting a subpoena to appear as a witness.

The trial lasted six weeks. Pearson could have won, he declared later. Senator Brewster had been willing to testify in his behalf if he agreed to drop his decades-long feud with Pan American Airways. Pearson would make no such agreement.

After considering the Dutch and Polish charges separately, the jury split on the Polish charge and granted $50,000 in damages on the Dutch charge. Pearson settled for $40,000 instead of appealing to a higher court when he learned that eleven of the twelve jurors had wanted a $100,000 verdict and that the sole holdout was the son of one of his old friends. To pay Littell he had to mortgage his Potomac farm.

2

During the early and middle 1960s Pearson increased his pressure on conservatives in Congress. Often he seemed to be daring opponents to sue. Two who separately accepted the challenge were Willis Carto and Philip Corso. Carto and Corso—they sounded like a dance team, but they made a determined effort for a while. They pursued Pearson in laborious pretrial examinations.

Asked at one of these sessions how much reliance he put on

his "associate," Jack Anderson, and other members of his staff, Pearson snapped: "I depend as much as anything on myself." Nobody, he said, edited his copy "except on spelling, dates or proper names—I have a girl [Marian Canty, of course] for that." He edited everybody else's copy, he added, and he made all policy decisions.

Carto had more to lose than Corso. Though he started as a propagandist using Birch Society sucker lists, Carto reached for respectability by organizing the Liberty Lobby, which he said spoke in Washington for 263 groups of "loyal Americans." His Congressional newsletter, while conservative, was not irresponsible. When Pearson called the lobby "neo-Nazi," exposed rabble-rousers on its policy board and named twelve Congressmen "who openly front for these subversives of the ultra-right," Carto felt obliged to file suit.

Fortunately for themselves, the twelve Congressmen who had been appearing on the lobby radio show or attending its conferences did not sue. Pearson had baited a trap. As a result of his success in a libel suit brought by Curtis Dall, policy board chairman of the lobby, he had acquired Carto's office correspondence. It had come to him not from the Anti-Defamation League—he had quarreled with the ADL—but from a patriotic stranger named Jeremy Thorne, a student of international affairs at Johns Hopkins University.

With copies of some very explicit letters in hand Pearson could safely discuss Carto's approach to "the Jewish problem," his plan to send blacks back to Africa, his passion for swastikas and his ceremonial observances of Hitler's birthday. Result: the Carto suit never came to trial.

Philip K. Corso, a tough little retired Colonel in Army intelligence who had handled dangerous wartime assignments in Italy, Germany and Japan, also found Pearson too tough to handle. The Colonel sued when the "Washington Merry-Go-Round" reported that he had been dropped from a job as investigator with the House Judiciary Committee on the basis of a secret report on his associates, record and character. He discovered that he could not face a trial because Pearson possessed a copy of a raw, unevaluated but quite revelatory FBI report on him.

Corso's previous employers on the Hill included Senator Strom Thurmond (D–S.C.), the white-supremacy advocate, and Representative Michael A. Feighan (D–Ohio). Pearson hit each in turn. Though they did not sue, they expressed some fresh and pungent reflections on Pearson from their respective Senate and House sanctuaries.

Feighan was a patsy for the column. He had, Pearson wrote, an absentee-junketeer record comparable to that of Adam Clayton Powell; he once called Eleanor Roosevelt a "nigger-lover"; he believed that the late President Kennedy was "soft on Communism" and that the State Department and the Central Intelligence Agency under President Johnson were "Communist-infiltrated."

Mentions of Feighan led by logical extension to the "fire-and-brimstone anti-Communists in Congress." Feighan himself had located more imaginary Communists than Senator Joe McCarthy, Pearson opined. Others included Representative John Rooney (D–Brooklyn), Speaker John McCormack (D–Mass.) and Senator Dodd.

Among these Roman Catholics, Dodd distinguished himself by the vehemence of his disapproval of the late Pope John for initiating improved relations between the Vatican and the Kremlin. When Pope Paul urged the opening of the United Nations to all countries, Dodd handed the Papal Nuncio in Washington a letter protesting to the Pope that his plan might be misconstrued as a reason for admitting Red China.

Pearson had been keeping an eye on Dodd ever since the Senator came oratorically to the rescue of Admiral Strauss, President Eisenhower's choice for Commerce Secretary in 1958. With his silver hair and chiseled profile, Dodd could have played the role of dedicated public servant in a TV serial. A Yale Law School graduate, former FBI agent and trial counsel at the Nuremberg Trials, a Congressman promoted to Senator, he projected the public image of a liberal Democrat, but Pearson found many conservative trails leading to him.

As head of the powerful Internal Security Subcommittee, Dodd had a habit of shielding people at whom Pearson was tilting. One was Frances Knight, a right-wing propagandist within the State Department. Miss Knight became a hero to Westbrook

Pegler during World War II by slipping information to Congressional committees to expose Eleanor Roosevelt's morale-building activities as "boondoggling." Much later, according to Drew Pearson, she provided Senator Joe McCarthy with his notorious list of supposed Communists in her own department.

Under the Hatch Act, federal employees are supposed to avoid political activities. Miss Knight fell into trouble with the Civil Service Commission over her inadequately concealed efforts to contribute to the defeat of Adlai Stevenson in the presidential election of 1952, but she was promoted to chief of the Passport Division during the Eisenhower administration and there she remained, taking periodic controversies in stride. Referred to as "The Dragon Lady" by Tom Wicker, she promptly dubbed the *New York Times* as "psychotic."

During the early 1960s, Miss Knight quarreled with Abba Schwartz, chief of the Bureau of Security and Consular Affairs. He had questioned State Department surveillance of distinguished Americans traveling abroad who aroused the suspicions of J. Edgar Hoover because of their attitude on the Vietnam war or some other issue. Miss Knight and the FBI Director appealed to Dodd, the Senator squeezed Secretary of State Dean Rusk, and the Secretary "bowed to pressure," according to Pearson, and fired Schwartz.

In writing critically about Miss Knight's triumph, Pearson noted that Schwartz had arranged for the inspection of American prisoners in North Vietnam by the International Red Cross. He had worked out deals with the Soviet Union for the release from Russia of aged Jewish relatives of Americans. These arrangements lapsed after Schwartz's departure.

Dodd's hawkishness on Vietnam displeased Pearson. So did his domestic political alliances. Dodd had backed the late Defense Secretary Forrestal. He was currently the Congressional spokesman for J. Edgar Hoover. Dodd even landed on Pearson's odd list of "heavy drinkers in Congress," along with Adam Clayton Powell of Harlem, Senator Russell Long of Louisiana and Representative L. Mendel Rivers of South Carolina, chairman of the House Military Appropriations Committee, who insisted on voting more money for the Vietnam war than Defense Secretary Robert

McNamara requested. Except for Powell, there were no liberals on that list.

Dodd exercised considerable influence as the No. 2 Democrat on the Senate Judiciary Committee. During the 1965 controversy over David G. Bress, President Johnson's nominee for U.S. Attorney in the District of Columbia, a spokesman for Tyler Abell visited the Senator to stress Tyler's greater eligibility for the post. Despite a promise not to disclose that Abell was Pearson's stepson, the spokesman blurted out the fact under questioning. That tore it: Dodd voted for Bress and strongly urged his colleagues to follow his example.

Though the "Washington Merry-Go-Round" did not deign to notice the Senator's role in Abell's defeat, it criticized Dodd regularly enough on other matters to signal readers that it would relish proof of a major slip on his part. Nothing happened until the Senator set the stage for his own downfall.

On the day of President Kennedy's assassination, Dood arrived in Washington by special plane from Hartford. He had been drinking heavily. To members of his staff who met him at the airport, he objected to the sentimental fuss over John Kennedy on the ground that the President had made as many "grave errors" as Pope John, who also had had a short stay in office. It would take fifty years, the Senator shouted, to correct the mistakes of those two men.

Hustled into his car, Dodd instructed his administrative secretary, James P. Boyd, Jr., to find out whether Congress or the President picked a new Vice President, since he himself might be picked. The Senator sang during most of the ride to his home. There he came on one of his sons and a schoolmate listening to a Canadian eulogy of the late President on TV. Irritably, Dodd switched the dial from station to station in search of something which did not concern the assassination. Finding nothing but some funereal organ music, the Senator stood swaying in front of his TV set, conducting the music with his arms and chortling, while Boyd, office manager Michael V. O'Hare and a secretary named Marjorie Carpenter looked silently at each other, wondering, they told Pearson later, how much longer they could continue working for such a man.

Boyd, Mrs. Carpenter and another secretary named Terry Golden were no longer employees of Dodd in June, 1965, when they volunteered to help the "Washington Merry-Go-Round" unmask the Senator's duplicity and chiseling. Pearson asked them to focus on thirty categories of information. They agreed to do so.

With the help of office manager O'Hare, who was still working for Dodd, they abstracted batches of official and personal papers from Dodd's office at every opportunity. During one weekend alone they made seven round trips to Jack Anderson's downtown office. Some six thousand documents were photostated, returned without detection to their cabinets, evaluated and checked over a six months' period.

Thomas J. Dodd was a formidable opponent. For one thing, he belonged to The Club, the inner group which handles the levers of Senatorial power. No populist orator, rampaging idealist or outsized personality of any kind is ever admitted to The Club. Its members are subtle, accommodating men who win their elections as tidily as possible and make deals among themselves over Scotch and soda or Bourbon and branch water. They show a united front against outsiders.

Despite The Club's traditional hostility to the White House, Dodd also held a strong position at the other end of Pennsylvania Avenue. As Senate Majority Leader, Lyndon Johnson gave Dodd a coveted assignment to the Senate Foreign Relations Committee ahead of other Senators. As President, Johnson seriously considered and almost chose him as his vice presidential running mate in 1964. Pearson displayed three photographs of LBJ at his office, one reading: "Drew has me listening"; but Dodd outranked him with four, one of which was inscribed: "To Tom Dodd, a courageous, competent and dedicated public servant from his friend, Lyndon B. Johnson."

Considering the strength of The Club, a frontal attack on Tom Dodd was not feasible unless White House neutrality could be assured. Pearson understood the lineaments of power: he had dropped an earlier drive against Speaker McCormack when President Johnson publicly and pointedly praised the man who was responsible for maneuvering his domestic legislation through the lower chamber. Arrangements were therefore made to present confidential proof to the President that his friend the Senator would soon become a political liability.

3

As usual, when he had a strong case to present, Pearson opened with a side issue. The first in the new series of anti-Dodd columns, dated January 24, 1966, was signed by Jack Anderson exclusively since Drew had gone out of town after it was written. The column declared that Dodd delivered Senate speeches ghost-written for him by Julius Klein, a $150,000-a-year Chicago lobbyist for right-wing German economic and military interests, thereby "skirting the intent" of the Foreign Agents Registration Act, which had been designed to identify the true sources of foreign propaganda.

Klein, an owlish, balding gentleman of great persuasiveness, denied writing speeches for Senator Dodd. The "Washington Merry-Go-Round" obliterated his denial by citing pages in the *Congressional Record* where speeches mentioned in quoted Klein-to-Dodd letters could be found. It added that Klein induced Dodd to lobby for him—shades of Norman Littell!—within the Department of Justice itself. "I am enclosing," Klein wrote to Dodd, February 12, 1965,

> a photostatic copy of the Registration Statement filed by a disgruntled competitor, Edwin Hartrich of Düsseldorf, Germany. I wonder if you have not written to the Department of Justice inquiring why Hartrich was permitted to act as a foreign agent without registering until finally forced to do so in December, and whether any disciplinary action has been taken against him. I think this move would do a lot to clear up the matter and you were good enough to tell me that you would do it.

Julius Klein showered gifts and cash on Thomas Dodd and provided luxurious quarters for his use in New York. The Senator, according to the column, reciprocated in his fashion:

> In 1961 and again in 1964, Dodd touted Klein for membership on the American Battle Monuments Commission. But each time the honor went to another.
>
> Having missed the opportunity to serve his country in the matter

of battle monuments, Klein sought an appointment in 1962 to the U.S. Advisory Commission on Information.

"I am sure you will want to add your endorsement," he wrote to Dodd on July 14. "But what is more important, couldn't you take this up personally with President Kennedy and with Lyndon Johnson so that we do not lose this opportunity by default, as happened last time?"

When this appointment, too, passed him by, he wrote bitterly to Dodd: "You know, Tom, friendship is a two-way street. I don't blame you for what happened, but what I am more disappointed in is that I didn't hear from you at all, either way."

Dodd replied testily: "I did what I said I would do, but I am sure you will understand that I cannot guarantee any performance."

Still sulking, Klein wrote back: "Tom, I never expected you to guarantee any performance. . . . Anyhow, this is water over the dam."

When the Army reprimanded Klein for falsification of his military record, Dodd intervened at the Pentagon to remove the tarnish from Klein's brass hat. More shattering to Klein, said the column, was a 1963–1964 Senate investigation of his behavior as a foreign agent:

When his industrial clients began canceling their contracts, Klein not only rushed over to West Germany but sent for Dodd to come help him impress the clients. Dodd readily agreed, but he had one misgiving.

"I have been thinking about this," he wrote to Klein in Germany on Feb. 14, 1964, "and I believe that I might be more successful with the people in Germany if I talk to them alone. I don't think it is at all necessary for you to accompany me, and there is a chance that it might be misunderstood. You know how anxious I am to help you, and it is for this reason that I want to present your case in the best possible light."

Later, Dodd made a remarkable mission to Germany on behalf of a registered foreign agent.

Using Klein's money, Senator Dodd wined and dined German generals, industrialists and bankers and reassured them on the governmental standing and influence of their American lobbyist. In return Klein sought the American dealership of a German auto for a friend of the Senator. The mutual hand-washing diverted attention from basic conflict-of-interest charges against Dodd. American newspaper readers, always rather insensitive to conflict-of-interest charges, virtually ignored Pearson's underlying heavy thesis that Klein and Dodd, by helping to expand West German industry in violation of the peace treaty between Germany and the United States, were shaping American foreign policy without any right to do so.

Meanwhile, public-relations man Klein, a retired major general and former national commander of the Jewish War Veterans, was trying to repair his reputation. Two particular friends of Pearson, Vice President Humphrey and Senator Jacob K. Javits (R,L–N.Y.), issued statements defending the integrity of "General Klein." Humphrey and Javits "hurt themselves" by sponsoring a man involved with reactionary and racist groups in Germany which were heating up the Cold War, Pearson snarled in print, adding: "When all the facts are out, their wounds may prove fatal." The Vice President and the Senator got the message.

When the Jewish War Veterans stirred up a wave of protest from Jewish readers, Pearson noted that the 1965 Klein-Dodd contacts in Germany included Dr. Hans Blobke and Hermann J. Abs. Blobke was "the name expert" who wrote the August 7, 1938, decree requiring Jewish Germans to add Israel to their names and the women to call themselves Sara. Abs was a banker who "participated in wresting away Jewish-owned property under Hitler" and who was currently intriguing, said Pearson, for the return of German property seized by the United States.

Julius Klein also supported conservative causes in the United States. He had, Pearson noted, actively promoted the presidential ambitions of the late General Douglas MacArthur. The Jewish protests died away.

Having cleared space around himself, rallied his following and aroused some expectation as to what he would do next, Pearson broadened his drive in March, not against Klein, whom many observers believed at this point was his chief target, but against Dodd. The deeper he dug into the Senator's affairs, he wrote, "the stronger is the odor of scandal." That oversized nose for news again! What he meant was that he had twenty-nine more categories of digested information to divulge.

The "Washington Merry-Go-Round" quickly limned Dodd as a cheapskate who obtained double, even triple, payments for the same speech by billing Congress as well as sponsoring private groups. The Senator got jobs for relatives and took gifts from companies he was supposed to be investigating; he accepted money and loans from people for whom he sought appointments in government; he allowed constituents to pay him for routine office services; and he interceded with the federal government—in one case actually fought the government in court—for private law clients.

Realizing his files had been raped, Dodd put the FBI on the trail. Pearson appealed to Attorney General Nicholas Katzenbach, who, in theory at least, had control over J. Edgar Hoover. Katzenbach listened courteously to Pearson's argument that the FBI should be investigating Dodd, not those who exposed the Senator's misbehavior. Before the two men parted, Katzenbach gave his visitor a private crumb of comfort: he had not, he said, received any instructions yet from the White House.

Pearson offered to provide the Senate Ethics Committee with details on issues already raised affecting Senator Dodd. He was informed that the committee, like the FBI, was chiefly interested in how he obtained his documents. Had he used informers? There was nothing wrong with informers, Pearson said. Without informers, he pointed out, the FBI could not have moved against the Ku Klux Klan in the Viola Liuzzo murder case. Tax informers were even paid by law.

"We paid no money and stole no documents," Pearson said in a news release. "We just talked to former members of Dodd's staff. If it is a crime to seek evidence documenting charges of corruption against a U.S. Senator, then the press must give up one of its important functions and Senators will remain a sacrosanct body. It's almost impossible to prove an indictable offense regarding a Senator without inside information."

To an editorial that he was seeking governmental status for the fourth estate, and that his informers should have gone to the FBI, Pearson had a ready answer. The intimacy between Senator Dodd and J. Edgar Hoover was well known to the Senator's staff, he pointed out. One of Boyd's functions was to write Dodd's glowing speeches about the FBI Director. Everybody in the office was aware that the FBI provided drivers for Dodd on his trips and agents to run his errands.

As the ex-employees who had talked, Boyd, Mrs. Carpenter and Miss Golden were questioned by FBI agents. They told what they had done without implicating office manager O'Hare. When news of their treachery circulated on Capitol Hill, sympathy for Dodd burgeoned. Legislators guilty in one degree or another of practices attributed to Dodd wondered whether they could rely on the absolute loyalty of their own staffs.

With frightened legislators added to hostile legislators added to The Club, how could Pearson get anywhere in Congress? His slight chance rested on arousing a ground swell of public indignation, yet the other Washington correspondents and the wire services showed no hurry in climbing on board another "Merry-Go-Round" exclusive. The Washington *Post*, the column's local outlet, had omitted the opening Klein column and several later ones. When the national desk of the *New York Times* queried its Washington Bureau on its failure to pick up the exposé, the bureau, which prized its autonomy, replied that it had little use for Pearson and Anderson and none for a story based on stolen documents.

Washington columnist William S. White finally broke the ice at the *New York Times* with a pro-Dodd story. Pearson noted acidly that White's daughter Lucia and one of her college classmates had previously held summer jobs in Dodd's office. He named and flatly contradicted the anonymous writer of a pro-Dodd story in *Newsweek*, the first magazine to touch the subject. Despite Pearson's deliberate provocation, he was not attracting as much publicity as a newly organized National Committee for Justice for Dodd, consisting of businessmen with obligations to the Senator.

Then it happened: Drew and Luvie Pearson were listed among the guests at a White House dinner for Ludwig Erhard, the visiting German Chancellor. Senator Dodd, the Senate Foreign Relations Committee specialist in German problems, was not on the guest list! That tipped off Dodd and Washington insiders generally where the President stood.

A letter from Jack Anderson addressed to somebody in Hartford and containing Dodd material for checking was removed from the mail collection sack in the lobby of Anderson's building, the material inside was inspected and the letter returned to the sack, according to a report by Postmaster General Lawrence O'Brien, implying that the FBI was responsible. O'Brien's report about this violation of the sanctity of the mails had gone directly to President Johnson. Pearson publicly challenged the FBI to find out how he had learned about O'Brien's complaint to the President. The FBI did not accept the challenge.

Senator Dodd had no alternative but to continue fighting. His investigators were already digging deeply for dirt on Pearson. One was James A. Lynch, of Wantagh, New York, a burly, red-haired private detective in his late forties. Lynch told employees in the Senator's office that he had rummaged through Anderson's wastepaper baskets. Pearson promptly accused Lynch of impersonating an FBI agent. Anderson rummaged through J. Edgar Hoover's *garbage* can and reported to the column the clues to the FBI Director's eating and other habits that he discovered there.

Morris A. Bealle went on Dodd's behalf to Reidsville, North Carolina, where Pearson had been arrested at the age of sixteen on a charge of indecent exposure. Investigators for the House Un-American Activities Committee and Senator Joe McCarthy had previously visited Reidsville. Neither the committee nor McCarthy ever made any public use of the incident, but McCarthy's private, socially circulated interpretation of the arrest may have played a role in countercharges emanating from Las Vegas about the Senator's alleged sexual fondness for boys, particularly elevator boys.

Pearson did not expect Dodd to stoop that low, but as a precaution he referred disarmingly to the matter in his March 30, 1966, column:

BATH IN NORTH CAROLINA

The other day I got a phone call from friends in Reidsville, N.C., that an agent friendly to Sen. Dodd had called to gumshoe on a bathing incident in 1915 when I was arrested at 2 A.M. for taking a sponge bath near the Southern Railway yards after working all night striking a Chautauqua tent.

It is an incident I have written about several times and has become quite a joke in North Carolina. I was even invited back to Reidsville by the Chamber of Commerce to celebrate the occasion.

Nevertheless, C. L. Oliver, publisher of the Reidsville Review, was cross-examined by a friend of Sen. Dodd's as to where he could get a 1915 newspaper describing the incident. Unfortunately, it had been destroyed in a fire a long time ago. Mr. Oliver assured the Dodd agent, however, that the newspaper, if available, would clearly show I was acquitted and that there was nothing sinister about the arrest and trial.

4

Pearson summoned his informants to a conference at his office. Despite indications of benevolent neutrality on the part of the President and a recent flurry of public interest over a columnar revelation that four-fifths of $500,000 raised for Dodd's political campaign in 1964 had been expended for things like a Florida vacation, a thirtieth wedding anniversary, a wedding for the Senator's daughter Martha and improvements to his house, the exposé seemed to be fading. Subscribers were complaining over a diet of too much Dodd, Pearson conceded.

His informants were unemployed and discouraged. They had been taking a steady beating in the news media. Nobody wanted to hear their story. During the three months since the first Klein column appeared only two of the hundreds of correspondents of various kinds in Washington had bothered to interview them.

Boyd, who had been earning $23,000 a year with Dodd, found lesser employment with the House Public Service Committee, only to be dropped abruptly as a result of a phone call to the committee chairman from Speaker McCormack. Mrs. Carpenter secured a job with the law firm of Arnold & Porter after leaving, but she was discharged when Senator Dodd complained. Miss Golden lost her secretarial spot with a judge as a result of similar pressure. All three were blacklisted throughout Washington.

Hoping to keep the "crusade" alive, Boyd pointed out that a lot of information about Dodd had not yet been tapped. One of the others mentioned several conflicts of interest which would make colorful reading. A more personal approach might stir the public, chimed in the third. Pearson smiled. It might not make much sense, he said, but they probably had to see it through. The next few hours were devoted to a painstaking consideration of tactics for a broadened campaign against the Senator.

Exasperated by fresh outbursts in the "Washington Merry-Go-Round," Dodd made two mistakes: He filed a $5-million libel suit against Pearson and Anderson and he demanded that the Senate Ethics Committee make a joint investigation of Pearson and himself. The committee had no jurisdiction over Pearson, but it agreed reluctantly to take a look at Dodd's proffered records.

Pearson welcomed the lawsuit. It provided an opportunity for him to document under judicial auspices complicated maneuvers of the Senator at which he had hinted in print. Dodd's lawyers soon decided that full disclosure was not in their interest. They refused to allow reporters to cover pretrial sessions. They dropped a number of counts, reducing the amount of damages sought to $2 million. Finally, they shelved libel entirely in favor of a desperate $1-million invasion-of-privacy action.

Journalistic campaigns used to stop dead upon the filing of a libel suit lest continuation be interpreted as malice and thereby multiply damages. Westbrook Pegler had taught Pearson to risk uninterrupted attack as a last-ditch measure. Dodd's lawyers tried to punish Pearson for this as a form of contempt of court. That did not succeed. They then sued for access to Pearson's files on the ground that he had stolen a look at those of the Senator. John Donovan knocked the case out in the U.S. Supreme Court.

Dodd did not live up to his promise to supply records. The Senate Ethics Committee was forced to initiate its own investigation before holding hearings. Since it proceeded slowly, with interruptions, a full year was required to reach the conclusion that Dodd had done at least one thing of which the public disapproved: He had converted to his personal use considerable sums contributed by gullible citizens to help him win elections.

Money flows so easily, invisibly, from one pocket to another in the same pair of pants. Most politicians dip into campaign funds to some extent for other purposes, when it is possible and not too conspicuous. They do not consider this practice reprehensible. Dodd had been a "shadow Senator" who performed unethical chores for business interests. Pearson was probably justified in accusing him of a half-dozen criminal acts, but the Justice Department had left the verdict in the hands of the Senate Ethics Committee, and the members of that committee, heeding their mail, did their minimal duty.

After nine days of debate, the U.S. Senate voted 92 to 5 on June 23, 1967, to censure Senator Thomas J. Dodd for using campaign and testimonial funds "for his personal benefit." He was sixty years old. Only five other Senators had been similarly condemned by their colleagues during the history of the upper chamber. The vote did not prevent Dodd from serving out the remainder of his term, but it stripped him of his dignity and led inexorably to defeat when he sought re-election in 1970, and to illness and death the following year.

A great deal could be written about the culminating months of controversy in the Dodd case which would not contribute appreciably to this account. Pearson's rubbing of conservative noses in the mud after he had the enemy on the run might be mentioned. He printed a private letter from Frances Knight to J. Edgar Hoover, dated March 21, 1966, in which she discussed their arrangements for State Department surveillance abroad of H. Stuart Hughes, a distinguished Harvard professor and former candidate for the U.S. Senate, because he had opposed President Johnson's policy on Vietnam. Secretary Rusk was "looking for suitable pretexts to put an end" to this kind of spying, the letter warned, adding:

> My own position in the department is such that I do not wish to commit too many details to paper for reasons that will be obvious to you. But I would willingly elaborate them for you personally if you wish to pursue the matter as I have no doubt you will. Forgive me if I sound alarmist but I am quite certain that a principle of vital importance is at stake. . . .

Despite the letter's internal evidence of authenticity, Miss Knight denied writing it. The FBI chief denied receiving it. Since the disclosure harmed Miss Knight by implying disloyalty and negotiation behind the back of the Secretary of State, she might well have sued for libel, but she did not do so. Pearson followed up this exclusive with another: an account of Hoover's surreptitious letters to key Congressmen opposing President Johnson's consular treaty with the Soviet Union on the ground that it would facilitate Russian spying.

Pearson told an embarrassing story about Jay Sourwine, counsel of the Internal Security Subcommittee. Sourwine persuaded Dodd to endorse a $2,500 check so Sourwine could cash it immediately. The check bounced. According to Pearson, Sourwine had to work out the money by ghost-writing a book on Dodd.

In a speech on the Senate floor on June 13, 1968, almost two and a half years after the initial Klein column, Senator Dodd made his first personal rejoinder. Starting with a reference to "the Rasputin of our Society," the inflamed Senator continued: "Drew Pearson is a liar. He is a monster. Those associated with him are thieves, liars and monsters. . . . His business is lying. He is a devil. It appalled me that he was honored as a Big Brother: a molester of children who had the records of his arrest destroyed. What is his strange power in this government?"

When a United Press reporter asked about the child-molesting charge, Pearson explained that he had been arrested as a boy at 4 A.M.—not 2 A.M. this time—for taking a bath in public. The judge, in acquitting him, had pointed out that the charge of "indecent exposure of person was so broad that it could be misunderstood by my future enemies." How did the judge know that the boy would have such persistent future enemies?

Pearson gave the dates of four columns in which he had previously discussed Reidsville, omitting the most recent, bland one of March 30, 1966. He mentioned again the testimonial dinner in Reidsville in his honor. That had been hurriedly arranged in 1948 to counter a reference to the incident by a North Carolina Congressman whom he had hounded for absenteeism following the death of his wife.

The fuse lit by Dodd continued to sputter. The Senator's comment itself was privileged. Suing the newspapers which carried the painfully impartial UP story would have advertised the libel. Pearson thought of *Parade*, a syndicated and widely circulated Sunday magazine of which Jack Anderson was Washington editor. The magazine included a section on people in the news under a blurb reading: "Want the facts? Want to spike rumors? Want to learn the truth about prominent personalities. Write . . ."

Pearson telephoned Lloyd Shearer, a friend who edited this section. Shearer was willing to spike a rumor. He did so by planting a question in *Parade* from an imaginary reader. The answer (supplied by Pearson) went as follows:

> Drew Pearson is not a child molester. In 1915 he was a member of a Swarthmore College Chautauqua tent crew working his way through college. In Reidsville, N.C., he had just finished taking down a large tent. It was 3 A.M. He was dirty, sweaty and along with other members of the crew, in need of a washup. The crew found a spigot alongside the Southern Railway tracks, took a towel, undressed and washed. A Negro citizen reported their semi-nudity. The boys were arrested as the sun was coming up. . . . A Reidsville attorney, Powell Glidewell, was appointed to defend them. Pearson and the others were quickly acquitted.

In a display of journalistic initiative, *Parade* had secured an affidavit, which it printed, from the clerk of the Reidsville Records Court. The date of the trial was given as July 9, 1914—not 1915. In the summer of 1914, Pearson was sixteen, with a year to go in an exclusive and expensive preparatory school. He was not working his way through college.

There were other discrepancies. The complainant was a white woman, not "a Negro citizen." Only Pearson and a local black boy of about the same age were arrested, not a crew of several boys of unremarked color. It was conceivable that the capering of two nude youngsters, one black and one white, in a Southern town in the middle of the night might have led to the arrest. However, when Morris Bealle first went to Reidsville for Senator Joe McCarthy, he reported that Judge I. R. Humphreys explained in an interview, "with a twinkle in his eye," that the boys were acquitted "because a nigger was involved; that made it trivial."

Bealle, whose venom against Pearson made him an unreliable witness, claimed in print that during his first visit to Reidsville he had learned from "another columnist," unnamed, that Pearson and an aide had been "moseying around" there and in Raleigh, the state capital, in an effort to conceal a "revolting situation." Inspection of the bound volumes of the local newspaper in

Raleigh, he said, showed that the issues of July 7 and 10, 1914, had been torn out.

In the second decade of the century, Chautauqua classed as a big event in a small town. It was sponsored by Baptist deacons, bankers, Main Street merchants and the intellectual élite. When the trial of Pearson and his local companion, D. C. Wideman, was held, Judge Ben Lindsey, the leading speaker of the Chautauqua troupe, sat on the bench alongside Judge Humphreys.

Bealle made a legitimate point in suggesting that the local bigwigs would have wanted to hush up a scandal—if one existed. He went overboard in implying a sexual angle to the incident. Interviewed closely in 1971 about his most recent visit to Reidsville for Dodd, he mentioned that editor Oliver of the local newspaper said "there was no moral turpitude involved."

"I hadn't said there was," declared Bealle.

Powell J. Glidewell, Jr., son of Pearson's lawyer at the trial, told Bealle "heatedly" that there was "no homosexual charge involved." Once again Bealle said: "I hadn't said there was."

The reasonable conclusion is that Drew took an innocent bath in the early hours of the morning and got tangled in his own later explanations. Dodd did not follow up his charge or produce any documentation. Interest in the controversy subsided. All it really demonstrated was that neither Dodd nor Pearson told the full truth about Pearson.

CHAPTER XVI

Final Crusades

Back around 1960 Pearson had begun to talk about establishing a library—like the Truman Library in Independence, Missouri, and other presidential libraries—as a repository for his personal and professional records. The sycophants who converged daily on his luncheon table at the Cosmos Club voiced their enthusiastic approval. The only question was where it should be located.

Over the years, in addition to his original 285-acre Potomac farm, Pearson had acquired two other farms in the same neighborhood: the 160 acres across River Road to the north, known as the Travilah farm; and another of more than 400 acres near Poolesville. Together these three farms were reportedly worth at least $2.5 million. The Poolesville farm had a run-down but noble colonial mansion which could be restored as the Pearson Memorial Library, it was suggested. This having been agreed upon, more than $50,000 was collected for the library in the name of the Foundation for the Expanding Freedoms, which was set up with several of Pearson's friends as trustees.

Pearson soon cooled on the idea of a rural cache for his memorabilia. He grumbled that the library would cost too much to set up and maintain. Actually, he wanted to reserve any disposition of the Poolesville farm until he could work out an equitable distribution of property between his wife and daughter. That would not be easy.

John Donovan urged that the intention of the foundation be carried out or the money returned to the donors. Pearson stalled. A Poolesville farm hand was already on the foundation payroll as caretaker of the mansion. The personal secretary who succeeded Margaret Laughrun was being paid by the foundation for several hours of work each week on Pearson biographical records. Pearson, in fact, never did turn over the Poolesville mansion to the Foundation for the Expanding Freedoms, which gradually dwindled into a tax shelter.

Pearson continued to ponder his future place in history. In 1963 he encouraged the writer of a biography of Westbrook Pegler to try one of himself. Nobody told the truth about him any more, he complained; his friends swung as wide of the mark as his enemies; readers viewed him in extreme terms as a crusader-in-shining-armor or a monster-in-disguise. What he wanted, said Pearson, was a balanced account which would credit his achievements without concealing the warts on his face.

He did not mean it any more than the first novelist who begs for a fair review in hope of receiving a few kind words. He acknowledged no real warts; he disapproved the use of any sources of information except himself; he became immediately suspicious over inquiry into suppressed aspects of his earlier scramble for position; he mislaid family memos which he had offered to deliver; and he referred questions about his controversies to close-mouthed trial attorneys. After two years of increasingly desultory effort, the writer—still an admirer of Drew Pearson—decided to forget the idea of an impartial biography for the time being.

Pearson had sound reasons for reticence. He depended on exposés to sell the column, yet they invariably created enemies. People expected him to be rough in print and on the air. "If you've made your name as the Boris Karloff of journalism, you can't come on like Marlon Brando," he said defensively. He often felt uneasy over the distant lidless scrutiny of those whom he could never convert and who were resolved to despise and hate him. He had no intention of giving them any fresh ammunition.

From the ultraright propaganda sheets which drifted sooner or later into his office, Pearson knew what his hidden enemies were saying. He also knew how he would reply if it were politic to do so. They said he hunted a fortune in marrying his first wife (whom he loved), that he stole his second wife from his best friend (though she came to him for refuge), that he cheated his daughter out of a valuable farm (as if he would ever do anything to hurt Ellen) and that he deprived his partner of a half-share of the column (after Bob deserted to fight in another war overseas).

Those and other libels were included in an abusive pamphlet, *All American LOUSE,* written carelessly and published obscurely by Morris Bealle in 1965. Pearson did not sue over this tirade. Similarly, he had not sued when Gerald L. K. Smith, the professional anti-Semite, issued a tract called *Drew Pearson, BLACK-MAILER.* Such things were poorly circulated. They were better ignored.

Out of a feeling that his public posture could stand a little refurbishing, Pearson did import Herman Klurfeld from New York. This former ghost writer for Walter Winchell was assigned a second-floor room at the office. Pearson made suggestions from time to time and Mrs. Kay Raley, the personal secretary specializing in Pearson biographical data, was assigned to help on newsbeats like the Gouzenko case and public-spirited gestures like the Friendship Train and the Pearson drives to collect food for needy blacks down South and to rebuild churches which had been bombed out by bigots.

Pearson himself displayed more and more interest in the image he would leave behind. He and Mrs. Raley pored regularly over the incredible detail of the office files. He had saved everything, even to carbons of love letters hurriedly typed at airports. Occasionally he stumbled on a tidbit for Klurfeld or one which he thought should be shared with the girls in the workroom.

Calling several secretaries into his study, he might read an old memo about how he, Luvie and their detectives had lurked for hours in bushes alongside a lonely country road on the island of Sark until Tyler Abell came by with his nurse and how Tyler, separated for months from his mother, looked up coolly and said, "Hello, Mommy, where you been?" Sometimes a group reading would be interrupted when he came on a reference to Cissy Patterson, Michael MacWhite or somebody else which he considered indiscreet.

Multimillionaire Pearson worried chiefly over the disposition of his property. He had never gotten around to drawing up a will with the aid of a lawyer, he told Mrs. Raley somewhat sheepishly, because he could not resolve the family conflicts. He asked Tyler in 1967 to suggest how to provide for Ellen. As a rival heir, Tyler quite properly sidestepped the request. Suspecting that whatever he did would turn out to be wrong, Pearson deferred action in the hope that something, somehow, would bring the family together.

He talked about retiring. He might fire his whole staff, he said, and produce only three columns a week or drop the column entirely, as well as his other activities, in favor of something more limited and challenging, like serving in a diplomatic post abroad or writing his biography. Staff members scoffed; they had heard such talk before. The "Washington Merry-Go-Round" would not let him retire, jeered one young assistant, who played with the notion that Pearson had become the slave rather than the master of his column. The columnist was deeper in politics than any Washington politician, he pointed out. Who ever heard of a politician voluntarily relinquishing his power base?

As he approached his seventieth birthday, which fell on December 13, 1967, Pearson went in for gestures to improve his appeal to posterity. He had spent most of the first three months of that year visiting South American countries and talking with their Presidents and chief diplomatic officials about electing Galo Plaza as the new Secretary General of the Organization of American States. In between trips he lobbied discreetly for Plaza at the State Department.

Pearson had been consistently critical of José Mora, the retiring OAS Secretary General. He blamed Mora particularly for standing by while U.S. Marines marched into the Dominican Republic in 1965, breaking a thirty-eight-year record of military noninterference in the domestic affairs of weaker nations in the Western Hemisphere. He believed that the OAS could not properly stimulate the economies or political processes of the countries south of the border unless it came into more creative hands.

Galo Plaza, a competent diplomat from Ecuador whom Pearson had known and admired since they were playboys together in Washington during the late 1920s, was duly elected. The "Washington Merry-Go-Round" took formal credit for a victory appraised as historic. Pearson conveniently forgot that Plaza could not have been chosen without U.S. support and that he remained at the mercy of the State Department. Within a year various countries were agitating for a reduction in the Secretary General's term of office from ten to five years. In 1970 Jack Anderson, running the column as Pearson's successor, noted that Plaza had retained many of Mora's cronies and that OAS back-scratching and bungling were proceeding as usual, with U.S. taxpayers paying the bills.

In the fall of 1967 Pearson revealed exclusively that a "homosexual ring had been operating" in the office of Governor Ronald Reagan of California. Two members of the Governor's staff, it seemed, had engaged in "gay orgies" in a cabin near Lake Tahoe. Governor Reagan had waited six months after he was told about the situation and had reluctantly discharged the homosexuals, Pearson claimed, only when they came under suspicion of being moderate in their politics.

During a hectic, highly emotional twenty-minute news conference in his office, Governor Reagan called the story "scurrilous and ridiculous." Asked whether there had been an investigation of homosexual behavior and if so whether anybody had been dropped from the staff, the Governor replied earnestly: "I just don't know what you are talking about."

Though Reagan applied the routine epithets of "liar" and "S.O.B." to Pearson, national excitement over the story built up in newspapers, news magazines, radio and TV. Challenging the Governor to back up his denials with a libel suit, Pearson invaded the West Coast. From Sacramento he fired an open telegram at Reagan warning that he would soon appear in San Francisco "to confront you with the record."

No confrontation took place. Reagan was vulnerable. The previous month he had gone on a Governors' Conference junket to the Virgin Islands. During the trip on the S.S. *Independence* his press secretary, Lyn Nofziger, had talked confidentially to several reporters in an apparent effort to discredit a former staff member who still presumed to speak for the Governor.

Reporters who had been on the *Independence* surfaced in various papers with versions of what Nofziger said. Governor Reagan adjusted his toga. He had let a couple of supposed homosexuals go, he conceded, but he had denied the "Merry-Go-Round" account "because I refuse to participate in trying to destroy human beings with no factual evidence."

On November 20, 1967, Pearson dictated a memo to Herman Klurfeld to add the Reagan exposé to his list of "recent stories which molded history." According to the memo, the incident had "pretty well knocked Reagan out of the box as a Republican candidate for President and as an attempt by the far right to take over the Republican party and the United States." There were several flaws in the memo. The exposé did not mold history. Reagan was not knocked politically out of the box, and he was too opportunistic a man to remain classified for long among the frustrated and disturbed radicals of the extreme right.

2

Half a century ago, in a foreword to *Come Hither,* an unexcelled collection of poems for the young of all ages, Walter De La Mare mentioned a nursery rhyme:

> "How many miles to Babylon?"
> "Three score and ten."
> "Can I get there by candle-light?"
> "Ay, and back again."

To illustrate the childish jingle, the poet drew a picture not of Babylon or a traveler or a candle but of a stone tomb.

Nowadays, of course, folks live longer than they used to. For many the Biblical allotment of years is a milestone rather than a tomb. As Drew Pearson liked to point out, the Soviet Union and Red China accord high ceremonial honors to prominent citizens who reach seventy. Even in the United States, an ordinary new septuagenarian still earning a living is entitled, even expected, to rejoice and reminisce in company with relatives and friends.

The "Washington Merry-Go-Round" published an annual list of Old Codgers in Congress. These were conservative Senators and

Representatives who by virtue of seniority of service—"the senility system," Pearson called it—had acquired important committee chairmanships. The Old Codgers, rated No. 1, No. 2 and so on in descending degree of political obnoxiousness, were held up to the public primarily as figures of fun. Legislative veterans considered progressive by Pearson—Senator Theodore Green of Rhode Island, for example, who played badminton out at the Potomac farm well into his eighties, or Senator Carl Hayden of Arizona, who lived to be ninety—did not qualify as Old Codgers. They received individual encomiums in the column.

Though Pearson urged various over-seventy opponents to retire for reasons of age, he no longer had any intention of quitting the fray. Conscious of his satisfaction over his continued effectiveness, Luvie Pearson collected some of his admirers to plan a surprise party for December 13, 1967. The ground-floor quarters of the Federal City Club at the Sheraton-Carlton Hotel were chosen as the site. A borrowed carrousel horse, placed in the center of the adjoining outdoor garden, with multicolored streamers leading to its four corners, helped to assure a festive atmosphere.

Invitations went to the two hundred most important Washingtonians who were not hostile to the birthday guest. Some relatives and staff people were also invited. Everybody who could come attended, including Joe Borkin, Ernest Cuneo, Art Buchwald, Herblock, Mrs. Katharine Graham, Mrs. Arthur Goldberg, Thurman Arnold, Warren Magnuson, Wayne Morse, Averell Harriman, Walter Lippmann, Walter Washington and Earl Warren. This was a party, chortled Joe Borkin, like the costume ball given in New York by Truman Capote, where not to be invited was to be branded a nobody! The guest of honor, lavishly praised, made a graceful and suitably modest response.

News about the party led to a spate of interviews. Though the intimacy of questions-and-answers offended Pearson's secretive nature, he felt obliged to honor requests from friendly correspondents. He tried to reduce the talk to anecdotes about Presidents he had known—President Johnson's precautions against the theft of White House cutlery, for example—but he was usually cornered in two areas: his relationship with the President and his attitude toward controversy.

Pearson denied being implacable or callous in his public quarrels. He cited the case of John Maragon. When General Harry Vaughan's favorite wheeler-dealer finished a sojourn in jail for perjury resulting from revelations in the "Washington Merry-Go-Round," nobody in Washington would give him a job. Finally, Maragon came to Pearson, who, believing in rehabilitation through punishment and penitence, found him a small post with one of the House committees.

Pearson had written columnar obituaries about such persistent critics as Senator Millard Tydings, Cissy Patterson and Senator Joe McCarthy. He cited these appraisals as evidence of his ultimate fairness without realizing how strongly his stress on Tydings' incurable shingles, Mrs. Patterson's drug-abetted disintegration and Joe McCarthy's alcoholism suggested that they, like Maragon, had paid the proper penalty for their offenses against an unspecified Quaker columnist.

Inevitably, the Forrestal case came up. In the course of their feud Pearson had blamed the Defense Secretary for running away in panic while four armed men despoiled his wife of her jewels and money. The holdup occurred as Mrs. Forrestal was being escorted home from a party by another man in the early hours of the morning. From one of his investigators, who spent months digging into various aspects of Forrestal's life, Pearson knew that Forrestal had not been at the scene of the robbery. He made and repeated the charge anyway.

To a man responsible for the safety of his country, a false accusation of personal cowardice came as a terrible blow. Instead of suing, Forrestal brooded over his injury. His meteoric rise from a home on the wrong side of the railroad tracks to the presidency of a Wall Street investment firm with world-wide interests, and then step by step up the governmental ladder, had created great internal stresses. He was plagued by long-standing domestic, economic and political problems. After a noticeable two-or-three-year period of nervous deterioration he resigned—or was forced by President Truman to resign—from government service.

Some months later, when Forrestal fell to his death, Pearson did not consider himself a murderer, but there were "awful moments," he told fellow correspondent Patrick Anderson during an interview, when he "woke up in the middle of the night fighting an almost paralyzing urge to join Forrestal."

In discussing Lyndon Johnson, Pearson labored under a handicap. He justified his truckling to the manipulative man in the White House on the ground that it enabled him to exert a little influence here and there in desired directions. He could not present proof of this to an interviewer without spoiling his presidential relationship. The best he could do was to concede minor differences between them on such subjects as Tyler Abell and the President's daughters.

During a visit to the Johnson ranch on the bank of the Pedernales in mid-1967 Pearson wrote a cloyingly sweet column about Luci and her baby. He reported the views of Lady Bird on the trials and rewards of grandmotherhood and ended with a denial of another correspondent's exclusive on the use of government labor to build Luci's nursery in Austin, Texas.

On the other hand, Pearson legmen foraged relentlessly within the Pentagon and the State Department for material to puncture the half-truths about the Vietnam war which were being fed to the public. The column uncovered the hidden struggle between administration hawks and doves, anticipating by years many of the revelations of the Pentagon Papers.

William P. Bundy, a hawkish Assistant Secretary of State, complained publicly at one point that Luvie told her husband confidential things he (Bundy) had blurted out when he was sitting next to her at a dinner party. Through the column, Luvie replied that she recalled Bundy's "style of dancing," but nothing he ever said. As Pearson's representative, she took his eldest grandson, Drew Pearson Arnold, a handsome six-foot-three red-haired undergraduate at George Washington University, to New York to march with her in a special contingent organized by Cyrus Eaton, the pro-Soviet Cleveland industrialist, in the first huge demonstration combining peace and civil rights groups.

Periodically, Pearson described Johnson's growing disillusionment over the struggle in Indochina. As early as 1966, long before anybody else, he predicted that the Vietnam war might preclude the President's running for re-election. However, he could not steel himself against LBJ's flattery or a White House exclusive. In 1967 he printed an account based on "a confidential digest kept by one of the participants"—meaning the President—of a secret conference on Guam between President Johnson and President Nguyen Van Thieu of South Vietnam. Without comment he relayed to the public a whole new set of unduly optimistic statistics about pacification of the South Vietnam countryside, adding: "The Vietnamese leaders brought to the Guam meeting a copy of their new constitution which had just been approved by the directorate. After President Johnson fondled a red-bound copy of the historic document, he mused happily: 'I looked at it just as proudly as I looked at Lynda, my first baby.'" Not until a later column did Pearson note that the South Vietnam countryside was as turbulent as ever and that a fair election was impossible even with a new constitution. As he knew better than anybody else, his record on Johnson was sadly mixed.

To raise money for the Washington Big Brothers, of which he had been president since 1957, Pearson agreed to a tardy additional birthday celebration at the Shoreham Hotel on May 3, 1968. More than fourteen hundred persons paid $50 each for the privilege of attending this testimonial affair.

Pearson persuaded his friend Frank Sinatra to bring up his show from the Hotel Fontainebleau in Miami Beach as free entertainment. Paying off Sinatra in publicity, Pearson noted in the column that this would be Frankie's first appearance in Washington since he sang at John F. Kennedy's inaugural in 1961. Sinatra had served as chief minstrel in Camelot until Bobby Kennedy let his brother look at some FBI reports on Sinatra's underworld connections. Then the singer was barred from the White House. Naturally, Pearson did not print this sordid detail.

President Johnson shied away from the Shoreham affair as soon as he heard about Sinatra's projected role. He did not intend to play second fiddle at another Kennedy inaugural. Moreover, he had been shaken by the temporary romance between Lynda Bird and George Hamilton, whom he vaguely associated with Sinatra and his Rat Pack. The President did suggest to Vice President Humphrey, who was attending the Big Brother celebration, that he "bring Drew around to the White House after the party."

Remembering Sinatra's exile from the White House, Pearson

decided to broaden the invitation to include the singer. The three men arrived at the Lincoln bedroom in the White House well past midnight. Lady Bird was already under the covers in the big four-poster Lincoln bed with its overhanging canopy. The President, bare above pajama bottoms, was lying on a table being pounded by a masseur.

After a quick glance, Johnson turned his head away from his visitors without saying anything. Humphrey's light conversation with Lady Bird gradually evaporated. The President finally threw a few words of greeting at Humphrey and Pearson, ignoring Sinatra, who had gone over to the famous mantelpiece, on which, Pearson had reported in the column, Jacqueline Kennedy had carved a strange record of her husband's tenancy.

President Johnson jumped off the rubbing table, grabbed an old souvenir booklet about the White House dating back to the Kennedy administration and thrust it at Sinatra. "I don't suppose you read," the President said, with an edge on his Texas drawl, "but this has lots of pictures." The pictures included Rat Pack members Eddie Fisher and Dean Martin.

"Here's something else," Johnson said, even more offensively, handing Sinatra a presidential trinket for women visitors, a lipstick with the White House seal on it. "It's a conversation piece," he said, glaring down at the uninvited guest. "It'll make a big man of you with your women."

Stiffening under the patter of insult, Sinatra turned and walked from the room without a word. Pearson and Humphrey followed after hurried farewells. Next day Pearson told Jack Anderson about the bedroom confrontation. Jack relayed the story to one or two members of the staff, who wondered whether Pearson might not have been demonstrating in his own way that even this particular President of the United States did not own him.

3

Throughout the 1960s Pearson's health had stood up pretty well. He continued to drive to the edge of his physical strength. During one of his increasingly rare visits to his sister Barbara, Mrs. Gordon Lange, dean of women at Swarthmore College, he dropped into a comfortable armchair in the living room after a heavy dinner. Despite the presence of company, his eyes closed and his chin fell to his chest.

A local professor of political science who often performed consultant chores in Washington had been brought in to meet the distinguished visitor. Lowering his voice so as not to disturb Pearson, the professor told a story of bureaucratic bungling in the national capital. To his surprise, the anecdote appeared word for word four days later in the "Washington Merry-Go-Round."

In addition to biennial trips to Israel and the Soviet Union, Pearson managed irregular jumps to other hot spots around the globe. He traveled through various parts of the United States three or four times a year on news-gathering and lecture tours. In the fall of 1965 he went to West Africa, leaving so hurriedly that Ellen, who had agreed at the last minute to replace Luvie as his companion, missed the plane in New York and had to catch up with her father in Liberia.

Following his African trip, Pearson spent time in a Washington hospital with malaria. He had skipped the usual precautions against the dapple-winged anopheles. "The boss thought he was too big a man to be bitten by a mosquito," joked one of his assistants.

Though Marian Canty and Luvie guarded news of any slight Pearson ailment like a state secret, word spread among the staff in 1967 that he had been operated on for ileitis. He reappeared in the office looking reasonably fit. His appearance had not greatly changed in recent years. His mustache, by now snowy white, was more overgroomed than ever. He had color in his cheeks, not the mauve tones of a heavy drinker—he was by now virtually a teetotaler—but a rosy, at times almost purplish flush which he attributed to outdoor work at the farm.

By the time he reached seventy, Pearson was reconciled to remaining a journalist. He still spaded his biographical ground at intervals, but he had rejected an offer from Arthur Goldberg to become Assistant to the U.S. Ambassador to the United Nations. He conjured up new projects in his own field.

Having done well with stray TV documentaries on such subjects as Israel and the Quakers, Pearson decided to produce a daily

TV political documentary out of Washington. Bill Neel, his journalistic handyman, was assigned to explore the idea. Pearson must be crazy, the experts said; no production manager on earth could handle the seven separate full TV crews which would be required. One agency said a single TV documentary a month might be feasible. Pearson rejected the idea out of hand. He disliked making small plans.

Herman Klurfeld, having completed the writing of *Behind the Lines*, his eulogy of master-journalist Pearson, received a new assignment. Pearson wanted to establish a confidential weekly newsletter resembling *Personal from Pearson* but devoted to Wall Street instead of politics. Klurfeld, who had considerable knowledge of the stock market, would ghost the newsletter in New York and Pearson would edit and sign it in Washington, according to the plan. Klurfeld began to work out the details.

When *Behind the Lines* was published in 1968, it did not do well because of its limited approach and compulsory lack of vitality. A similar fate met a contrary exercise in propaganda, an anti-Pearson book by Frank Kluckhohn and Jay Franklin, two Washington correspondents who had swung right after retirement from the *New York Times* and who were out to avenge columnar insults in the Morris Bealle manner.

The literary sensation of the year, so far as politically oriented books went, proved to be *The Senator*, a novel by Drew Pearson. An opaque foreword expressed "gratitude to Scott Meredith, Kenneth McCormick and Gerald Green for their assistance in the preparation of this book." Meredith was Pearson's literary agent, McCormick was editor-in-chief of Doubleday & Company, the publisher, and Gerald Green was the ghost. According to a later statement by McCormick, Green wrote most of the novel.

Public interest was undoubtedly whetted by Pearson's flaying of Senator Dodd. Pearson had opened his political files to Green. Even so, the book would not have hit the best-seller list without the dramatic writing of Green, who had several excellent novels to his credit. When word of Green's role reached the press and Pearson was asked to comment, he said stiffly that he had "given some credit to Green" and that he intended to give more. At no time did Green object: he had shared a $150,000 advance on *The*

Senator, and he had already been assigned to work on a successor
to be called "The President."

Another ghostly tour de force, *The Case Against Congress,* appeared in 1968. Jack Anderson had contracted to write this non-
fiction book, but, being busy, he turned the chore over to sprites
named William Haddad and George Clifford. At the last minute
Pearson wrote the concluding chapter and agreed to be listed as
author, with Anderson as co-author, to boost sales.

When *The Case Against Congress* also landed on the best-seller
list, Pearson joked about his magic touch on the typewriter keys.
Since he had already been involved with radio, TV and movies,
all he needed to conquer the literary world, he said, was a successful play on Broadway.

4

Like fire alarm bells, presidential election years excited Pearson
politically. Nineteen sixty-eight was no exception. He began the
year on January 5 by printing in the "Washington Merry-Go-
Round" sensational excerpts from secret tapes made five years
earlier during an investigation of Bobby Baker. The FBI had
bugged the suite of one of Baker's friends, a gambler named Fred
Black, at the Sheraton-Carlton Hotel. The surveillance had been
authorized by Attorney General Robert F. Kennedy, Pearson
wrote, in hope of discrediting another friend of Baker, Lyndon
Johnson, then Vice President, and preventing him from running
with President John Kennedy on the 1964 Democratic national
ticket.

Bobby Kennedy, already in hot water with President Johnson
for making disrespectful noises as a possible presidential contender
in 1968, phoned Pearson in acute distress to deny that he had
authorized the Black bug, or even knew about it, in 1963. Pearson
printed the denial along with word that President Johnson had
been assured by FBI Director Hoover that the tap order came from
Kennedy. The former Attorney General entered another denial;
he had been Hoover's official superior five years ago and the President might hold him responsible, he said, but in fact the order had
not come from him.

Pearson pointed out that Black's suite—No. 438—had been next door to No. 436, the hospitality suite used by the State Department to entertain Prime Ministers, Kings and Presidents who were about to visit the White House. Over a period of months the FBI had illegally listened to some of the country's most influential friends and enemies! In the resulting public uproar, Pearson encouraged Hoover, an old enemy, and Kennedy, a newer one, to exchange mutually incriminating assertions of innocence.

One recording cited by the column came close to home. It caught Fred Black telling a friend that a man associated with the "Washington Merry-Go-Round" had visited the suite to ask if he were, as rumored, a "liaison man and bagman for the Las Vegas gamblers." Black had denied the rumor.

"Pearson could murder you," commented the friend.

"No, he couldn't murder me," replied Black.

"He could give you bad publicity!"

The gambler conceded that much. He and his friend then joined in cursing Kennedy on the theory that he had tipped off Pearson.

After exploring the subtleties of the Kennedy-Hoover and Kennedy-Johnson relationships, the "Merry-Go-Round" noted that Joseph P. Kennedy had placed a $300-million fortune at the political disposition of his several sons. "The Kennedy family conceived the idea that it could buy primaries." John F. Kennedy bought one in West Virginia in 1960 and Bobby Kennedy had just bought one in Indiana in 1968, Pearson declared.

"Big spending" made a U.S. Senator out of inexperienced, not-well-known Edward Kennedy at the age of twenty-nine, the columnist continued. When Murray B. Levine, a professor of government at Boston University, documented Ted's expenditures, Pearson revealed, the family put "terrific pressure" on large contributors to the Unitarian-Universalist Church in a vain effort to force the church-owned Beacon Press to suppress Levine's book.

In judging a presidential aspirant, Pearson theorized, liberal sentiments and achievements were less important than a tendency to crucial error. This permitted him to comb the career of Robert Kennedy, the chief immediate political threat of his family, for "mistakes." Bobby had been such an hysterical anti-Communist that when as a young man he became sick in Moscow he refused to go to a hospital and almost died as a result. He suppressed cabinet dissent prior to the Bay of Pigs fiasco. He never repudiated Senator Joe McCarthy. Finally, he was "the man who really started the eavesdropping vogue."

In the spring Pearson announced possession of a copy of an order signed by Robert F. Kennedy as Attorney General for the surveillance of Martin Luther King prior to the black leader's assassination. J. Edgar Hoover, who carried out the surveillance, was known to have subsequently furnished taps bearing on King's private life to Representative John Rooney and other Congressional chums.

Kennedy by this time was out on the presidential campaign trail with strong minority-group support. His spokesman tried to minimize the damage by associating Pearson with Hoover's alleged effort to destroy King's character. He hinted that the copy of the document, which Kennedy did not remember signing, must have come from President Johnson, who, having announced his own decision not to run again, was backing Vice President Humphrey for the nomination.

Partly, perhaps, because of the Pearson bombshell, Kennedy was defeated in the Oregon primary. He won California and in his moment of triumph was fatally shot by a fanatic Arab. Hurriedly, Pearson covered his controversial tracks with an open letter in the column to one of his grandsons praising the loyalty, idealism and courage of the lost leader.

For months Pearson had been convinced that Richard Nixon had the Republican nomination sewed up and would coast to victory in the general election, because of the Democratic factionalism created by Kennedy. The death of Kennedy did not change this opinion, but it dulled Pearson's political writing. He had lost a preferred target. He could not drum up much enthusiasm for the national conventions that summer, in which Nixon and Humphrey were predictably selected as candidates by their respective parties.

In September, following the Russian invasion of Czechoslovakia, Pearson made a tour of East Europe. Luvie having begged off once again, John Donovan came along as companion. Shelving his old anticolonialism, Pearson reached the uninspiring conclusion that those countries in the shadow of the Soviet giant more or less had to be controlled by their neighbor much as countries in the Western Hemisphere had to be dominated by the United States.

In October Jacqueline Kennedy married Aristotle Onassis. Though she was only "half-a-Kennedy"—Bobby Kennedy's phrase for Sargent Shriver when President Johnson considered Shriver as a possible running mate in 1964—Pearson made her an overnight stand-in for the sins of the whole family. His first column about her began in this fashion: "At the same time Aristotle Onassis married Jacqueline Kennedy he also purchased a Swiss bank. . . ." There was no truth, the columnist went on to assure his readers, in a report that Kennedy International Airport would be renamed Onassis International Airport.

In succeeding short essays, Pearson discussed the economic and political maneuvers of the Greek shipowner and his well-known liaison with Maria Callas, the opera singer, before returning to the international jet set of which he and his bride were members. During a visit to her sister, Princess Lee Radziwill, during the summer of 1962, Pearson recalled, Jacqueline cruised along the Italian coast on the yacht of John Agnelli, heir to the Fiat auto millions. The following summer she cruised on Onassis' yacht through Greek and Turkish waters until, Pearson revealed, the President reached her by telephone in Morocco and "ordered her home."

Day after day the column reviewed Jacqueline Kennedy's behavior in the White House. She once held a "Twist Party" there for the jet set which lasted until 4 A.M. Nothing like this had happened at the White House, Pearson wrote, "since Andrew Jackson's frontiersmen from Tennessee stomped their square dances in muddy boots on the inlaid oak floors in 1829." For the first time Pearson revealed that Mrs. Kennedy had cursed him out personally for implying that she had desecrated her own home.

Jacqueline "inherited her vituperative vocabulary," Pearson explained, "from the days when she was a photographer for the Washington Times-Herald and held her own with any cameraman." Even as a President's wife, he added, she could not restrain "a temper as explosive as the first Queen Elizabeth of England."

At one White House reception attended by Pearson, Jacqueline Kennedy displayed a diamond, emerald and ruby necklace worth at least $100,000 which she had received from the President of Pakistan. She showed displeasure at the columnist's suggestion that she sell the bauble at auction and donate the proceeds to a particularly neglected local orphanage.

"I'll give it to Luvie," exclaimed Mrs. Kennedy. Pearson shied away from letting his wife be responsible for auctioning off the necklace. In the column he urged Mrs. Kennedy to put the necklace in a museum as Eleanor Roosevelt had done with jewelry from the President of Brazil. Furious over the airing of their discussion, Jacqueline kept the necklace.

Conceding that Jacqueline Kennedy was "the nearest thing to American royalty the country has ever seen," Pearson catalogued her imperious gestures: she sent her horse halfway around the globe in an Air Force plane; she pleaded illness to avoid a Washington reception for the President of Ecuador, only to be trapped by pictures in the newspapers next day showing her water-skiing off Cape Cod; and she refused to see a large delegation of American women who were worried over the nuclear race with Russia, though Nina Khrushchev had welcomed these women and treated them to tea.

After John Kennedy's death, Pearson noted, Jacqueline permitted William Manchester to write derogatory things about the new President in White House quarters considerably set aside for her use by Lyndon Johnson. Her later row with Manchester gave Pearson more openings to link her with the Kennedy brothers, whom he kept kicking in their graves.

Bobby Kennedy was Jacqueline's "closest adviser" between the time of his brother's death and his own, Pearson wrote, as if he were linking her with a member of the Mafia. Two months after the assassination of President Kennedy, Pearson declared, Jacqueline dined at the Jockey Club with Marlon Brando and "had to be spirited out through the back door amid garbage cans to avoid photographers." The garbage cans were a nice gratuitous touch.

Aspersions which Pearson did not dare or care to ventilate in the "Washington Merry-Go-Round" appeared under his signature in *Die Zeit,* a West German newspaper, in an article calling Jacqueline "the discothèque girl who roamed the pleasure spots of the world." The article mentioned quarrels between Jacqueline and Jack Kennedy which kept them apart during their marriage for weeks and months and once for almost a year. On the night of his inaugural Kennedy misbehaved with another woman in some fashion not spelled out in the abridged version of the German article which appeared in the *National Enquirer,* a sensational American weekly.

The new President, declared the *Enquirer,* "spent the early morning hours at the house of a friendly newspaperman. Jackie was so indignant that she picked up the children and walked out. She went down to Middleburg, Va., then Florida, and it was two or three weeks before the President of the United States was able to entice her back." Since Mrs. Kennedy became "reasonably philosophic about her husband's amours" after that, the article added, "she reserved considerable freedom for herself."

Mrs. Onassis made no reply to the things Pearson wrote and said about her. She did not sue him or acknowledge his existence. Her implied disdain infuriated Pearson, yet he could hardly extradite her to face his Dodd-like barrage on matters which were largely personal, not public, in nature, and which did not seem to ordinary observers to be worth so much attention.

To carry his annoyance to a wider audience, Pearson decided on a more striking format. He sent a detailed outline of a play about Jacqueline to David Merrick, Abe Burrows and other producers. One after another they returned the manuscript with tactful comments designed to conceal their opinion that it was more venom than drama.

Insisting that the play would make his reputation as a playwright, Pearson took to reading bits of it out loud to members of the staff. On his assumption that Jacqueline had at one time been unduly friendly with a well-known Washington artist, the play depicted a romance between a President's wife and a house painter —assigned, of course, to paint the interior of the White House— who shared her interests in astrology and the Twist.

To his secretariat, Pearson's preoccupation had something odd and unhealthy about it. He had previously jabbed female enemies, from Vivien Kellems to Frances Knight, but always with a political purpose. Jacqueline Onassis, though a subject of international gossip, was not running for President. She was no longer a political figure of any kind in the United States.

When Pearson persisted in tinkering with his play to the detriment of his regular office work, staff members consulted informally on how to let him know that it was a waste of time and energy. Klurfeld was picked to bell the cat. Given the news without preamble, Pearson stared in silence at Klurfeld for a long moment. Then he put the manuscript in a desk drawer. So far as anybody in the office knew, he never referred to it again.

CHAPTER XVII

Finish at the Top

DURING THE 1968 PRESIDENTIAL CAMPAIGN Pearson printed story after story about the big clients of Richard Nixon's New York law firm—investment banks, railroads and oil companies—whose interests would be carried into the White House if the Republican candidate won. Then, several weeks before election, he received a tip that Arnold Hutschnecker, a New York psychiatrist, had treated Nixon secretly for a year following his humiliating defeat for Governor of California in 1962 and his hysterical postelection outburst against reporters.

After talking by telephone with Dr. Hutschnecker, Pearson made an uncharacteristic last-minute check with the candidate's public-relations staff. Hutschnecker revised his earlier statement and Pearson delayed until the election slid past. A week or so later he told a luncheon meeting of the National Press Club about his unwritten exclusive. The correspondents made extensive use of the tip. Hutschnecker defined himself as a "specialist in psychosomatic medicine" and stressed that he had detected no signs of mental illness on the part of the President-elect.

Pearson had been writing hostile articles about conservative presidential candidates every four years as far back as anybody could remember. Some had come so close to election day that rebuttal was difficult. One reason he did not write about Hutschnecker, Pearson told his Washington colleagues, was that he remembered the unfavorable reaction of many of his editors to a previous revelation about Nixon a few days before the 1960 election. This concerned a $205,000 loan by Howard Hughes to Donald Nixon, the then Vice President's brother, in a vain effort to save Donald's sagging chain of drive-in restaurants in Southern California which featured three-decker sandwiches called Nixonburgers.

Donald Nixon never repaid the loan. Howard Hughes gained federal favors worth millions through tax exemption for his dubious Medical Institute and changes in his airplane routes. No clear connection between the loan and the favors was established, but Noah Dietrich, executive vice president of the Hughes Tool Company, eventually told how he visited Richard Nixon before he paid the money in a circuitous fashion to Donald. Though Hughes had already approved the loan, Dietrich warned the Vice President it would become known sooner or later and cause a scandal. Nixon, he said, responded stiffly: "Mr. Dietrich, I have to put my relatives ahead of my career."

In retrospect, the reception of the Donald Nixon exposé did not seem to be a valid excuse for sidestepping the Hutschnecker story. Pearson had been distracted by his pursuit of Jacqueline Onassis and more personal matters. He conceded he had not worked as hard as usual to harpoon Nixon in 1968. Friends wondered whether he was mellowing or losing his competitive edge.

Professionally, Pearson faced a cost-price squeeze. Column expenses were going up and radio show revenues were going down. *Personal from Pearson*, once a gold mine, was barely breaking even because profits over the years had not been plowed back into promotion. A Pearson moving picture company had gone broke and the farm deficit grew every year. Were it not for lecturing and extraordinary book profits, Pearson would have been in real trouble.

A certain discouragement was perceptible in the column. The root cause of political corruption in the United States, Pearson wrote, was the unchecked rise in campaign expenditures. Back in the 1920s, he recalled, Congress used to expel members who floated

into office on a flood of cash. Despite the pious new talk about
ethics, that no longer happened. All large business contributions
to campaigns, in Pearson's opinion, were bribes. Their proliferation, he believed, was turning Congress "into an agent of the
private enterprise system."

Pearson once told a group of Capitol Hill interns that his
function was "keeping Congress honest." His syndicate used the
phrase as a slogan without much justification. Though Tom Dodd
had been demolished, more shadow Senators than ever were ply-
ing their trade. Senate Minority Leader Everett Dirksen, one of
the most flagrant, expressed amusement whenever Drew made a
new list of his legislative services to law clients.

"Drew was certainly in fine form this morning," Dirksen would
tell Capitol Hill reporters with a tolerant chuckle—and make no
further comment.

Representative L. Mendel Rivers picked up the Dirksen tactic.
When the "Washington Merry-Go-Round" carried a fresh story
about his periodic benders, he told cheering colleagues on the
House floor that he had been on the wagon but that the continuing chatter of an unnamed columnist might yet drive him to drink.

Even Luvie Pearson, thinner, wittier than ever under the strain
of controversy, took a faintly irreverent attitude toward the sacred
column. Stories about "the tobacco-chewers in Congress," she told
friends, were what really kept the "Merry-Go-Round" revolving;
Drew should write more of them, she said.

Frances Knight, J. Edgar Hoover, John McCormack and others
in the conservative bloc who had been subdued during the Dodd
exposé were back at their old stands. One of the worst was Senator
John McClellan (D–Ark.), who appeared on Pearson's Liberty
Lobby and Old Codger lists and who was generally known in the
column as "Dour John." As chairman of the Senate Investigations
Committee, McClellan had gotten his hands on potentially damaging personal information about Pearson himself.

Drew's former personal secretary, Margaret Laughrun, had re-
married in 1967. She and her new husband, Alan McSurely, a tall,
college-educated man about her own age who shared her radical
views, had gone down to Pike County, Kentucky, to agitate against
strip-mining for the Southern Conference Educational Fund. On

August 11, 1967, their house in Pikeville was raided by a group of armed men led by Sheriff Thomas Ratlif, a publicity-hungry coal-mine owner who was running on the Republican ticket for Lieutenant Governor.

The McSurelys were arrested on a charge of sedition against the Commonwealth of Kentucky. Their books, pamphlets, notes and letters were seized. Among the documents carted off was a copy of a letter Margaret wrote to Drew during the 1964 Democratic National Convention in Atlantic City to explain why she was leaving him; also a letter written to her by Drew on a Central Airlines plane in October, 1964, addressed affectionately, "Dearest Cucumber"; a later Drew-to-Margaret letter and her diary.

Margaret and Alan McSurely spent a week in jail. Meanwhile, an investigator for McClellan's committee came down from Washington to inspect the seized documents. Margaret wrote to Pearson in alarm. Two of her friends in Washington visited him to reinforce her plea for drastic action. All he ever did, she complained later, was discontinue references in the column to "Dour John."

Through a lawsuit, the McSurelys knocked out the ancient state sedition statute as unconstitutional and recovered their papers. By this time Southern staff members on Capitol Hill were quoting tidbits from copies of the letters. On the ground that the McSurelys attended a 1967 meeting of the Southern Conference Educational Fund in Nashville addressed by SNCC leader Stokely Carmichael the night before a riot there, Alan and Margaret were subpoenaed to testify before a closed hearing of the McClellan Committee in October, 1968, on subversive influences behind urban disorders in the South.

"Get off your butt and do something," read a peremptory wire from Margaret which was opened at Pearson's office during his absence. He did nothing unless it could be said that his annoyance at being placed in such a position played an unconscious part in his vendetta against Jacqueline Onassis.

On the ground that they were victims of a fishing expedition against Drew Pearson, the McSurelys refused to testify at the closed hearing. They were resubpoenaed for a larger public hearing to be held in the spring and warned that their continued defiance would result in a citation for contempt of Congress.

Bess Abell's father, the former Kentucky Governor, still subscribed to home-state newspapers. He knew about the "Dearest Cucumber" phrase of agricultural endearment long before it delighted the Washington press. He and his wife and Bess and Tyler Abell tried to be discreet, but inevitably the story spread.

The developing edginess toward Drew in the office was based to some extent on his rudeness toward those working for him and his reported rejection of a Donovan suggestion that a regular will be drawn up at once to take care of the family and provide pensions for older employees. Pearson yielded to some extent to Donovan but, with his passion for secrecy, which had progressed to the edge of paranoia, including periodic new changing of all the locks in his office-home, he told nobody about it. He asked Sheldon Cohen, a lawyer skilled in estate matters, to work out a plan for providing a fixed annual sum for Ellen, who had been wasteful, he said, with previous allowances. Cohen said he would need a full statement of assets. Pearson promised such a statement, but he never produced it.

Pearson seemed to be increasingly isolated. He had quarreled with his former partner, Bob Allen, following a speech Drew delivered in 1966 before a Cleveland civic group at the request of Cyrus Eaton. Somebody in the audience with a grievance against the local Scripps-Howard paper asked about an old columnar charge that Roy Howard, head of the chain, had cheated on his income taxes during the 1930s. In evading the question in the presence of reporters, Pearson blamed the item on Allen, though Allen had actually opposed its use at the time.

Since Ruth Finney still wrote a national column out of Washington for Scripps-Howard, Allen complained by phone that the falsehood might cost his wife her job. When Pearson tried to justify himself, Allen cursed steadily until the other man hung up. The former partners never spoke to each other again.

For some reason Pearson had not been on speaking terms with his beloved younger brother, Leon, when Leon died in 1963. He saw less and less of his sisters, whom he prized above others in the family. He had friends like Katharine Graham, publisher of the Washington *Post*, Cyrus Eaton, Averell Harriman, Hubert Humphrey and John Steinbeck, most of whom attended his testimonial parties, but they were primarily friends who appreciated his political views.

A tightening spiral of work had gradually excluded such non-political friends as Andy Simpson, who had been with him in Yugoslavia. If he squeezed out time for somebody like Simpson, who lived in Croton-on-Hudson remote from the parochial quarrels of Washington, his abstracted behavior soon made the occasion painful.

Dorothy Detzer had become Mrs. Ludwell Denny after the death of her close friend Josephine, the first Mrs. Denny. The Dennys lived in Monterey, California. During a Washington visit they were invited by Drew out to the Potomac farm one summer weekend. Luvie had a cold and did not join them for dinner. Toward the end of the evening Denny urged Pearson to retire.

"Your name is a household word," Denny said. "What more do you want? Go plow your acres or look at the river and forget the imprisonment of deadlines. . . ."

"I can't do it for financial reasons," replied Pearson. Denny looked skeptical. "I've been active so long I can't stop," continued Pearson. Denny shrugged. "I'm not like you, Lud," Pearson said finally, in confession. "I can't retire because I have no inner resources."

On the way home Ludwell Denny told Dorothy he was "sad" about Drew. "He's afraid to keep house with himself," he said. "That's pitiful."

As a result of his preoccupation with politics, which included some aspects of economics and history, Drew had gradually neglected other fields which formerly interested him, such as philosophy, music, art, poetry and sociology. At a formal dinner one evening he sat alongside an opinionated middle-aged woman who said things which caught his attention. "Who is that woman?" he demanded later.

"That's Margaret Mead," he was told.

"I caught her name," he replied, "but what does she do?"

Washingtonians who had been on friendly terms with Drew for decades found him more easily irritated. He cooled toward Ernest Cuneo, for example, because Cuneo complained that a particular column, while not Communist or pro-Communist in tone, sounded "pro pro-Communist" to him. As one long-time associate said: "Drew had a wonderful, lovely feeling for friends, but toward the end of his life he seemed to have less and less need of people."

Early in October, 1968, as one of his final official acts, President Johnson appointed Tyler as State Department Chief of Protocol at the White House. Liz Carpenter, Lady Bird Johnson's press secretary, gave Tyler a party at Thompson's Boat Center. Lady Bird and Supreme Court Justice Abe Fortas were among those present. Tyler appeared wearing a blue turtleneck sweater and a gold chain marked "HHH" to indicate his choice for the presidency.

Humphrey's defeat by Nixon meant the quick end of Tyler's job. He cast around and arranged to join the law firm of Eddie McCormack, nephew of Speaker John McCormack, one of Drew's chief targets on Capitol Hill. Tyler would be working as government liaison man for some of the largest and toughest industrial clients in the country.

As Chief of Protocol, Tyler had been the boss of his father, George Abell, who was Assistant Chief of Protocol for some time. George was delighted to work with his son, however temporarily. Whatever their differences in the past, the Abells had grown increasingly close. When Tyler needed $10,000 to invest in the Gangplank, Washington's only floating restaurant, he went not to his stepfather, Drew, but to George, who handed over the money without question. George and Tyler Abell kissed in public when they met. In a sense George had won back his son from Drew Pearson.

Ellen had an encounter with George Abell which she mentioned in all innocence to her father. One afternoon little Felicia wandered into the backyard of a Georgetown neighbor. In time the neighbor returned the child by the front door and introduced himself. Ellen invited him in for tea.

"You—let—George Abell—into *my* house?" exclaimed Drew.

"Why not?" rejoined Ellen. "He's a wise and sweet old man."

Drew could not get over it.

A more crushing blow to his family pride was the arrest of Leon's daughter, Anne, on a charge of homicide in the first degree. Anne, thirty-seven, a former stage and TV actress in New York, had divorced her actor-husband and moved with her three children to Annapolis, where she found a job doing publicity for a housing project. She became emotionally entangled with a large, friendly, alcoholic tavern owner who had been married and divorced three times. When he turned violent one evening, she plunged a paring knife, by accident, she said, into his heart. Two brothers—Andrew (known as Drew) and Paul (who at one time managed the Potomac farm for his Uncle Drew)—hurried to Anne's side.

That December Drew Pearson the elder was supposed to go to Chicago to run the midwinter conference of the International Platform Association, a trade association of lecturers founded by his father. The session had to be canceled on word that he was too sick to attend. Nobody in the office seemed to know where Drew was. For the first time the staff grapevine was unable to learn the nature of his illness.

At her trial Anne Pearson told how she was fixing a roast in her kitchen when her fiancé stumbled toward her, roaring and "holding his arms out, like an animal does, like a bear does." She raised her arms in self-protection, she said, with no thought of the knife in her hand, and he backed off, mortally wounded, crying: "You cut me! Nobody ever cut me before."

Anne's lawyer called a dozen character witnesses of great political and business prominence in Annapolis, including Mayor Roger Moyer. The Mayor praised the defendant as "very responsible and very forthright," adding that anything she said under oath could be believed. It took the jury only three hours on January 1, 1969, to decide that Drew Pearson's niece was not guilty of murder.

2

At the start of a presidential administration Pearson followed a ritual known as "coming to grips with the man in the White House." His theory was that a new Chief Executive, having been married by popular opinion to his high office, deserved a honeymoon regardless of how heavily he had been belabored in the past. For a certain period developments were measured with conspicuous fairness against the incumbent's past behavior. Readers were intrigued by this process even as they were led by the hand toward fresh appraisal. Eventually, conclusions were reached with sufficient persuasiveness to enhance the "Merry-Go-Round" 's reputation for making mass opinion.

Pearson had encountered Richard Milhous Nixon in three previous incarnations: as a naked conflict of interest; as a government salesman for private enterprise; and as a difficult-to-gauge public-relations kind of a politician.

Always an opportunist, Nixon had been a New Dealer in New Deal days. He was a Democrat who became an obscure official in the Office of Price Stabilization. When the war began, he found a desk job in the Navy. He did not actually come to Pearson's attention until 1946 when he was negotiating a war contract with the Erco Company of Maryland for the government just prior to leaving the service.

Hearing that a group of millionaires in his native state of California had advertised for a conservative young activist to run as a Republican for Congress in their district, Nixon borrowed $150 from the manager of the Erco Company—who was in no position to refuse the loan—flew West, sold himself to the millionaires and returned to Washington to award a sizable refund to Erco. Nobody seemed to remember whether he repaid the loan— he probably did—but the conflict of interest was clear.

By crying Red in a manner later known as McCarthyism, Nixon upset Representative Jerry Voorhis, a liberal anti-Communist Democrat, and took his seat in the House of Representatives. Similar tactics a few years later against Helen Gahagan Douglas, who had voted for the Marshall Plan and for military aid to South Korea, propelled Nixon into the U.S. Senate. He made himself better known by helping to expose real Communists like Alger Hiss who had burrowed into the New Deal.

In 1951 Nixon climbed on the presidential bandwagon of General MacArthur. Next year he slid off artfully enough to land second place on the more moderate Eisenhower ticket. During the campaign Pearson heard of an $18,235 fund created by rich Californians to make Richard and Pat Nixon comfortable in Washington. He decided to tell the story on his radio program. William P. Rogers, a lawyer friendly with both Pearson and Nixon—he later emerged as Nixon's Secretary of State—warned Pearson that if he broke the story first, Nixon might support Senator Joe McCarthy's charge that Pearson was a Communist agent.

Pearson made truculent noises, but he did not break the story first. He delayed until Leo Katcher, a West Coast scriptwriter and novelist serving as a stringer on the New York *Post*, rushed the details into print. The touch of caution paid off: Nixon blamed Communists generally for writing about his nest egg, but he did not try then or later to pin a Marxist tag on Pearson.

Nixon's lachrymose version of the fund satisfied General Eisenhower and many rank-and-file Americans. It did not satisfy Drew Pearson, who displayed his dissatisfaction by an unrelenting scrutiny of the methods used to reward Nixon's helpmates.

Dana Smith, the lawyer who set up the fund, had explained to Leo Katcher that he selected Nixon as "the finest salesman of the American free-enterprise system." Pearson was able to translate this into concrete terms: Nixon intervened with the Justice Department to seek a $100,000 tax refund for the altruistic lawyer! More remarkably, Nixon sought help from the American Ambassador to Cuba when Smith welshed on a $4,200 gambling debt at the Club Sans Souci in Havana.

Bankers, builders, real estate men, cheese and dairy producers on the succor-Nixon list, Pearson revealed, got their money's worth. Oil men Tyler Woodward and William O. Anderson, for example, had been refused permission to explore for oil at Camp Roberts, a military reservation in California. Nixon came to their rescue with a Congressional bill to give them permission. Herbert Hoover, Jr. was another oil man on the list. He benefited generally from Nixon votes on tideland oil and the oil depletion allowance.

Except for the time he risked his career to help brother Donald, Richard Nixon seemed to tailor his actions to the needs of his image. From Pearson's point of view this was not entirely bad. As Vice President, he noted, Nixon had surprised critics and admirers by championing the rights of blacks and by prodding President Eisenhower into sending troops to meet the challenge to school integration in Little Rock.

By this time Pearson was a professional Quaker. He contributed money to the Society of Friends, but he did not attend church on the excuse that his meeting was in Swarthmore and he was virtually never in Swarthmore. Nevertheless, the yardstick he chose for measuring the new President on Inauguration Day, January 20, 1969, was Nixon's standing as a Quaker. Whereas that other presidential Quaker, Herbert Hoover, had gone regularly to the Friends' meeting house on Florida Avenue during his term in the White House, Nixon had been seen there only once, Pearson reported.

"Peace is the No. 1 tenet of the small religious group which fled from England in 1680 to found Pennsylvania," he pointed out. "Since then the members of the Society of Friends have stood so fast on this issue that they are automatically given noncombatant duty in time of war."

Nixon had been a hawk who "favored sending troops to rescue the French in Indochina in 1954," but he subsequently vacillated on war and peace, Pearson wrote. On the basis of his own visits to Poland and Rumania in the fall of 1968 and his reading of the Soviet newspapers, the columnist assured the new President that the Russians and their East European satellites were willing to "do business" with him.

The President was open-minded on China, Pearson assured his readers. Nixon's campaign funds had been sweetened heavily at one time by the Nationalist China Lobby, but he told the Prime Ministers of India and Burma early in his term as Vice President that he favored recognizing the Mao regime, Pearson recalled.

In March the "Merry-Go-Round" reminded the President that he had not yet revealed "the plan to end the war in Vietnam" which he promised during his campaign. Some weeks later the column revealed exclusively that Nixon had told Congressional leaders in private about "Vietnamization," a plan to beef up South Vietnam's military strength to permit gradual withdrawal of U.S. forces from Indochina.

On the domestic front Pearson found less reason to be pleased. Nixon appointments were generally disappointing. Pre-election promises to the oil lobby were being fulfilled. Not enough was being done to check inflation.

"The United States today has more economic safeguards than

existed in President Hoover's day," he wrote in June. "Nevertheless some of the same 1925–29 ingredients exist and they are causing political and economic uneasiness not only on Wall Street but all over Europe. Once depression starts it isn't easy to stop."

In July Pearson called a staff conference to consider whether to end the evaluation process with a blast against Nixon for inactivity. A national news magazine had just carried an article on the lack of constructive achievements by the administration which would make any similar "Merry-Go-Round" piece sound imitative, one assistant pointed out, but majority opinion strongly favored opening up on the man in the White House. After listening to everybody in turn, Pearson decided to give the President a little more leeway.

"Nixon was working for his ambition until he became President," he said. "Now he is working for the history books. It may be premature to dismiss him as just another Herbert Hoover."

That was Pearson's final staff conference.

3

He complained of vague symptoms which persisted until he overcame them with some fresh burst of energy. On top of his regular column-and-radio-and-newsletter work he kept up an enormous correspondence, managed his own three farms and four smaller rented ones, delivered lectures and went to occasional parties. He showed signs of weakness, irritation, even confusion, and he spoke longingly of a vacation in August which, unlike his usual working trips, would be devoted to relaxation and rest.

His flow of exclusives was unimpaired. On the domestic front they ranged from disclosure that Senator Eugene McCarthy, an unsuccessful Democratic aspirant for President the previous year, would get a divorce from Abigail, his wife of twenty-four years, to the revelation that J. Edgar Hoover possessed a list of two hundred Congressmen and ex-Congressmen who had patronized a classy Washington bordello. The implication of the column was that Pearson also had the list and might use it if Hoover did not.

"The State Department can be expected to issue a diplomatic denial but . . ." began a typical foreign exclusive, "the United

States has a secret understanding with Laos that American air-power will be available in case Communist forces attempt to take over the country." Other exclusives included:

"The Army is testing war germs at the desolate Dugway Proving Grounds West of Salt Lake City. . . ."

"For five months the Navy searched the ocean bottom in vain for the wreckage [of the *Scorpion*, American nuclear submarine which had disappeared in the Atlantic], until the Russians pointed out where the *Scorpion* had gone down. . . ."

"It has been established that the young Army lieutenant who killed Brezhnev's chauffeur last January was aiming at Brezhnev. . . ."

Though he himself was sinking, the Scorpion-on-the-Potomac continued to sting enemies. Frank Kluckhohn—"in white tie and tails," Pearson reported derisively—had attended President Nixon's dinner for Australian Prime Minister John Gorton and was under consideration for appointment as U.S. Ambassador to Australia. For the benefit of readers who might not be fully informed, he explained that Kluckhohn was notable for writing "scurrilous books," listing some of them but not the one about himself by Kluckhohn and Jay Franklin.

On the pretext that Kluckhohn had accepted chairmanship of a press ethics committee established by Willis Carto, Pearson devoted a series of sizzling columns to Carto's earlier "subterranean society called the Francis Parker Yoskey movement, named for a neo-Nazi philosopher who committed suicide in a San Francisco jail in 1960." This outfit, he said, hoarded Nazi war relics, sang Nazi songs, displayed swastikas at meetings and promoted *Imperium*, a book calling for the revival of Hitlerism.

"While not known as a Nazi," Pearson added to avoid libel, "Kluckhohn is definitely on the payroll of Carto's Liberty Lobby." The columnist then browsed through Kluckhohn's career as a correspondent for incidents to demonstrate that his antagonist was "irresponsible and unbalanced." Two previous Liberty Lobby suits having failed to get anywhere, Kluckhohn did not sue. Abandoning hope of a diplomatic career, he went into semi-seclusion in his cubbyhole of an office in the National Press Building. Within a year he was dead.

Reverse treatment was meted out to T. Lamar Caudle, former head of the Criminal Division of the Justice Department. When Caudle completed his prison term that spring for his income-tax case fix during the Truman administration, Pearson undertook to rehabilitate his onetime informant.

"Caudle came home to raise his $10,000 fine and pay his lawyers," declared the "Washington Merry-Go-Round" in sympathetic fashion. "His wife had died and his children wouldn't speak to him. Making a living when you're old and tired isn't easy. The thing that kept him going was that the neighbors in Wadesboro, N.C., believed in him." Negro neighbors brought Caudle homemade soup and other gifts, Pearson continued, "because they knew that long before the Supreme Court issued any of the race equality rulings he had championed justice for black men as well as white."

Pearson may have been thinking of himself when he wrote how hard it was to earn a living "when you're old and tired." He could not escape the strain of his controversies. During a pretrial session, in June, 1969, of a suit brought by Representative Eugene Keogh (D–Brooklyn), the Congressman responded to a formal question by shouting that Pearson was a son-of-a-bitch. John Donovan had to file a legal motion to obtain a more proper answer.

A physical scuffle developed during a pretrial session in a different case that same month when a photographer named George G. Ortiz tried to snap Pearson's picture despite an agreement that there would be no photographs. According to Ortiz' subsequent $115,000 damage suit, Pearson "grabbed plaintiff by the neck with his left hand with great force and pressure and while holding the plaintiff helpless in this position proceeded to viciously pound the plaintiff in the stomach with an object in his right hand"—apparently a briefcase.

The description recalled Senator Joe McCarthy's manhandling of Drew at the Sulgrave Club. In Pearson's entire career there is no other recorded instance of physical aggression on his part. His formal answer is not available because Ortiz did not succeed in effecting service of his complaint.

Though Tyler Abell by this time was lobbying for such influential clients of Eddie McCormack's law firm as American Airlines, Pearson planted a Trojan Horse in the office of Eddie's uncle, Speaker John McCormack. The Trojan Horse was a young reporter from the staff of *Parade* magazine, disguised as a volunteer worker, whose salary Pearson and the magazine agreed to share while he tried to uncover evidence that McCormack's office had become a clearinghouse for influence-peddling.

Another indication of expanding purpose on Pearson's part was a conference in June with Cass Canfield and John Jay Iselin of Harper & Row, Publishers, Inc. They had come to Washington at Joe Borkin's suggestion to bid for Drew's memoirs. Because of the illness of Margaret Brown, Drew's cook, the breakfast conference was shifted to the Cosmos Club.

The original proposal of Harper & Row was for five or six volumes to appear at two-year intervals. Without any stress on the fact that Pearson was approaching seventy-two, the discussion focused gradually on one or two volumes. Pearson spoke jubilantly of the kind of revelations he had in mind: the cabinet member who was a homosexual, the Congressman who kept a female lobbyist as mistress, the Senator influential in foreign affairs whose plane was blown up in mid-air on orders from British intelligence.

While Pearson did not say how far he would go in discussing his own misadventures, the Harper & Row men became convinced that the memoirs would make him, as they put it, "the political Pepys of twentieth-century America." They presented a check for the first of ten $25,000 payments, to be spaced out for tax purposes, but they never received any copy for their money.

More difficult for Pearson to endure, perhaps, than the strains of authorship or controversy was the rising tension in his office-home. Alan and Margaret McSurely had again been brought before the McClellan Committee. Through their lawyer, Morton Stavis, they publicly refused to testify on the ground that the real purpose of the committee was to smear Drew Pearson by disclosing the contents of the "Dearest Cucumber" letter and other personal material known to the committee.

The McSurelys were duly cited for contempt of Congress. Their case was referred for prosecution to David G. Bress, the

United States Attorney for the District of Columbia whom Pearson had tried so hard to supplant with Tyler Abell. The question eagerly debated around town and in the office was whether Margaret would crack in court when faced with the prospect of imprisonment if she continued to be discreet about her relationship with her former boss.

Over the years factions had coalesced gradually in Pearson's office behind Luvie-Tyler and Ellen-Canty-Donovan. Lesser individual animosities crisscrossed from one side of the house to the other. More than once police had been called in to quiet quarreling since Pearson declined to intervene. No arrests were made.

To cover family discord, the concerned patriarch wrote more frequent open letters in the "Washington Merry-Go-Round" to his grandsons, giving equal treatment to Tyler's children and Ellen's. Thus in May, Joseph P. Arnold, one of Ellen's boys, heard in simplistic terms—along with forty million other Americans—about the progress made by blacks in America during Pearson's lifetime. In June, Dan Tyler Abell was treated to an Horatio Alger version of the life of Earl Warren which might have been sticky for Pearson to deliver in normal fashion.

In July, young George Arnold got an escorted trip to the moon. "When I asked your Aunt Luvie whether I should go all the way down to Cape Kennedy to see only 15 seconds of the moon launching," Pearson wrote in the column, "she said: 'Of course. It'll give you something to write your grandchildren about for years.' "

After describing events at the Cape, Pearson moralized: "We were so anxious to beat the Russians that for once we forgot politics and states' rights and the Congressional habit of interfering, but in inner space the big question is can we apply the same teamwork for solving our urgent problems at home." Nothing, he wrote, was being done to clean up the polluted river which ran alongside the Potomac farm. A badly needed Washington subway was being delayed because the concrete, tire, gasoline and trucking lobbies were forcing Congress to build highways first. "If this continues," he concluded, "some day we may have to go and live on the moon."

That was Pearson's final story.

4

When a car containing Senator Edward Kennedy and a star-struck young Congressional secretary named Mary Jo Kopechne plunged off the Chappaquiddick bridge on Friday evening, July 18, 1969, it created a crisis for Drew Pearson. Whether or not the local assumption was correct that the couple was headed for a midnight swim at a secluded beach, Mary Jo's death in the submerged car and the Senator's panicky flight from the scene left Kennedy in no shape to deliver the featured address the following week at the annual Washington convention of the International Platform Association.

As general chairman of the IPA convention, Pearson needed an immediate replacement for Senator Kennedy. Despite a strange lassitude which had hit him at Cape Kennedy, he worked the telephone until he won a promise of appearance from Wernher von Braun, the former German scientist who played so large a role in the American moon shots.

Relatives of Drew wondered later how he kept going through the six-day convention. He was obviously on the edge of exhaustion when, appropriately clad in white dinner jacket and black tie, he delivered a reminiscent talk at the annual banquet. He was ashen-faced but jaunty in shirtsleeves and slacks as he played his traditional role of host at the weekend barbecue at his Potomac farm which always wound up IPA conventions.

When it was over, he took to his bed in Georgetown. A doctor who was called in did not dispute the patient's firm opinion that he had acquired a virus of some kind. The next weekend Pearson returned to the Potomac farm.

Since Luvie was attending a social affair in Newport, Pearson invited John Donovan to keep him company. Realizing at once that Pearson was in worse shape than he knew, Donovan was able by Monday, August 3, to persuade his friend to go to the Georgetown University Hospital.

As usual Pearson's illness was concealed as far as possible. When his condition did not improve, Luvie rationed visits by relatives and staff members. Ellen complained bitterly that her father's requests to see her were being ignored. Luvie retorted that Ellen had upset Drew too much during her first visit to be allowed to come again. When Kay Raley appeared to take a half-hour's dictation one day, Drew lamented that he had not been able to decide how to dispose of his property in fairness to his wife and daughter. He would settle that question as soon as he was up and around again, he said.

On August 18 he told Joe Borkin he was getting well. "We've got to live a long time," he added. "We've got so much to do."

On August 20, in response to inquiries from several reporters, a member of the staff issued a statement that the columnist had conquered his virus and would soon return to work. The statement did not satisfy John Donovan, who had not been added to the guest list until Bill Neel raised a fuss, or George Vournas, Pearson's neighbor and least selfish friend, who thought he looked worse than ever. Vournas wrote for medical help to William G. Helis, Jr. of New Orleans, whose father, known as the Golden Greek, had risen from penniless immigrant to millionaire oil baron and racehorse owner.

Years ago Pearson had devoted several columns to the elder Helis, identifying him as a silent partner of Dandy Phil Kastel of New Orleans and Frank Costello of New York. That was another generation, almost another country. By this time the builder of the family fortune was dead and his heir had sufficient status to lunch occasionally with that other exalted Greek, Spiro Agnew.

Avowing unlimited admiration of Drew Pearson, Helis arranged at his own expense for Dr. Alton Ochsner, director of the renowned Ochsner Clinic at Tulane University, and three of Ochsner's department heads to fly north at once. Vournas met the medical missionaries at the airport. Driving to Georgetown Hospital, they found Pearson sitting in a chair reading a newspaper. The doctors talked to him, examined him, pored over his cardiograms and other records.

That evening, Dr. Ochsner reported to Mrs. Pearson at dinner in her home. Drew, he said, had suffered "a very serious heart attack." If he understood the necessity of taking very good care of himself for at least six months, he could leave the hospital as he so ardently wished. However, he must avoid all exertion and excitement. He must not even walk up or down stairs. The inference was that Pearson, temporarily at least, must forget the newspaper column, the farm, the newsletter and all the other activities in which he was engaged. Dr. Ochsner gave a similar report to George Vournas. It was the first time Vournas had heard the word "heart" mentioned in connection with his friend's illness.

Before his discharge from the hospital on August 28, Pearson dictated a full column—which appeared posthumously—praising the New Orleans specialist as the farsighted man of genius who first alerted the nation to the health menace of cigarettes. The Helis-financed visit was never disclosed.

The day Pearson returned home the local newspapers carried stories about the McSurelys being indicted for contempt of Congress. Concealing any distress he may have felt over this psychological blow, Pearson summoned Jack Anderson and promised he would soon resume his regular writing schedule for the column.

Though Pearson gave no sign of facing up to Dr. Ochsner's alternatives of retirement or possible death, he did go to the farm that weekend for a rest. On Monday morning, September 1, 1969, he asked Tyler to drive him around the farm on an inspection tour. He had the car stopped at the bean patch for a chat with a farm hand. There was a flurry of excitement over a poacher glimpsed running from the far end of the field.

Suddenly, Pearson slumped forward fighting for breath. He became unconscious before he reached the stone mansion on the farm, and he was pronounced dead shortly after arrival at Georgetown Hospital.

The next morning the Washington *Post* described him as a muckraker with a Quaker conscience, in print fierce, in life courtly and gentle, a man who for almost forty years had done more than any other to keep the national capital honest. The *New York Times* said he was a descendant of Lincoln Steffens and Upton Sinclair who had "adapted the untiring and often merciless skill of investigative political reporting to the modern idiom of the insider's gossip." During a memorial service in the Washington Cathedral Senator Morse called him "a citizen-statesman dedicated to the service of mankind," which would have pleased his parents more than anything else.

"He could have been saved," mourned George Vournas. "He just couldn't reconcile himself to sitting idly in a chair." Out in Monterey, California, Ludwell Denny turned from his newspaper to his wife, Dorothy. "Thank God," he said. "Drew went out with his boots on!"

In accordance with a wish expressed privately to his sisters, Drew's ashes were placed in a bronze urn, which was inserted in a high rock at the farm overlooking the Potomac upriver. There was no inscription. After the ceremony, Drew's daughter, Ellen, spoke of spending all night by the rock, but she was dissuaded from her sentimental vigil by Tyler Abell.

Cracks began to appear in Pearson's journalistic structure. *Personal from Pearson*, the confidential weekly newsletter which Bill Neel had been writing for more than a decade in Drew's name, was discontinued. *Pearson on Wall Street*, which Herman Klurfeld was to have ghosted starting September 1, never appeared. Pearson's radio show was dropped. His controlling share in his newspaper syndicate was soon sold by Luvie. Jack Anderson took over the "Washington Merry-Go-Round" itself under a private arrangement with Drew that Luvie was to receive $1,000 a month from its revenue. Anderson later secured a radio program in his own name.

Luvie Pearson swept out the occupants of the office side of her house. When they were gone, she separated that area from the residential side and rented it as a separate dwelling to a private family. Drew's personal lawyer, accountants, investigators, assistants and secretaries, most of them with decades of service, were let go without warning. No severance pay or pensions were provided. Several of the employees were given tryouts of varying length by Anderson, but in the end none caught on with him. Tyler Abell changed the locks on the Pearson house in Georgetown to prevent unexpected visits by Ellen, which, he said, might upset his mother.

Drew had left seven conflicting and largely out-of-date expressions of testamentary intent. Six were holographic, that is, unwitnessed and untyped, hence unacceptable as wills in the District of Columbia. The seventh was thirty-one years old. Ellen and Luvie soon went to court in a struggle over an estate estimated to be worth between $4 and $5 million. Startling assertions were made in dry legal affidavits.

Noting that a codicil which she remembered placing in a safebox had not been produced, Marian Canty implied improper conduct by Tyler Abell as personal attorney for his mother. Blaming Ellen for Miss Canty's attack, Tyler asserted that Ellen had often exhibited irrational and bizarre behavior. Ellen told friends she would sue Tyler for libel as soon as the estate was settled.

Despite the cluster of a dozen or more high-priced attorneys around the estate like ants on a piece of honey, the family tried to conceal the contest from the public. Claims against the estate included one by John Donovan, the former family lawyer. Luvie added a complication by contesting the federal claim for estate taxes.

Luvie called together the trustees of the Foundation for the Expanding Freedoms. They decided to rename it the Drew Pearson Foundation and to expend its income on annual Drew Pearson prizes for excellence in investigative reporting. The first $5,000 prize, awarded on December 13, 1971—Drew's birthday—went to Neil Sheehan of the *New York Times* for his reporting on the Pentagon Papers. In 1972 three reporters from the Washington *Post*—Carl Bernstein, Robert Woodward and Barry Sussman—shared $6,000 for their revelations of Republican espionage at Democratic Party headquarters the previous June. Three reporters from the New York *Daily News*—Joseph Martin, Martin McLaughlin and James Ryan—shared a $1,000 honorable-mention award for exposing corruption and favoritism in New York City government. Luvie Pearson awarded the prizes. She also took an active role that year in local political efforts for the McGovern-Shriver national Democratic ticket.

Margaret and Alan McSurely were tried in Washington for contempt of Congress in June, 1970. Special Prosecutor Bress insisted that "this simple little case" revolved around technicalities: whether the defendants had been subpoenaed to testify before a Senate committee and whether they had complied. Alan argued that the committee had really been investigating his wife's love life "in a personal vendetta against Drew Pearson." Love letters supposedly kept under lock and key had been "spread all over the Capitol," he testified, denouncing the members of the committee as "crooked men with sick minds." The jury quickly found the McSurelys guilty.

On October 20 Alan and Margaret came before U.S. District Judge John L. Smith, Jr. for sentencing. "Your job is protecting the U.S. government," Margaret told the judge in open court. "It's a government whose present purpose is to serve the interests of the owning class; a government that is responsible for the murders of millions of working people in Southeast Asia and Latin America; a government that thrives on apartheid and racism in South Africa, South Carolina and New York; a government that has perpetuated male supremacy and denied equal status for women, thereby oppressing us."

Judge Smith sentenced Alan to a year in prison and Margaret to three months. They appealed. On December 20, 1972, the Court of Appeals reversed the conviction and ordered dismissal of the case against the McSurleys on the ground that it stemmed from an unconstitutional search and seizure of their records.

As of February, 1973, more than three and a half years after Drew Pearson's death, the struggle over his estate was still unsettled. This and the dispersal of his staff had left a sour taste among many prominent Washingtonians who knew him well. Nevertheless, one outstanding political figure in the capital attempted an impartial appraisal from the vantage point of anonymity.

"Don't forget," he said, "that Drew conducted his life with very great skill. Considering the things he wrote, he had far fewer enemies than you would expect. Once you enjoyed a relationship with him, you were safer than with any of your more pretentious modern liberals.

"The flaw in Drew, and I suppose in most persons who get ahead in the world, was that he wanted things both ways—to be a pacifist, for example, and a warrior, too; a leader of radical thought and a member of the establishment; a good husband with a mistress on the side and a kindly patriarch without enough time or patience for those dependent on him.

"On his small scale Pearson operated like a Great Man. If you call him that, remember what E. M. Forster said of Great

Men, that they 'produce a desert of uniformity around them, and often a pool of blood, too.' Perhaps it boils down to Lord Acton's familiar comment that power tends to corrupt and absolute power corrupts absolutely. The next sentence in that quotation, which nobody, including me, ever remembers precisely, is that the mere exercise of great influence, not to speak of power, has a damaging effect on personality.

"What I have said should not obscure the fact that Drew was the most important writer in the United States, perhaps the world, during his period. Oh, I know that Walter Lippmann reached the intellectuals and that others had pretensions, but the one with the greatest impact on ordinary Americans for the longest time was Pearson, and that impact enabled him to influence Congress, cabinet members and Presidents. He will be missed."

Index